TOOLKIT *for* MENTOR PRACTICE

PATTY J. HORN
KRISTIN METLER-ARMIJO
Foreword by Lois Brown Easton

CORWIN
A SAGE Company

For information:

Corwin
A SAGE Company
2455 Teller Road
Thousand Oaks,
    California 91320
www.corwin.com

SAGE Ltd.
1 Oliver's Yard
55 City Road
London EC1Y 1SP
United Kingdom

SAGE Pvt. Ltd.
B 1/I 1 Mohan Cooperative
    Industrial Area
Mathura Road, New Delhi 110 044
India

SAGE Asia-Pacific Pte. Ltd.
33 Pekin Street #02–01
Far East Square
Singapore 048763

Printed in the United States of America

Library of Congress Cataloging-in-Publication Data

Horn, Patty J.
Toolkit for mentor practice / Patty J. Horn, Kristin Metler-Armijo.
    p. cm.
Includes bibliographical references and index.
ISBN 978-1-4129-7651-0 (pbk. : alk. paper) 1. First year teachers—United States.
2. Mentoring in education—United States. I. Metler-Armijo, Kristin. II. Title.

LB2844.1.N4H68 2011
371.102—dc22   2010017632

This book is printed on acid-free paper.

10   11   12   13   14   10   9   8   7   6   5   4   3   2   1

Acquisitions Editor:	Dan Alpert
Associate Editor:	Megan Bedell
Editorial Assistant:	Sarah Bartlett
Production Editor:	Veronica Stapleton
Copy Editor:	Tomara Kafka
Typesetter:	C&M Digitals (P) Ltd.
Proofreader:	Dennis W. Webb
Indexer:	Sheila Bodell
Cover Designer:	Scott Van Atta

TOOLKIT
for MENTOR
PRACTICE

This book is dedicated to my family—to those who have gone before me, to those who are with me now, and to those who will come after me. I am who I am because of each of you. Especially, I dedicate this book to my Mother, Aleda Raidt Terrell Craig, who led by example to trust in God and taught me. "You can do anything you wish as long as you follow the Lord and are willing to work for it." To my husband, Ronnie; my son, Rod; my daughter and son-in-law, Lori and Manny; and my five grandchildren, Harleigh, Bryce, Kaden, Brooklyn, and Brandi—the loves of my life.

I also dedicate this book to those I have worked with throughout my career. Dr. John Renner from the University of Oklahoma was my first mentor who taught me how to teach. My students from the first grade to the university level gave me new insights and challenged my own thinking. My many colleagues who provide a pathway for collaboration and our mentors past and present who have allowed us to transform our own practice as we were teaching them to transform the teaching of others.

—Dr. Patty J. Horn

I would like to dedicate this book to my family and friends who have helped support me with creative ideas and time to think. Each of you inspires me to continue my ongoing journey of learning and growth as an educator. I would especially like to thank my father and mother for being the perfect role models of life-long learners. To my husband and daughters, thank you for providing me the loving support you have given me as I reach for my dreams. To my sister who is my best friend and advisor, thank you for always being there. To all of my fellow educators I have worked with over the course of my career, thank you for providing me with thought provoking conversations and encouraging me to dig deeper.

—Kristin Metler-Armijo, M.Ed

Contents

List of Resources

Foreword

The book you are holding in your hands is a compelling book, compelling for a number of different reasons and uses and for educators in a variety of roles.

This book is rooted in the real world of classrooms, schools, and districts. It is rooted in the work of beginning teachers, beginning and veteran mentors, principals, supervisors of mentors, those who want to start a mentoring program, and those who want to improve their mentoring programs. This is also a book I would rely on if I were working with student teachers.

This book is compelling because the United States is edging closer each year to a drought in the teaching profession. The authors comment, "Teachers do not leave the profession due to lack of content knowledge but rather due to lack of support within the system." They cite credible resources about school staffing problems, including Ingersoll (2007), who "asserts that school staffing problems are not a result of a deficit in the supply of teachers, but rather a result of the excess demand for teachers resulting from a 'revolving door' within the profession." The retirement of "baby boom" teachers in the next decade is enough of a challenge to those who lead our educational systems. What's more challenging is the fact that their replacements aren't staying long because they are insufficiently supported by their colleagues and their supervisors and because they face instructional problems the prim marms of a century ago could hardly have imagined.

This book is compelling because it's not enough that we merely replace the numbers of exiting teachers; we must replace them with quality teachers. What was good enough for that marm in 1910 is not good enough today. The damage a "bad" teacher can do to one child (never mind the 27 in his class) is one reason that "quality" must be added to our "Help Wanted" ad for more teachers soon.

This book is compelling because it represents the real work of the authors, over time, as professional partners working with mentors and the beginning teachers they guide. The processes and forms these authors created and used have been honed. It is clear that the authors have worked in classrooms and schools—they know the language of support; they know the hallways of schools; they know the demands students today make of first-year teachers. This is not a hypothetical book.

This book is compelling because it does not ignore the problems and pitfalls that can beset mentoring relationships. There are even processes and forms that deal with these problems, such as a tool that helps prevent things from going bad, the Mentor-Teacher Agreement, and what to do when they do go bad: the Breaking Confidentiality Protocol:

The model undergirding the work of the authors—as constituted in this book—is an inspiring one. It posits that mentors need support and mentoring as much as the new teachers they mentor. Even for veteran mentors each new teacher presents a new mentoring context, so the veteran mentor must continue to be a learner.

I am an advocate of professional learning, as differentiated from professional development. Not all professional development is bad—far from it—but teachers who are learners need to feel safe and respected; they need to feel as if they are among learners themselves, and this book and its processes and forms help them feel that way. Professional learning is collaborative, not isolated, and the authors understand deeply the power of collaboration, a side-by-side stance that invites "quality" into the conversation. I am reminded of one of the 10 Common Principles from the Coalition of Essential Schools. One of them calls for a culture of "unanxious expectations," and that's the culture mentors and their teachers need for learning (essentialschools.org).

This is a compelling book because it makes sense of matters that can be quite complicated. Through the Transformational Learning Stages and the Conference Data Conference (CDC) Cycle, the authors set up a vehicle that carries all of the processes, strategies, and tools a mentor needs to do a superb job working with beginning educators. The use of data is authentic, driven by need and exercised through reflection. As the authors claim, "Through the use of these tools, teachers have an opportunity to view the classroom through an objective lens." I would add that the mentor, too, has a lens through which to view the classroom and real information to share and puzzle over with the beginning teacher.

The Transformational Learning stages alone will help you understand what new teachers (and all learners, including yourself) go through. Who am I as a teacher learner? How can I affect the context or environment for learning so that all, including myself, learn? How can I focus on individual learning needs, including my own? The first is a role question; the second is about the possibilities within the role; and the third focuses on impact. These are important questions, and the authors use the stages as a way to organize the processes and tools that help people learn.

Other words can be used to describe this book—"forceful, "convincing," "pragmatic," but the best word is "compelling." This is a book that professionals who care about the future of education cannot afford to ignore.

—Lois Brown Easton

Acknowledgments

We wish to acknowledge the following people, as they have been instrumental in the development of this book.

Dr. Ron Richards, superintendent of the Pendergast School District, for being our colleague and friend and providing a place for us to practice our craft.

Dan Alpert, our editor, who is always cheerful, encouraging, and challenges our thinking.

Dr. Heidi C. Blair who was a collaborative partner who contributed to the development of ideas, significant language, time, and effort in helping us successfully complete our manuscript.

Phyllis Lussier was a mentor in the past and is a continuing colleague who works with us on an ongoing basis.

Lorin Sempkowski, one of our mentors and our colleague, who conducted a peer review and offered advice and feedback. Thanks to all the mentors we have worked with in the past as well as the present who continuously challenge our thinking and helped transform our practice.

We offer our thanks to our partner superintendents, management council members, administrators, beginning teachers, and evolving teachers who provided the foundation upon which the teacher induction program was built.

Duke Photography provided us with the portraits through their representatives Dan Fisher and David Willkie.

PUBLISHER'S ACKNOWLEDGMENTS

Corwin gratefully acknowledges the contributions of the following reviewers:

Karen Brainard, Intervention
    Coordinator
Hilliard City School
    District
Hilliard, OH

Rosemary Burnett, District
    Mentor Consultant
School District of
    La Crosse
La Crosse, WI

Lisa Casto, Curriculum and
Staff Development
Director
Allen Independent School
District
Allen, TX

Kim Fontana, Director
Staff Development and
Research
Ithaca City School
District
Ithaca, NY

Arthur Foresta, Director
Principal Mentoring
Program
New Visions for Public
Schools
New York, NY

Mary Ellen Kotz, Education
Associate
Professional Accountability—
New Educator Mentoring
and Induction
Delaware Department of
Education
Dover, DE

Debra Long, Mentor
Coordinator
Merced Union High School
District
Merced, CA

Jeanne Ross, Teacher/Mentor,
Special Education
Chariho High School
Wood River Junction, RI

Cathern Wildey, Teacher
Gulf High School
New Port Richey, FL

About the Authors

Photo by Duke
Photography, Inc.

Dr. Patty J. Horn is a professor and director of the Teacher Induction Program at Northern Arizona University. In her 43 years in education, she has served as a classroom teacher, department chair, an associate dean at Northern Arizona University, and the dean of the College of Education at Grand Canyon University. Graduate work has been completed at Arizona State University with a major in elementary education and a specialization in math and science. She has conducted research and evaluation for mentoring and induction programs. As a team member with Cooperative Services International Education Consortium, she has traveled to Tibet; Hong Kong, Guilin, and Chengdu, China; Tunisia, Africa; Bangkok, Thailand; and the Soviet Union.

She has held the office of president in Arizona for the Association of School Administrators, Science Teachers Association, and the Association of Teacher Education. Dr. Horn has also served as secretary for the Staff Development Council of Arizona and the Association of Liberal Arts Colleges for Teacher Education as well as served on the board of directors for the American Association of Colleges for Teacher Education and the Arizona Rural Schools Association.

Awards include the Distinguished Higher Education Administrator; Plank Holder of the Arizona Alliance for Math, Science, and Technology Education; Outstanding Contributor to Teacher Education in Arizona; Environmental Educator of the Year; Distinguished Professor of the Year; and Arizona Rural Schools Association Hall of Fame Inductee.

Dr. Horn's mission is to work with teachers and students so that all reach their full potential for success.

Photo by Duke
Photography, Inc.

Kristin Metler-Armijo is currently the project director for the Teacher Induction Program at NAU. She was a former Academic Services Consultant team member in the Pendergast School District. Her previous experiences include developing and implementing the district induction program, curriculum development, staff development, and teaching 7th and 8th grade reading, writing, and social studies.

Kristin earned a bachelor of science degree in secondary education with a social studies emphasis from the University of New Mexico in Albuquerque, New Mexico. She earned a master's in educational leadership from Northern Arizona University, and currently teaches for NAU. Kristin's professional interests have been reflected in her presentations at national, state, and local conferences on various topics ranging from curriculum development to differentiated instruction. She has been on several state level committees including the Statewide Induction Committee. She is the former president for the Staff Development Council of Arizona and was part of the governing board that worked to revive the council. Her passion is building lifelong learners who recognize that we all must continue to grow for the betterment of students.

Introduction

A high school teacher walks out of the district office on a Monday afternoon with textbooks piled high in his arms. It is January; the sun shining in the southwest. He is new to the state and to the teaching profession. His hometown is in Michigan, where snow covers the doorsteps. He is a confident novice science teacher who, despite having no experience working with Native American or Latino learners, is looking forward to meeting his class composed of 86% Native American, 11% Latino, and 3% Caucasian students.

On his way to the school, he sees the high desert backed by tall mountains. A herd of sheep grazes in the distance while an elderly man sits under a mesquite tree with his dog. What a different environment from his native Midwest. He wonders if he is prepared to teach these students. How will he begin to understand each of their cultures? How will he fit into the community?

Will this teacher return for a second year of teaching in this environment? Will he stay in the teaching field but look for a different situation? Will he be successful wherever he accepts a teaching position? Teachers do not leave the profession due to lack of content knowledge but rather due to lack of support within the system. How can teachers be retained in this environment or any other one existing across this nation? This is a perfect example of a beginning teacher which exemplifies the need for support, the support of a full-time mentor.

The U. S. Department of Education (1999) projects the nation will need more than 2,000,000 new teachers by 2010. The attrition rate of teachers during the first five years of teaching is reported to be between 40–50% (Ingersoll, 2007). A majority of these teachers leave during their first two years in teaching (Hope, 1999). Ingersoll (2007) asserts that school staffing problems are not a result of a deficit in the supply of teachers, but rather a result of the excess demand for teachers resulting from a "revolving door" within the profession. Teachers face many difficulties, which lead to job dissatisfaction and may eventually cause them to leave the profession. The more problems a teacher encounters, the more likely one is to leave teaching. Large numbers of teachers depart their jobs for reasons other than retirement, specifically lack of administrative support, classroom management issues, and a lack of support and collegial interaction (Ingersoll & Perda, 2006; National Commission on Teaching and America's Future, 2006). Education in the United States accounts for 4% of the entire civilian workforce. Within the first three years, approximately 33% of teachers in the workforce leave the profession. Within five years, 50% leave. This is a significant number of individuals who are in transition either entering or leaving the profession (Ingersoll, 2007). Without a support system for new professionals, the education system and the children it serves are at risk.

Teacher recruitment efforts will be unable to prevent the staffing problems if school systems do not deal with systemic sources of low teacher retention. Losing a teacher is expensive. The cost per lost teacher is between $4,366 for a small rural district in New Mexico to an average cost of nearly $18,000 for a large urban district such as Chicago (National Commission on Teaching and America's Future, 2007).

It is not enough to retain teachers; schools must develop and retain *quality* teachers. Research substantiates the crucial link between high levels of achievement and the quality of instruction (Ingersoll, 2007; Hanushek, Kain, & Rivkin, 2004; Wang, Coleman, Coley, & Phelps, 2003). In 2004, Carey stated that the effect of a teacher's instruction on student achievement accumulates over time. If a child has an ineffective teacher three years in a row, his chance of overcoming a deficit is low (Jordan, Mendro, & Weerasinghe, 1997; Sanders & Rivers, 1996). The challenge is to induct teachers in ways that rapidly promote high levels of practice and ensure that all students have effective teachers.

According to Moir and Gless (2001), new teachers who participate in systematic professional development through an organized program with full-time mentors remain in the profession at a significantly higher rate than the teachers who do not. Horn, Lussier, Metler, and Blair (2007) found that the retention rate of first-year teachers in districts with full-time mentors increased. This type of support develops instructional proficiency at a faster rate. When an induction program provides specialized professional development to all beginning teachers, students ultimately benefit from having effective teachers who are competent in the classroom.

For teachers who are in collegial settings with their peers, experience tends to help those teachers improve throughout their careers (Darling-Hammond, 2000). The key benefits of experience are that the teacher has time to

- Develop an increased depth of understanding about the content and how to teach it to students (Covino & Iwanicki, 1996).

- Learn and use various strategies to meet students' needs (Glass, 2001, & Durall, 1995).
- Learn how to maximize his or her usage of instructional materials, management of the classroom, and working relationships with others (Reynolds, 1992).
- Incorporate reflective practice (Allen & Casbergue, 2000).

Providing a full-time mentor for the beginning teacher in a collegial setting allows that teacher the opportunity to gain these benefits in their first year of teaching. The two hours per week that the mentor spends with the beginning teacher in a collegial setting is congruent with Darling-Hammond's beliefs about experience.

Full-time mentors should be carefully selected and intensively trained to work collegially with first and second-year teachers. The mentor meets with each teacher for two hours per week, and that time with the teacher is well protected.

The relationship that exists between the mentor and the teacher focuses on transforming the teacher's practice in order to improve student success. Research conducted by Villar, Strong, & Fletcher (2008) found that greater student achievement gains are realized as a result of intensive induction sustained over two years. The research that has been conducted over the past four years by Horn, Blair, & Metler-Armijo (2008) confirms that beginning teachers who participated in an induction program that featured full-time mentors evidenced student achievement scores that were equal to or greater than those of the veteran teachers with whom they were compared. This induction program, which incorporated the tools and recommendations featured in this book, has been shown to be effective in transforming the practice of early-career teachers.

Keys to the success of this induction program are

- Full-time mentors hired by the district to collaborate with first-year teachers two hours per week and second-year teachers for one hour per week.
- Workshops for beginning teachers and second-year teachers are conducted monthly.
- Workshops for administrators are conducted quarterly.
- The management council representing each of the partner districts meets semi-monthly.
- The tools themselves, which were initially developed by the authors and the participating mentors to be used with first- and second- year teachers. Conversations with mentors, whose primary work is that of transforming beginning teacher practice, has served as the genesis of many of the tools over the past four years. Each tool has been refined to increase its simplicity and

effectiveness and has been successfully used in the field. Quite simply, the tools work!

The purpose of this book is to provide a toolkit for beginning mentors who provide support to beginning teachers; however, the tools can be used by other educational professionals as well. These include mentors who would like to refine their practice, principals or site supervisors working with the veteran teachers, or coaches working with veteran teachers who find themselves in a new grade level that they have never taught.

We do recognize that everyone does not have the opportunity to work in an optimum environment of full-time mentors working with a small number of 15 beginning teachers. The district may be in a position of only providing a buddy mentor that teaches next door or a part-time mentor who assists a limited number of beginning teachers or a full-time mentor who assists a large number of teachers. Whatever the circumstance of working with mentors and teachers, the tools can be selected based on the knowledge of the mentors and the needs of the teachers.

In the process of designing the tools, we identified two critical components to serve as the foundation for working with novice teachers. These two components are Transformational Learning stages and the CDC Cycle. Teachers who are new to the profession or who experience a shift in practice go through Transformational Learning stages. Mentors mirror those stages as they develop into their new role of mentor. The CDC Cycle is the process that allows mentors to facilitate collaborative conversations which enhance the transformation of practice. These two critical components are detailed in Chapters 1 and 3.

When working with beginning teachers, many programs utilize tools for collecting evidence but do not go any further toward analysis and change. The tools in this book were designed with the deliberate intention of fostering the concepts of formative assessment within novice teachers from day one of their instructional practice for the purpose of transforming their practice. We agree with Popham (2008) when he defines formative assessment as the planned practice of collecting a body of evidence, analyzing that evidence, and then making decisions for change based on growth. The data collection tools provide beginning teachers and mentors with an artifact and evidence of what behaviors are occurring in the classroom. Through the use of these tools, teachers have an opportunity to view the classroom through an objective lens.

The book provides an overview of key concepts for mentoring as well as classroom data tools that are applicable to the everyday work of the mentor, the administrator, the supervisor, or the professional development

Figure I.1 Transformational Learning Stages

Stage 1: Role Focused

Teacher
- Chapter 4: CDC Journal Record
- Chapter 5: Beginning Conversations
- Chapter 7: Professional Teacher Growth Process

Mentor
- Chapter 1: Transforming Practice
- Chapter 2: CDC Cycle
- Chapter 3: Foundations for Mentoring
- Chapter 4: CDC Journal Record
- Chapter 5: Beginning Conversations
- Chapter 6: Administrator and Mentor Conversations
- Chapter 8: Professional Mentor Growth Process

Stage 2: Practice Focused

Teacher
- Chapter 11: Observing a Master Teacher
- Chapter 12: Student Data Mapping
- Chapter 13: Planning for Instruction
- Chapter 14: Lesson Design
- Chapter 15: Videotaping as a Process for Reflection
- Chapter 17: Probing Higher Level Thinking

Mentor
- Chapter 9: Collecting Evidence: Teacher and Student Behaviors
- Chapter 10: Collecting Evidence: Teacher and Student Verbal Interactions
- Chapter 11: Observing a Master Teacher
- Chapter 12: Student Data Mapping
- Chapter 13: Planning for Instruction
- Chapter 14: Lesson Design
- Chapter 15: Videotaping as a Process for Reflection
- Chapter 16: Collecting Evidence: Student Engagement
- Chapter 17: Probing Higher Level Thinking

Stage 3: Learner Focused

Teacher
- Chapter 18: Analyzing Student Work
- Chapter 19: Planning for Differentiated Instruction
- Chapter 20: Analyzing Student Assessments
- Chapter 22: Reflecting on One's Practice

Mentor
- Chapter 18: Analyzing Student Work
- Chapter 19: Planning for Differentiated Instruction
- Chapter 20: Analyzing Student Assessments
- Chapter 21: Planning for Differentiated Mentoring
- Chapter 22: Reflecting on One's Practice

provider. These tools were designed to foster the concepts of transformative learning within teachers and mentors from day one of the beginning teacher's instructional practice. However, they can be used in a variety of programs to meet a variety of needs.

Depending on the parameters of the program, such as full-time mentors versus buddy mentors, the developmental timeframe of mentors and teachers varies. In order to assist readers with a visual explanation of the tools and provide a connection between mentor transformational growth and beginning teacher transformational growth under the parameters of full-time mentorship, we have created the graphic organizer shown in Figure I.1. As a reader, it would be important to recognize what elements of the Transformational Learning stages can be implemented according to the constraints of your program.

Each chapter will contain the following to represent a specific section.

- *Purpose* for the rationale, process, or tool will be clarified.
- *Description* will describe the tool to be used followed by the tool itself.
- *How to Use* the tool will include specific instructions on implementation.
- *Tools in Action* will be samples of the tools that a mentor has used while working with the beginning teacher in the collaborative cycle.
- *Notes for Implementation* will include a short paragraph that may align the content of the chapter with the Transformational Learning stage, may suggest the time of year for the mentor to introduce the tool to use with the beginning teacher, or may provide the rationale for why the tool would be introduced at this particular time of the year.

The research base for our work is presented as a Research Summary in Resource A. The topics include Full-time Mentors, Induction Program, Mentor Responsibilities, Professional Development, Quality Teaching, Student Achievement, Teacher Development & Performance, and Teacher Retention.

The tools and practices that are introduced in each chapter are listed in Resource B. Many of the tools we developed are produced on no carbon required (NCR) paper in order to provide the teacher with instant feedback. We have found this to be the most efficient means for the mentor in a variety of settings. Often, mentors do not have the availability of a copy machine nearby. We have also found that laptops, when used as a means for data collection or collaborative documentation, often present a barrier between the mentor and teacher and therefore impede the trusting relationship.

Resource C provides the reader with the rubric used for the Framework of Professional Growth Teacher Practice that is used with the Professional Practice Teacher Self-Assessment Checklist found in Resource D.

The Framework of Professional Growth Mentor Practice rubric is found in Resource E that is used with the Professional Practice Mentor Self-Assessment Checklist in Resource F.

Section 1

Role Focused Transformational Learning Stage

The first stage we identified as being *role focused*. Individuals who are new to a practice spend the greater part of their time developing their roles as mentors or teachers. The majority of their focus is spent acclimating to new environments and creating foundations on which they can build relationships. During this orientation period, novice mentors work on establishing routines that are not bound by classroom structures and begin developing trusting relationships with their teachers. Novice teachers concentrate on creating effective classroom management and establishing themselves as leaders in the classroom. Both the novice mentor and novice teacher focus on centering learning around professional growth goals and student objectives and goals. The experienced mentor refines her practices every time they begin working with a new teacher.

Each chapter in this stage becomes the foundation for the mentor or teacher roles determined by how they personally fit into their respective roles. Chapters 1–8 set the precedent for how to work with beginning teachers and establish a skill set for collaboration. These chapters answer the questions: How do you transition from being teachers to becoming mentors? How do you have conversations with beginning teachers and others? How do you focus those conversations? How do you document those conversations? What process do you use to establish continuity and thereby transform teacher practice?

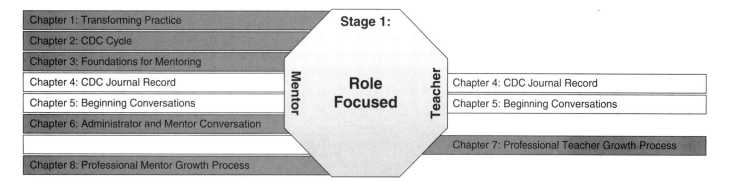

Chapter Introduced	Practices and Tools
	Section I: Role Focused Stage
Chapter 1	1. Transformational Learning Stages
	2. Managing Transformational Learning
Chapter 2	3. Conference, Data, Conference (CDC) Cycle
Chapter 3	4. Mentor Stances
	5. Mentor Roles
	6. Mentor Language
Chapter 4	7. Conference Data Conference (CDC) Journal Record – NCR
Chapter 5	8. Mentor–Beginning Teacher Confidentiality Agreement – NCR
	9. Breaking Confidentiality Protocol
	10. Teacher Profile – NCR
	11. Mentor Profile – NCR
	12. Community and School Resources – NCR
Chapter 6	13. Administrator and Mentor Journal Record – NCR
Chapter 7	14. Framework of Professional Growth Teacher Practice Standard 1
	15. Professional Practice Teacher Self-Assessment Checklist Standards 1–3
	16. Establishing Professional Teacher Growth Priorities
	17. Professional Teacher Growth (PTG) Plan – NCR
	18. Professional Teacher Growth Plan Data Summary – NCR
	19. Professional Teacher Growth Plan Reflection
Chapter 8	20. Framework of Professional Growth Mentor Practice Standard 2
	21. Professional Practice Mentor Self-Assessment Checklist Standards 1–3
	22. Establishing Professional Mentor Growth Priorities
	23. Professional Mentor Growth (PMG) Plan – NCR
	24. Professional Mentor Growth Plan Data Summary – NCR
	25. Professional Mentor Growth Plan Reflection
NCR = No Carbon Required paper. NCR copies are made for the mentor and the beginning teacher to provide each with a copy of the tool.	

1

Transforming Practice

PURPOSE FOR TRANSFORMATIONAL LEARNING STAGES

Today's educational landscape is a fast-paced, structure-bound, results-driven arena that predicates educators become lifelong learners who embark on a journey of ongoing professional change. This process of change requires two levels of learning: informational and transformational (Kegan, 2000). Informational learning consists of professionals acquiring procedural and structural information related to work and life issues. As educators enter the profession or face change, they either have this knowledge or that knowledge can be readily acquired. This type of knowledge, as important as it is, typically does not change one's way of thinking (Kerka, 2001).

Garavuso (2010) states, "Transformational learning, on the other hand, seeks to change how we know, 'altering our existing frame of reference, [and] our ways of making meaning'."

Joellen Killion (2008), deputy executive director for the National Staff Development Council, describes how educators must experience

deep learning, often called transformational learning, occurs at the level of beliefs, values, and motivation rather than only at the level of knowledge and skills. Transformational learning is long-term and results in behavioral changes. Transformational learning is deep change that occurs at the core of the learner. Learning at this level promotes a change in practice. (p. 7)

It is with this foundational belief that we created our induction program to support new educators embarking on a journey of change.

Educators who enter the profession or experience a shift in practice that occurs as a result of a change in job expectations or reassignment undergo a tremendous professional transformation. Fuller and Bown (1975) identified three stages of teacher development characterized by their concerns: survival, teaching situation, and pupil. All three stages are evident in the process of transformational learning. As educators take on a new role as teacher, mentor, or leader, they move through a process where their first concerns are who they are within their new role. They then begin to examine more thoroughly what they do within their new role, and finally, they begin to focus on who they are impacting as a teacher, mentor, or leader.

This shift in practice is especially true for new educators who arrive at their first job with utopian ideas as to what they will do with their first set of students or who have no idea at all where to start. As these educators prepare to take over their first classes or new assignments, they must be ready to question their practice based on what they believe and envision in order to impact the future. They must be prepared to see themselves in their practices as they really are and reflect on their experiences over a period of time. They must be ready for the challenges necessary to accelerate their practices and perform to the highest expectations required by today's educational system.

Here are some reasons why induction and mentoring are necessary during transformational learning:

- It is difficult to see ourselves in our practice as we really are. We need a trained mentor to guide us through self-analysis and to self-discovery.
- Transformational change cannot happen without reflection. Reflection is not an innate skill for most individuals.
- Transformational change takes time.
- Resisting change is ingrained in human behavior.

In the process of designing an induction program that ensures professional transformation and accelerated practice, we identified three *Transformational Learning Stages* for new mentors and beginning teachers. Each stage is comprised of professional learning components that help learners acclimate and transcend to the next learning level.

The following graphic (Figure 1.1) is a visual representation of the *Transformational Learning Stages 1–3*. The left side of the graphic depicts the learning stage components that mentors experience as they transform their practices. The right side of the graphic shows the learning stage components for teacher transformation. Common components that are shared between mentor and teacher are portrayed with a similar color palette.

Figure 1.1 Transformational Learning Stages

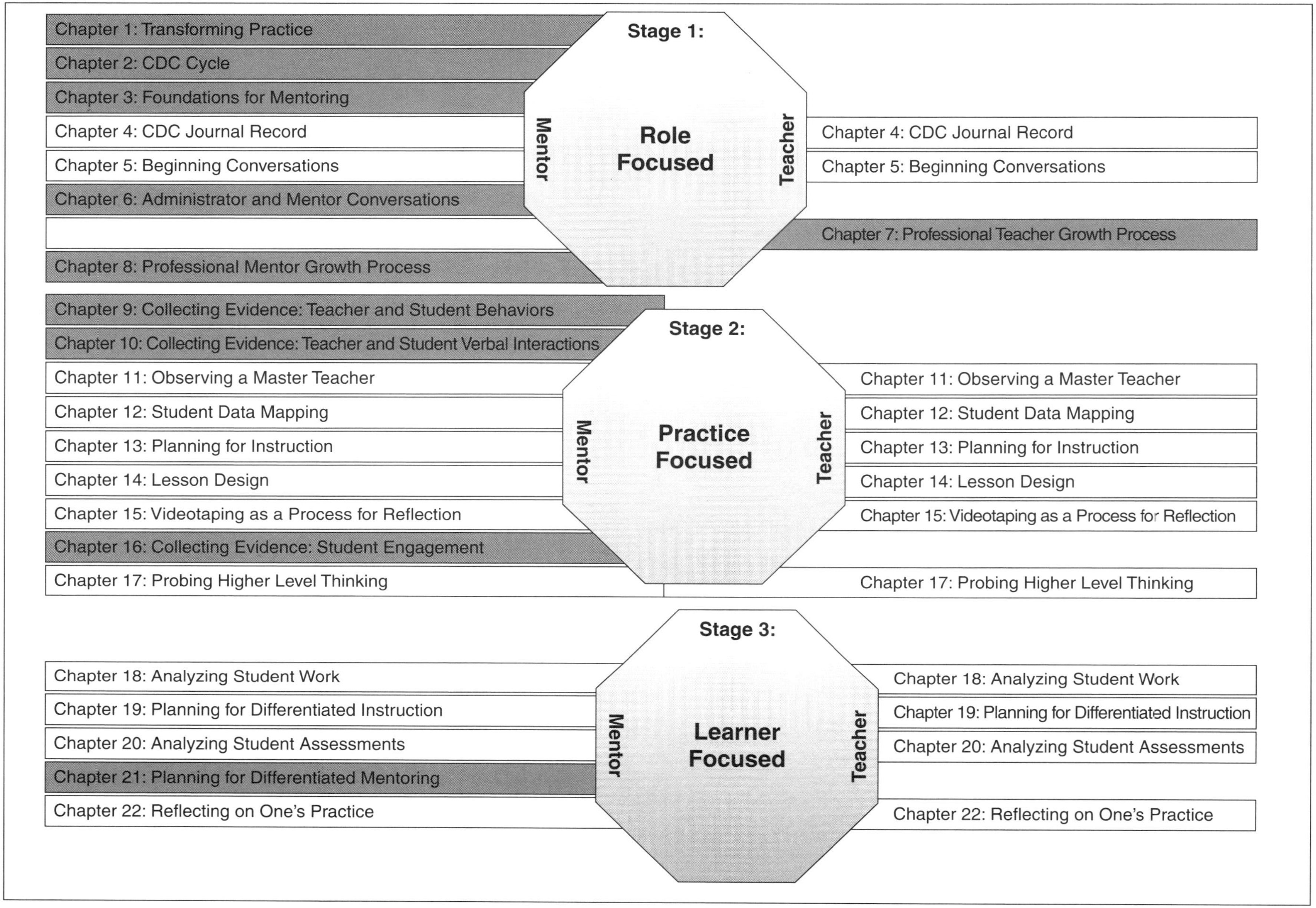

Chapter 1: Transforming Practice

Chapter 2: CDC Cycle

Chapter 3: Foundations for Mentoring

Chapter 4: CDC Journal Record

Chapter 5: Beginning Conversations

Chapter 6: Administrator and Mentor Conversations

Chapter 7: Professional Teacher Growth Process

Chapter 8: Professional Mentor Growth Process

Chapter 9: Collecting Evidence: Teacher and Student Behaviors

Chapter 10: Collecting Evidence: Teacher and Student Verbal Interactions

Chapter 11: Observing a Master Teacher

Chapter 12: Student Data Mapping

Chapter 13: Planning for Instruction

Chapter 14: Lesson Design

Chapter 15: Videotaping as a Process for Reflection

Chapter 16: Collecting Evidence: Student Engagement

Chapter 17: Probing Higher Level Thinking

Chapter 18: Analyzing Student Work

Chapter 19: Planning for Differentiated Instruction

Chapter 20: Analyzing Student Assessments

Chapter 21: Planning for Differentiated Mentoring

Chapter 22: Reflecting on One's Practice

Stage 1:

Role Focused

Teacher

Mentor

Chapter 4: CDC Journal Record

Chapter 5: Beginning Conversations

Chapter 7: Professional Teacher Growth Process

Stage 2:

Practice Focused

Teacher

Mentor

Chapter 11: Observing a Master Teacher

Chapter 12: Student Data Mapping

Chapter 13: Planning for Instruction

Chapter 14: Lesson Design

Chapter 15: Videotaping as a Process for Reflection

Chapter 17: Probing Higher Level Thinking

Stage 3:

Learner Focused

Teacher

Mentor

Chapter 18: Analyzing Student Work

Chapter 19: Planning for Differentiated Instruction

Chapter 20: Analyzing Student Assessments

Chapter 22: Reflecting on One's Practice

DESCRIPTION OF TRANSFORMATIONAL LEARNING STAGES

Just as becoming a classroom teacher involves making a transition from being a student to being a professional, so does becoming a mentor teacher involve making a transition from classroom teacher to teacher leader.

—Dobbins and Walsey

The first stage we identified as being *Role Focused*. Individuals who are new to a practice spend the greater part of their time developing their roles mentors or teachers. The majority of their focus is spent acclimating to new environments and creating foundations on which they can build relationships. During this orientation period, novice mentors work on establishing routines that are not bound by classroom structures and begin developing trusting relationships with their teachers. Novice teachers concentrate on creating effective classroom management and establishing themselves as leaders in the classroom. Both the novice mentor and novice teacher focus on centering learning around professional growth goals and student objectives and goals. Experienced mentors and teachers look for ways to continually refine their practices.

The second stage we identified as being *Practice Focused*. During this stage, individuals spend the greatest part of their time enhancing their practices and skills. They become more familiar with the tools and resources that are available to them in their roles as mentors or teachers. Mentors increase their organizational skills, develop the expertise necessary for capturing evidence during observations, and hone their data analysis skills to expand beyond student work to teacher development. Teachers focus their energy on examining student data in order to get to know their students better. They spend time developing effective lesson plans, organizing their time more efficiently, and implementing instructional strategies that engage students.

The third stage is *Learner Focused*. During this stage, the transformation occurs when the teacher and mentor begin to realize the impact they have had on the individuals with whom they have been directly working. Both individuals are able to move toward more abstract concepts, such as differentiation. Mentors examine how to meet the needs of individual teachers through self-assessment of practices and reflection. Mentors utilize tools to plan how to differentiate for their teachers based on evident growth. Novice teachers recognize the importance of focusing on the academic and social needs of a class as a whole and students as individuals. Teachers begin to see their practices of analyzing student work, differentiating instruction, and using formative assessment as effective practices to meet student needs.

By providing mentors and novice teachers support through the *Transformational Learning Stages*, deep learning can occur paving the way for professional transformation and accelerated practice. Educators who are left to their own devices seldom experience true transformational change. Practices might change for a time but beliefs and paradigms do not shift resulting in lasting and impactful learning. Joyce and Showers (1988) discuss the necessity of support for teachers who are undertaking new learning. Their research indicates that new learning must be accompanied by modeling, practicing with low-risk feedback, and mentoring. As Joyce and Showers determined, mentoring is necessary for the transfer and application of new learning into new contextual situations. However, the process of change through the *Transformational Learning Stages* is a larger undertaking and requires a thoughtful and carefully planned process of *Managing Transformational Learning.*

PURPOSE FOR MANAGING TRANSFORMATIONAL LEARNING

Teachers need to participate in a planned process in which they follow a series of steps designed to promote change. Initial growth goals for professional practice should be established by the teacher. The mentor provides support to the teacher through collaborative conversations and reflective dialogue. Observable data is collected either by the mentor capturing classroom interactions or by student achievement scores. Together the mentor and teacher analyze the data for areas of strength and areas of growth. As a result of the analysis, teachers make decisions as to what adjustments will be made to their instruction that will change their practice and impact student learning. Finally, the teacher and mentor develop an action plan to further promote the growth of the teacher.

One of the critical factors to consider in order for transformational growth to occur is the process of *Transformative Assessment.* James Popham (2008) describes transformative assessment as a "planned process in which assessment-elicited evidence of students' status is used by teachers to adjust their ongoing instructional procedures or by students to adjust their current learning tactics" (p. 6). When examining teacher or mentor growth, the same philosophy can be applied. Formal induction programs can provide a structured method for transformative assessment that accelerates the practice of novice teachers through transformational learning. It is when teachers are assessing their current practice and planning for future practice in a structured manner that transformational growth happens.

DESCRIPTION OF MANAGING TRANSFORMATIONAL LEARNING

The planned process we have identified as *Transformative Assessment* parallels Ambrose's process of *Managing Complex Change* (1987). We have identified five key components that an induction program should contain in order to promote desired transformational growth. Each component is a powerful aspect of the change process. However, it is when all five are combined as part of the learning process that transformational learning will occur. When absent from the learning process, each component results in a different form of resistance and blocks growth. All five components— *Mentor Support, Growth Goals, Data Collection, Data Analysis,* and *Action Planning*—need to be continuously integrated in order for the mentor and teacher to experience true *Transformational Learning* (Figure 1.2).

Figure 1.2   Managing Transformational Learning

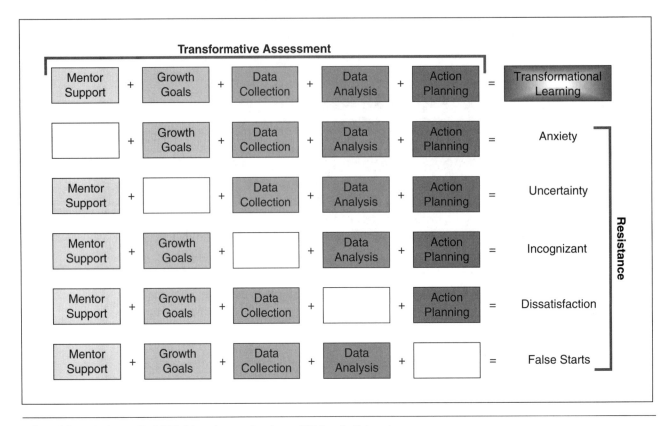

Adapted from Ambrose, D. (1987). *Managing complex change.* Pittsburgh: Enterprise.

The first component is *Mentor Support*. Mentors who are trained and attentive to the needs of the teachers they support are essential to the transformational learning process. We found that full-time mentors who have no other job expectations are able to support teachers in a more meaningful and productive way. If mentor support is nonexistent, there is a lack of learning-focused, collegial interaction for the teachers. Teachers experience high anxiety due to the pressures to change and fail to grow in their practice.

The second component is establishing *Growth Goals*. Teachers who desire transformational growth must have a clear focus for where they will go and how they get there. If growth goals are not established, there is a lack of vision by the teachers. They cannot see how their practices could look differently and approach learning with uncertainty and apprehension.

The third component is *Data Collection*. Teachers need to see evidence of classroom behaviors performed by themselves and students. If data collection is missing, teachers do not have specific evidence to determine areas of success and areas for growth. They cannot see their practices as they currently exist and therefore experience little dissatisfaction. Teachers who are satisfied with the status quo are unwilling to change the current state of instruction and are incognizant.

The fourth component is *Data Analysis*. Teachers need to have a structured way to look at the evidence of classroom behaviors. If data analysis is lacking, teachers approach learning and change with a lack of direction and a sense of dissatisfaction. They may identify areas that need to be modified but do not have a clear idea of the specificities of the changes that need to be made and how those changes might impact their practice.

The fifth component is *Action Planning*. Teachers need to determine how they will move forward in their practices. If action planning is not present, teachers will experience a series of false starts. They will approach learning with a clear vision of where they want to be and why they need to be there, but they will have no plan for how they will get there.

When all components of *Transformative Assessment* are integrated, transformational learning manifests itself allowing mentors and teachers to manage their own learning. Those mentors and teachers who partake in the process of transformational learning develop into lifelong learners who are continuously seeking ways to improve their practices and impact the lives of students. The stages of transformational learning illustrate the need for a planned and structured induction program.

NOTES FOR IMPLEMENTATION

In a full-time mentor induction program, the initial focus for the first three months of a beginning mentor and beginning teacher's practice is to provide support. By the third month, mentors and teachers are well on their way to Managing Transformational Learning. The tools and ideas presented throughout this book provide the structure and guidance necessary for mentors and teachers to transform their practice and impact others. Identify what support elements your system can provide and implement critical to your own needs.

2

Conference Data Conference (CDC) Cycle

PURPOSE FOR THE CDC CYCLE

The many roles a mentor plays during the process of mentoring teachers were described in chapter one. The complex role of a mentor and the limited amount of time a teacher has to meet with her mentor demand a framework for managing the varied interactions required to accelerate the teaching practice of teachers. The *Conference Data Conference (CDC) Cycle* was developed in response to this need. The CDC Cycle provides both mentor and teacher the opportunity to collaborate in the development of the teacher's instructional practice. It provides a process they can follow that leads them through collaborative conversations and classroom data analysis.

The development of the teacher as an autonomous reflective practitioner is one goal of the mentoring process. During each phase of the CDC Cycle, the mentor assists the teacher in recognizing what is actually happening in the classroom through conversation, classroom data examination, and reflection.

Professional teacher standards serve as the foundation of the CDC Cycle. In today's educational environment, student success is determined by looking at one's achievement compared to a set standard. This is no different for teachers. Standards articulate the specific skills expected of an effective teacher. They serve as a common language for discussing classroom practice. The mentor and teacher reference these standards throughout process of conferencing and data analysis.

The success of this process in accelerating a teacher's classroom practice depends on the existence of a trusting relationship between the mentor and the teacher being mentored. At the core of the process is the belief that, through self-evaluation and critical reflection, a teacher can improve the multiplicity of the instructional strategies in her teaching practice. A teacher must be able and willing to identify areas of need, a position of vulnerability. A teacher will only feel comfortable doing this in a trusting and nonjudgmental relationship. For this reason, trust is at the center of the CDC Cycle. This trusting relationship is strengthened over time. Each time the teacher and mentor repeat the cycle trust is strengthened and the teacher's practice accelerates. Once initiated, the CDC Cycle continues throughout the mentoring relationship.

Confidentiality is an important component of the trusting relationship. Any anecdotal notes, documentation, completed tools, and personal conversations between the mentor and teacher are to be used exclusively to support the professional growth of the teacher. A confidentiality agreement is signed at the beginning of the year by the administrator, mentor, and teacher. All conversations and documentation are held in confidence with the exception of unprofessionalism on the part of either party. Unprofessionalism can be inappropriate behavior or language, danger to self or others, failure to keep scheduled appointments, and failure to participate. If unprofessionalism occurs, the mentor follows the Breaking Confidentiality Protocol (see Chapter 5) in order to provide opportunities for change. This applies to everything except safety issues which are reported immediately to the supervisor.

DESCRIPTION OF THE CDC CYCLE

The CDC Cycle is comprised of three phases: a planning conference, classroom data collection, and a reflective conference. Therefore, the acronym CDC represents the three phases of the cycle (Figure 2.1). A basic cyclical support process is not unknown in the field of mentoring. In 1969, Goldhammer discussed supporting developing teachers via multiphased cyclical processes of conferencing and observation. In 1994, Costa and Garmston discussed a condensed process comprised of two phases. The two conference phases require the self-examination of a teacher's practice and open discussions with the mentor. Our model is different from that of Costa and Garmston in that it includes a distinct phase for data collection that serves as the basis for the reflective conference.

Figure 2.1 CDC Cycle

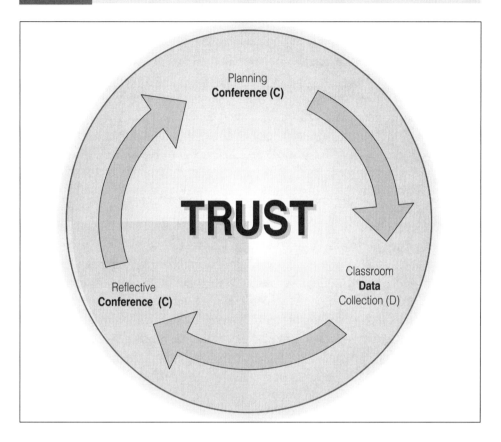

Phase 1: The Planning Conference

During the planning conference, the initial phase of the CDC Cycle, the teacher and mentor participate in a collaborative conversation regarding the teacher's practice. The goal is for the teacher to identify an aspect of her practice for improvement. Based on this focus, the teacher and mentor determine the appropriate classroom data for the mentor to collect. In many situations, several tools can be used to collect the data. Together they select the most suitable data collection tool. In order to accomplish this goal they must answer four overarching questions.

First, what is the teacher's goal for her next observed lesson? The teacher describes the instructional objectives and context of the lesson. The mentor asks questions to assist the teacher in thinking critically about this lesson. Questions regarding alignment to academic standards, instructional context, and individual student learning needs are asked.

The second overarching question is how will the teachers know they have met a goal? The teacher must identify the evidence, including product, test score, and performance, that documents student success. Mentors pose a variety of questions to assist the teacher in clarifying the type of evidence that aligns with academic expectations.

Third, what strategies will the teacher use to enable students to meet the learning goal? The teacher explains the instructional strategies and methods to be used during the lesson. The mentor poses a variety of questions to assist the teacher in clarifying these strategies.

Finally, what behaviors will the mentor document during the lesson? To assist the teacher in answering this question the mentor may offer statements and questions to clarify the specific teacher or student behaviors to be documented. Together they determine the data to be collected. It is important that the collaborative conversation between the teacher and mentor determine what is to be observed and which tool will be used to collect the data. It is the effective use of these data collection tools that are the focus of this book. These tools are described in detail in the following chapters.

Phase 2: The Classroom Data Collection

During the classroom data collection phase, the next CDC Cycle phase, the mentor uses selected tools such as seating charts, logging engaging behavior, and scripting to document data collaboratively agreed upon between the mentor and the teacher. The teacher trusts the mentor to collect data on one area of her teaching practice. This allows the teacher to focus on that one area as well. Whether or not the mentor leaves a copy of the data with the teacher is decided during the planning conference. The analysis of this data is a key component of the reflective conference, the third phase in the CDC Cycle.

Phase 3: The Reflective Conference

In preparation for the reflective conference, the mentor reviews the data as it relates to the agreed upon focus. The mentor identifies evidence related to the teacher's focus. The analysis of the collected data will be most effective if the teacher identifies the patterns and evidence within the data. However, the mentor must prepare to guide the teacher by identifying guiding questions prior to the reflective conference.

In the reflective conference, the data is analyzed as it relates to the observation focus decided upon in the planning conference. To start this conference, the mentor encourages the teacher to reflect upon the observed lesson. The teacher shares these reflections with the mentor. Next, the mentor supports the teacher in identifying specific data elements that support her impressions of the lesson. The mentor guides the teacher in a review of the data by posing a variety of questions as needed. These encourage the teacher to look at the data for patterns, indicators of successes and challenges, and possible foci for future data collection. The mentor may ask the teacher to reflect on the mentoring process itself and propose refinements. In this cyclical process, the reflective conference naturally leads into the planning conference phase. The CDC Cycle continues unabated until the end of the mentoring working relationship.

Mentors and teachers use the CDC Journal Record as a tool to guide the planning and reflective conferences. It is an artifact of the conversation, which can be referred to by both the teacher and mentor. It is an integral part of their collaborative effort to push the teacher's practice forward. The CDC Journal Record is discussed in detail in Chapter 4.

NOTES FOR IMPLEMENTATION

The CDC Cycle is the heart of a teacher-directed mentoring program focused on accelerating a teacher's instructional practice. At the heart of the CDC Cycle is a trusting relationship between the mentor and teacher. This trust is created by nurturing a deep sense of respect for one another as professional colleagues. From the first meeting, the mentor must model the practice of assisting the teacher through collaboration rather than *fixing* the teacher. The mentor's use of nonjudgmental language further cultivates the trusting relationship. One technique for correcting judgmental language is to ask a question rather than make a statement. Replace a judgmental statement such as "You ignored the children at the back of the room" with the question "What was happening in the back of the room?" The mentor shows respect for the teacher's view when asking a nonjudgmental question. Creating this kind of collaboration builds a trusting relationship.

With trust at the center, teachers feel comfortable with honest explorations of their teaching practice during the conferencing and data collection phases of the cycle. Knowing that all that occurs during the activities of the cycle is confidential and will never be shared with anyone gives the teacher a safe feeling in identifying areas of their practices that might need improving or refining. It is within this trusting relationship built on mutual respect and nonjudgmental feedback that transforms teachers' practices.

3

Foundations for Mentoring

Perhaps the most essential component needed for Transformational Learning to occur is mentor support. Mentors provide the assistance and guidance necessary to help novice teachers become successful practitioners and lifelong learners. Mentors encourage teachers to see themselves in their profession as they really are. Mentors guide teachers through self-analysis to self-discovery. Through comprehensive support, mentors help teachers become reflective in their practice and initiate transformational learning.

We have found three fundamental skill sets necessary for mentoring and supporting teachers though the transformational learning stages: *mentor stances*, *mentor roles*, and *mentor language*. When striving for deep learning, mentors must have an understanding of what the three key skill sets are and how to utilize them when working with teachers. Each of these skill sets apply to new mentors and mentors who are refining their practice regardless of the time spent between mentor and teacher due to program differences.

PURPOSE FOR MENTOR STANCES

During the transformational learning process, mentors develop their teachers to become independent problem solvers and thinkers. Throughout collaborative conversations, mentors adopt stances, or attitudes, that allow for this development to occur. When mentors utilize a specific stance, they take on the behaviors associated with each attitude. We have implemented the use of *instructive, collaborative,* and *facilitative* stances for mentoring.

The purpose of the mentor stances is to interact more effectively with teachers during conferencing conversations. Each stance is reflective of a set of purposeful behaviors and actions that mentors take to deepen teachers' skills and knowledge and thereby transform their practices. Mentors intentionally utilize the instructive stance to share specific expertise, exemplar models of practice, or strategies that a teacher might use. Mentors employ the collaborative stance to build, develop, analyze, or problem solve together with a teacher. Mentors purposefully use the facilitative stance to help teachers probe deeper into their own thinking, build reflective practices, and increase problem solving skills.

DESCRIPTION OF MENTOR STANCES

Lipton and Wellman (2001) describe the stances as a *continuum of interaction* that mentors move through during conversations with teachers. On one end of the continuum is the instructive stance. In this stance, mentors typically adopt the attitude and behaviors of instructional specialist. Here they transfer their knowledge and experiences to their novice teacher. Mentors might provide specific information regarding school policy, district curriculum, parent teacher conferencing, and specific instructional strategies or methodologies.

In the middle of the continuum of interaction, is the collaborative stance. In this stance mentors adopt the position of co-worker and collaborator. Costa and Garmston (2002) describe a collaborator as a mentor and teacher "working together as equals to achieve goals. Thus, teacher and [mentor] plan, reflect, or problem solve together. Both are learners, offering ideas, listening deeply to one another, and creating new approaches to student-centered outcomes" (p. 12).

At the opposite end of the continuum is the facilitative stance. In this stance, mentors assume the attitude of facilitator. Senge (2006) describes a facilitator as a person whose, "functions include helping people maintain ownership of the process and the outcomes" (p. 229). Mentors provide question prompts and reflective stems during conversations to mediate teachers' thinking. They allow teachers to make connections between problems and potential solutions, thus empowering teachers with ownership of the problem-solving process.

HOW TO USE MENTOR STANCES

The mentor stances are intended to be used during conference conversations with teachers. Lipton and Wellman (2002) share how "versatility across this continuum provides [mentors] with options for response patterns that are developmentally and situational appropriate" (p. 20). The most effective mentors are able to move through the instructive, collaborative, and facilitative stances easily and instinctively to get the most out of their teachers.

The stances are not meant to be used in isolation but rather in conjunction with each other. During a conferencing conversation, the mentor makes a decision as to what stance to adopt in order to better meet the needs of the teacher. Most often, all three stances are used together depending on where the teacher is developmentally within the transformational learning stages.

Many novice teachers struggle with generating solutions and ideas of their own during the role and practice focused transformational learning stages. Teachers are often stuck and have no idea what steps to take next. Therefore, the instructive stance can provide a way for mentors to further teacher growth by sharing specific strategies. During the instructive stance, the mentor is doing most of the talking. In this stance the mentor uses the pronoun "I" to indicate she is sharing a particular support strategy. A mentor might suggest several options for the teacher to select from by stating, "Here are three strategies that I have seen work in other teachers' classrooms." In this stance, the mentor might suggest resources for the teacher to try.

In order to maintain a trusting relationship and promote teachers as independent problem solvers and thinkers, mentors should employ the collaborative stance following the use of the instructive stance. A mentor should never conclude a conversation by giving directions on what the teacher should fix and how she should fix it. The teacher needs to have input as well as ownership of solutions in order for change to occur.

During the collaborative stance, the teacher and mentor are doing equal talking and problem solving. The pair is generating ideas and solutions together. The pronoun "we" is often used by the mentor to establish a collaborative tone. A mentor might state, "Let's find a spot on your table where we can analyze your student work together and identify which of the three strategies will work best for your students."

During the facilitative stance, the mentor uses mediational questions to guide the conversation and prompt the teacher's thinking. In this stance, the teacher is doing the majority of the talking. The pronoun "you" is often used by the mentor to help reinforce the teacher's ownership of the conversation. A mentor might state, "It seems that you really value your students. How important will the strategy you selected be to the success of your students?" Once teachers transition into the learner focused transformational learning stage, mentors use the facilitative stance more frequently.

MENTOR STANCES IN ACTION

In this scenario, Pam, the mentor, is meeting with Sue, a beginning teacher, who is having difficulty with designing lessons. Sue is concerned that her lessons are not what her principal expects and they are not engaging for her students. Below is the conversation between Pam and Sue in which Pam moves from the instructive to collaborative and then finally to the facilitative stance.

Pam initiates the conversation by stating, "Last time we met you were going to meet with your principal about your lesson design. How did that go?"

Sue replies, "Not so hot. My principal said my lessons were cumbersome and showed a lack of design. I am not sure what he meant by that. I am very frustrated. I spent a whole weekend just writing lessons for the week!"

Pam initiates the instructive stance by responding, "It sounds like you are very concerned about meeting your principal's expectations and those of your students. Would it help to see some examples of lesson plans that meet your principal's expectations?"

"It sure would."

"This time of year, it seems like all of our teachers are really concerned with lesson design. So I came prepared with examples of lesson plans. Why don't we spend some time looking at these and then compare them to your lesson plans to look for areas of improvement?"

"Okay. At least now I can see what my principal means by well-designed lessons," Sue states.

"From talking to your principal about what he expects for all teachers on his campus, he is looking for the Essential Elements of Instruction (EEI). Are you familiar with that lesson structure?"

"Well I have heard of EEI before but I never knew that it pertained to writing lesson plans. I feel so lost," Sue shares.

Pam utilizes the instructive stance to briefly describe and teach the basic components of EEI to Sue. She then arranges the sample lessons on the table before them and moves into the collaborative stance. "Let's look at these sample lessons together and describe what we see that represents the EEI." Together the pair analyzes the sample lessons and identifies key components of the lesson.

"I see that the all of teachers have included modeling in their lesson plans," observes Sue.

"I see that all of the teachers have listed ways they will check for understanding throughout the lesson plan," notes Pam.

Once the pair has examined the sample lesson plans and identified the key components, Pam shifts into the facilitative stance. "When you compare your lesson plans to the sample plans we just looked at, what do you see?"

Sue pauses for a moment and says, "I see that I do not have modeling written into my lesson plans at all. It is something that I know I need to do, so I don't feel I need to write it down all of the time in my plans. I just do it."

"When you think back to your best lessons, did you include modeling as a component? When you think back to your least successful lessons, did you include modeling as a component?" Pam questions.

"Well my best lessons did have modeling written into them. And I guess if I have to admit it, my lessons that did not go so well did not. Wow, I know I intended to model, but I guess that I just don't leave myself enough time during the lesson if I don't write it in the plan," Sue admits.

Pam asks several further facilitative questions during the rest of the conversation to help guide Sue's thinking, "If modeling is relevant to the success of your lesson, is it important to have that component included in your plans? If your principal has said that the samples we looked at are exemplar lessons, and they all contain modeling, is that something that you want to make sure you include in your lesson design? How are you going to continue to develop well designed lessons?"

NOTES FOR IMPLEMENTATION

The mentor stances are one of the foundation blocks for transforming teacher practice. However, if a trusting relationship is not established first, then the stances can often be misinterpreted by teachers. The stances must also be used in conjunction with each other. The instructive stance is often misused in isolation. Teachers do not like to be told what to do and how to do it. They do not like to be told how to fix their problems. However, a suggested strategy that is followed by collaborative development for implementation and facilitative questions can produce powerful changes within teachers.

Mentors use the instructive stance more prevalently at the beginning of the year. A mentor would not ask mediating questions to the novice teacher if they were not developmentally ready for the questions or if there is no specific point to asking the question. For example, a mentor would not respond to a teacher asking, "Where is the copy room?" with "Well how do you think you might find the copy room?"

The instructive stance is natural for mentors who are new to the role of mentoring because they are used to instructing students. New mentors should focus on becoming more proficient at the collaborative stance and then move toward the facilitative stance. Like any other skill set, the mentor stances take time to develop and become proficient at using.

PURPOSE FOR MENTOR ROLES

Mentor programs and coaching models have identified and labeled roles for mentors as a way to clearly communicate how mentors and coaches support teachers. Killion and Harrison (2006), "believe the success of a coaching program depends on making smart decisions about the roles of coaches" (p. 28). It is important to label and define roles so that there is consistency in how the roles are implemented.

When working with teachers, mentors often adopt various roles to help build a professional growth environment grounded in inquiry and problem solving. The mentor roles are intended to be utilized by mentors to help support teachers and transform their practice. They are important to the success of the teacher due to the functional differences of each role. Killion and Harrison (2006) have identified four specific reasons why mentor roles are important to the success and support of novice teachers. Mentor roles are important because they:

1. Define mentor job expectations

2. Frame mentor professional development

3. Help mentor consider how best to serve teachers

4. Provide a measure of effectiveness

Establishing mentor roles provides a concise description of how mentors will assist in the development of novice teachers. It is necessary that all stakeholders of the induction program have an appreciation of the work that mentors do. A clear understanding of how the mentor is expected to support teachers is important to the success of any induction program.

Mentors use the roles to personally identify where they need to grow professionally. Innately most mentors are great resources but often need to develop their understanding and fine-tune their skills of the other support roles. Those providing professional development for mentors can create learning events that enhance their growth towards the mentor roles.

In preparation for meeting with a teacher, a mentor considers how to best meet the needs of her teacher. The mentor reflects upon the previous meeting and develops strategies to successfully work with the teacher. Often during a conversation, an evident need for a specific role might present itself and the mentor may adopt a particular role in order to solve a problem.

Those who are evaluating mentors also utilize the roles to determine how mentors are meeting the needs of teachers. Mentors who spend too much time in one role are not meeting the development needs of novice teachers and are not supporting their growth. Mentors also self-evaluate their effectiveness to determine where they need to continue to grow professionally.

DESCRIPTION OF MENTOR ROLES

Each of the 12 mentor roles can be used to provide support to teachers and are an integral part to managing transformational learning through transformative assessment. These roles can stand alone or can be used in conjunction with each other because each role serves a different function. The roles are not hierarchical or intended to be used sequentially. The roles we have identified as being most critical to novice teacher success are *advocate, catalyst, collaborator, data collector, demonstrator, facilitator, instructor, leader, learner, problem solver, resource provider*, and *trusted listener*.

An *advocate* is somebody who acts or intercedes on behalf of another. A mentor adopts this role to help beginning teachers when she feels that the teacher cannot act on their own behalf. This role is most often used at the beginning of the school year during conversations with teachers or administrators. A mentor might have a conversation with administrators to support supplies and materials that a novice teacher needs in order to be successful with students.

A *catalyst* is somebody who initiates action or accelerates the rate of practice. A mentor adopts the role of catalyst when the teacher is perhaps hesitant or unsure about beginning a specific course of action. This mentor role is most often used during collaborative conferences between the mentor and teacher. When the mentor senses that a teacher is tentative about starting a plan of action or change initiative, she channels the teacher's energy toward that new undertaking.

A *collaborator* is somebody who works with others to achieve goals. A mentor adopts the role of collaborator when the teacher asks for assistance and is willing to cocreate instructional matter for the classroom. This mentor role is most often used to develop instructional materials, lesson plans, or analyze student work.

A *data collector* is somebody who collects observable student and teacher behaviors. A mentor adopts the role of data collector during classroom observations as part of the Conference Data Conference (CDC) Cycle. It is important that mentors adopt the role of data collector during observations so that they collect observable student and teacher behaviors only and do not place judgmental remarks on data collection tools.

A *demonstrator* is somebody who models effective classroom and instructional practices. A mentor adopts the role of demonstrator when the teacher needs a visual example of a specific instructional strategy. This strategy is most effective when the mentor and teacher have a trusting relationship and the teacher invites the mentor to model a lesson. The teacher should observe the mentor and use data collection tools to capture evidence of the desired behaviors.

A *facilitator* is someone who encourages others to find their own solutions to problems or tasks. A mentor adopts this role when the teacher is ready to problem solve on her own but still needs guidance towards solutions. The mentor uses mediational questions to prompt the novice teacher's thinking.

An *instructor* is somebody who teaches others, content, a process, or a practical skill. This role is used when teachers cannot find a solution to a problem or challenge. It is used primarily to assist novice teachers who do not yet have experiences from which to draw upon. Mentors should be conservative in using this role as it can prevent teachers from moving toward independence. If we are always providing the answers to problems, then teachers do not have to find solutions on their own.

A *leader* is somebody who influences others toward a specific direction during a change process. As mentors transition through their own transformational learning stages, the role of leader emerges. Mentors begin to see themselves influencing their novice teachers as well as the system in which they work. Self-recognition of this role empowers mentors to continue to make a difference.

A *learner* is somebody who is continuously gaining skills or knowledge to improve practice. Effective mentors continue to present themselves as lifelong learners. They continue to seek ways to grow professionally in order to understand how to better meet the needs of their teachers. As learners, mentors model how to be reflective practitioners and how to keep current in skill and knowledge.

A *problem solver* is somebody who finds solutions to challenging situations. In this role, mentors actively pursue answers to difficult challenges and issues their teachers are facing. A mentor assumes this role when the teacher cannot determine a resolution on his own. This role is utilized best in the collaborative stance where mentor and teacher are working together.

A *resource provider* is somebody who can be used as a source of help or information. In this role the mentor shares resources that the teacher has asked for and will help support her. Resources can be books, lesson ideas, articles, websites, a personal contact, or another teacher. This role is used throughout all of the transformational learning stages.

A *trusted listener* is somebody who respects confidentiality and listens attentively. When meeting the teacher for the first time, the mentor begins to build trust by listening and assuring that all conversations are confidential. This role is essential to the development of the relationship necessary for transformational learning.

HOW TO USE MENTOR ROLES

Depending on the needs of the teacher, the mentor determines which role would best help to accelerate the teacher's practice. Mentors implement different roles for different purposes. For example, if a teacher is having difficulty seeing what a particular instructional strategy might look like, the mentor might adopt the role of demonstrator in order to model a particular instructional strategy or skill. Often during a conversation, several of the roles are used in conjunction with each other.

A mentor who is flexible in the use of the roles can sense the needs of the teacher and adopt the most appropriate roles to move a teacher through the ascending stages of transformational learning. If mentors remain in one support role, they will not provide differentiated support to meet the varying needs of their beginning teachers. Mentors who use these roles effectively are more credible with teachers and administrators, and that enhances the trusting relationship.

NOTES FOR IMPLEMENTATION

The mentor roles are essential to helping teachers transform their practice and require time for mentors to become proficient. Mentors should focus on developing one role at a time. Those who provide support to mentors should center professional development on the skills and knowledge of the mentor roles.

PURPOSE FOR MENTOR LANGUAGE

Using specific mentor language allows mentors to direct and focus the conversations with novice teachers. Knowing which prompt to use in specific situations will make a difference not only in conversations but in the mentoring relationship. Being able to direct and focus conversations also accelerates the practices of the teachers.

DESCRIPTION OF MENTOR LANGUAGE

There are eight different mentor language components we have adopted as essential for accelerating teacher practice and transformational learning. The components consist of *questioning prompts* including probing questions, clarifying questions, and mediational questions; *paraphrasing prompts* including acknowledging, summarizing and organizing, and shifting conceptual focus; and *ways of communication* including teachable moments and nonjudgmental language.

Questioning prompts are intended to further the conversation between mentor and teacher. Mentors should use three types of questions to further the development of teachers: probing questions, clarifying questions, and mediational questions.

Clarifying questions are asked to further the mentor's understanding. These types of questions convey to the teacher that the mentor is paying attention but is unclear about what was said.

Probing questions are asked to help the teacher think more deeply about the concerns and challenges present. These questions are intended to guide the responder to search for specificity where there are generalizations.

Mediational questions as described by Costa and Garmston (2002) are "intentionally designed to engage and transform the other person's thinking and perspective" (p. 86). The questions help guide the responder to clearer understanding of the issues and challenges at hand.

HOW TO USE MENTOR LANGUAGE: QUESTIONING PROMPTS

Clarifying questions should be asked as basic questions of fact. Questions should be straightforward and easy for the responder to answer. When asking clarifying questions, mentors need to be careful that they are not seeking information that is irrelevant to the conversation. Mentors should not be seeking for the teacher to come to a new depth of understanding. Mentors might ask a clarifying question if they need more information, want to discover the intent behind a statement, or want to guide the teacher toward connecting concepts they have presented. Examples include

- Can you tell me more about . . . ?
- Is there more . . . ?

- Can you give me an example so I can better understand . . .?
- Are you suggesting . . .?
- What do you mean when you say . . .?

Probing questions are useful in moving teachers from reaction to reflection thus creating a paradigm shift and generating transformational learning. These types of questions are generally asked after a sweeping statement. For example, a teacher might say, "All the students are out of control in my classroom," and the mentor might respond by asking, "Can you think of someone who is not out of control?"

Mentors should be patient and wait for an answer when they ask probing questions. Give teachers adequate time to respond. If teachers respond too quickly, they are reacting versus reflecting. Mentors should ask probing questions in response to generalizations stated by the teacher. For example, a teacher might state, "My students are unmanageable!" A mentor might respond with the following probing question, "Is it all students? Is there a specific area in your classroom that seems more unmanageable than the rest?"

Mentors ask mediational questions most often when using the facilitative stance in order to help teachers become independent problem solvers and thinkers. Answers to these types of questions are intended to help responders synthesize and evaluate and therefore require a higher cognition level. Some examples:

- What would happen if . . .?
- What would it look like to . . .?
- What do you think about . . .?
- What's another way you could . . .?
- How will that impact . . .?
- What criteria could be used to . . .?
- How was . . . different from . . .?
- What's another way you might . . .?
- What might you see happening in your classroom if . . .?

NOTES FOR IMPLEMENTATION

Using the three questioning prompts depends on the situation and the need of the mentor to seek additional information. It is often easy to understand what teachers are saying, and yet mentors finds themselves in situations where they thought what they heard was not what was said. It is during this time that mentors need to ask clarifying questions. When the mentor asks the teacher, "Could you explain to me what you meant when you said . . .?," the teacher has the opportunity to clarify the comment and provide a deeper understanding for the mentor.

When teachers use generalizations such as "the students," it is important for the mentors to ask probing questions such as, "Which students specifically?," in order to get the teachers to be more focused in their conversations. When the conversation is specific rather than generalized, it becomes easier to solve problems.

Mediational questions are used by mentors to push the thinking of the teacher forward. It is easy to say, "Here is my grading scale." But when a mentor asks, "What criteria did you use to determine each scale?" the teacher has to analyze her own thinking and therefore reach a high cognitive level. The teacher at this point might decide the grading scale being used did not align with the intended outcomes and decide to use a rubric instead.

Paraphrasing prompts help mentors establish trusting relationships with their teachers because it communicates that they are listening to the speakers. This type of mentor language works in conjunction with questions. Paraphrasing following questioning helps to establish a safe environment. It also helps the speaker hear again what it is that she has said and therefore make deeper connections. The three types of paraphrasing prompts that Costa and Garmston (2002) suggest mentors use are *acknowledging, summarizing and organizing,* and *shifting conceptual focus.*

Acknowledging paraphrase is a brief statement reflecting on what was said in the listener's words. Using this type of paraphrase indicates that the mentor has heard the teacher and can relate to what the teacher is communicating.

Summarizing and organizing paraphrase is a statement revealing themes and categories that connect to the speaker's words. This type of paraphrase is effective in helping teachers make connections to a variety of issues and topics they may be sharing.

Shifting conceptual focus paraphrase is a statement where the mentor helps beginning teachers sort through their thoughts. This type of paraphrase helps teachers shift their thinking. For example, if the teacher is focused on the big picture, the mentor may use this type of paraphrase to help narrow the teacher's thoughts and ideas. In contrast, if a teacher has a very narrow focus, a mentor may use this type of paraphrase to broaden her perspective.

HOW TO USE MENTOR LANGUAGE: PARAPHRASING PROMPTS

Acknowledging paraphrase also helps clarify any misunderstandings or misinterpretations that the mentor may have about what the speaker has said. One way to think about this type of paraphrasing is of a mirror that reflects thinking. Examples of acknowledging paraphrase prompts:

- You're concerned about . . .
- You would like to see . . .
- You're pleased with . . .
- We're feeling badly about . . .

- You're trying to figure out . . .
- You know it can be . . .

One way to think of *summarizing and organizing paraphrase* is a set of kitchen containers. Ideas shared are separated and organized into meaningful categories. Some examples include:

- So you are concerned about several issues here. One is . . . another is . . .
- You have two goals here; one is . . . and the other is . . .
- So on the one hand . . . , on the other hand . . .
- There seem to be three themes: (1) . . . , (2) . . . , and (3) . . .
- So, we have a list of ideas here. They are . . .

Shifting conceptual focus paraphrase helps teachers move to a lower logical level when abstractions and concepts need a concrete description and higher logical level when concepts, goals, values, and assumptions are named. A way to think about this type of paraphrase is steps or an elevator. Some examples include:

- So . . . might include . . .
- So a major goal here is . . .
- So a . . . here is . . .
- So a value here is . . .
- So an assumption is . . .
- So a belief here is . . .
- So a concept here is . . .
- So an intention here is . . .
- So a perspective is . . .

NOTES FOR IMPLEMENTATION

Costa and Garmston (2002) state that "to structure an effective paraphrase, begin by carefully listening and observing to calibrate the content and emotion of the speaker" (p. 80). Mentors should use voice inflections and body language to signal they are about to paraphrase. This helps initiate collaboration between the mentor and teacher.

Mentors should avoid using the first-person pronoun "I" when paraphrasing. For example, "What I think I hear you saying . . . ." The "I" transfers emphasis from the teacher to the mentor and suggests that the mentor is now directing the conversation instead of the teacher. Instead, the mentor should use a paraphrasing prompt to help focus the conversation on what the teacher is saying and not on what the mentor thinks the teacher has said.

Using the various acknowledging, summarizing and organizing, or shifting conceptual focus prompts are dependent on situational circumstances within a collaborative conversation. Extracting meaning from teachers allows mentors to move the conversation to a different level and allows mentors and teachers to transform their practice.

Ways of communication is the third component of mentor language we have identified as essential for supporting novice teachers. How a mentor communicates with a teacher is critical to building the trusting relationship necessary for moving practice forward. There are two specific modes of communication a mentor should consider when working with a teacher: *teachable moments* and *nonjudgmental Language*.

Teachable Moments are opportunities for mentors to share insight with their teachers. These moments are unplanned and spontaneously arise in the moment.

Nonjudgmental Language is a manner in which mentors communicate with teachers based on evidence and not on personal opinion. Mentors who use this type of language increase the level of trust with their beginning teachers because they are communicating in a non-evaluative way.

HOW TO USE MENTOR LANGUAGE: *WAYS OF COMMUNICATION*

A mentor typically identifies a teachable moment when the novice teacher introduces an entry point of conversation. The mentor recognizes this as an ideal chance to convey an idea that will add to the teacher's skill or knowledge level. Mentors should not use teachable moments as the primary way to convey information to the teachers with whom they work but rather as ways to collaborate and motivate teachers. Some examples of teachable moment prompts mentors might use:

- One thing to consider is . . .
- I have seen other teachers do . . .
- Some other teachers have tried . . .
- One thing to keep in mind is . . .
- It can be helpful to . . .
- From my experience, I have noticed . . .
- There are a number of approaches . . .
- If you are interested in . . . then it is important to think about . . .

The New Teacher Center at the University of California, Santa Cruz (2004) states that nonjudgmental language "helps to build trust, promotes an internal locus of control, encourages self-assessment, develops beginning teacher autonomy, and fosters risk-taking" (p. 20). Some examples of prompts mentors can use to initiate responses that are nonjudgmental:

- When you did . . . the students responded by . . .
- You have several strategies to try. It'll be exciting to see which one works for you.

- How do you feel the lesson went today?
- What part did you have in the success of the lesson?
- I'm interested in hearing more about . . .

NOTES FOR IMPLEMENTATION

Building trust is essential when working with teachers. How the mentor communicates and conveys a trusting relationship is heavily dependent on how the mentor communicates with the teacher. Using teachable moments as a means of collaboration and motivation, rather than a means of sharing expert advice, promotes a collaborative, trusting relationship.

Using nonjudgmental language during the conversation with the teacher is challenging at first for the mentor during their *role focused stage* of transformational learning. It is important for the mentor to focus on evidence rather than personal opinion during conversations with the teacher. This builds a trusting relationship and serves as the foundation for their future work together.

NOTES FOR IMPLEMENTING FOUNDATIONS FOR MENTORING

As mentors become more skillful in implementing mentor stances, mentor roles, and mentor language, it becomes easier for them to support their teachers through the transformational learning stages. These skill sets will assist the mentor as they introduce the various tools that the teachers and mentors will use throughout the year and enhance the weekly, collaborative conversations between the mentor and the teacher. Mentors will become more proficient in using the foundations of mentoring while transforming their own learning from role focused to practice focused and ultimately learner focused.

Differences in programs will determine not only the amount of time a mentor meets with a teacher, but also the amount of professional development provided for mentors to acquire each of the above skill sets. We suggest that mentors begin with the knowledge and practice of mentor stances and proceed through mentor roles and mentor language as time permits.

4

Conference Data Conference (CDC) Journal Record

PURPOSE FOR THE CDC JOURNAL RECORD

The *Conference Data Conference (CDC) Journal Record* is one of the most important tools for transforming teacher practice. This tool is used to facilitate and record each conversation between the teacher and the mentor during the planning and reflective conferences of the CDC Cycle.

The mentor can facilitate effective goal setting and use of time by guiding the dialogue through the five sections of the CDC Journal Record. The CDC Journal Record allows the mentor the opportunity to keep the conversation focused and on target by recording what was said during the conference. It is important for the teacher, the mentor, and the administrator to recognize the confidentiality of all CDC Journal Records. These journal records are only to be shared between the teacher and the mentor. No one else will have access to the information or to the tool itself including the administrators at the site or district level. Trust between the mentor and the teacher is enhanced due to the confidentiality of the journal records and the conversations.

The CDC Journal Record is one of the key components of the mentoring relationship between the teacher and the mentor as the journal record provides documentation of the conversation. The journal record also allows the mentor and the teacher the opportunity to review progress over time through reflection.

There are six basic reasons for the mentor to use the CDC Journal Record.

1. To help the mentor focus and clarify the conversation with the teacher

2. To track ongoing data the mentor is collecting for the teacher

3. To identify possible solutions, actions, and next steps for the teacher

4. To keep the mentor and the teacher accountable during their meeting time

5. To use as a tool for reflection

6. To follow the CDC Cycle of conferencing

DESCRIPTION OF THE CDC JOURNAL RECORD

The CDC Journal Record can be used during both the planning and reflective conference. The professional teacher standards are listed on the side of the journal to remind the mentor and the teacher of their current goal as well as providing a focus for future growth. The sample journal record that follows uses professional teacher standards (Horn & Metler-Armijo, 2010): (1) managing the learning environments, (2) designing and planning instruction, (3) facilitating student learning, and (4) assessing student learning. Any state standards or professional teacher standards that are the foundation of a program can be used.

HOW TO USE THE CDC JOURNAL RECORD DURING THE PLANNING CONFERENCE

The CDC Journal Record has five basic sections. The mentor is able to build trust by listening and recording what the teacher is saying throughout the entire process. As stated by Moir and Gless (2002), "Begin by encouraging your beginning teachers to share recent examples of successful practices." Therefore, the focus in Section 1: Success is on classroom accomplishments. The conversation begins by the mentor asking the teacher questions such as, "What is going well in the classroom?" or "How would you describe the successes in your classroom?" The teacher responds by describing what successes are happening in the classroom (Figure 4.1).

Figure 4.1	Conference Data Conference Journal Record

Teacher: _Bryce_   **Mentor:** _Lori_

Grade/Subject Area: _9th English_ **School:** _Horizon HS_ **Date:** _8/14_ **Time:** _9 AM_

Professional Teacher Standards	1 Success:	2 Focus:
Standard 1: Managing the Learning Environment O 1. Establishes expectations for student behavior O 2. Establishes and maintains a respectful and nurturing learning environment O 3. Promotes student responsibilities and self-discipline O 4. Recognizes and values differences among individuals O 5. Facilitates collaboration among learners O 6. Establishes an environment for student success O 7. Utilizes active participation strategies ⊖ 8. Arranges and manages the classroom environment for student success	Samuel talked about the success of his lesson plan. He likes the way he presented the grammar section using cooperative groups.	While Samuel's lessons are going well, the students are not quiet or productive during the cooperative group time. He doesn't know if it is just one group or all of them. He is also concerned that maybe his lessons are not as well planned as he thought since the students are not completing the assignment.

Standard 2: Designing and Planning Instruction O 1. Utilizes academic standards to plan instruction O 2. Utilizes student assessments to plan instruction O 3. Plans instruction to meet the diverse needs of learners O 4. Links learning to students' prior knowledge and experiences O 5. Plans short term learning objectives and long term curriculum goals O 6. Includes a variety of methods in instructional plans O 7. Includes a variety of technology, materials, and resources in instructional planning O 8. Develops learning experiences that are developmentally appropriate for learners O 9. Develops learning experiences that address the cognitive levels of learners O 10. Plans for experiences that align with learning objectives that accurately represent content

3 (Data To Be Collected) or Data Shared:

During cooperative groups, data will be collected to see which group(s) is on and off task. On task = students working on assignment while in group and off task = students not working on assignment while in group

(Data Tool Selected) or Data-Based Reflection:

On-Task/Off-Task Seating Chart

Standard 3: Facilitating Student Learning O 1. Utilizes a lesson plan to guide student learning O 2. Communicates high expectations for learning O 3. Demonstrates skills, knowledge, and thinking processes O 4. Uses correct grammar, mechanics, and developmentally appropriate language to communicate with learners O 5. Uses instructional strategies that are appropriate to the developmental levels of learners O 6. Uses strategies to address the diverse needs of learners O 7. Promotes critical thinking O 8. Makes connections between learning and real life situations O 9. Uses a variety of instructional strategies to engage learners O 10. Uses instructional time to maximize learning O 11. Ensures students apply new knowledge and skills O 12. Uses technology and instructional resources	4 Teacher Action: • Provide the names of students in cooperative groups • Provide lesson plan prior to observation (by 8/19)	5 Mentor Action: • Complete room arrangement on On-Task/Off-Task Seating Chart • Compare lesson plan with school site lesson plan template

Standard 4: Assessing Student Learning O 1. Aligns formal and informal assessments to instruction O 2. Designs student assessments to measure progress O 3. Promotes student self assessment O 4. Maintains records of student performance and respects privacy of student records O 5. Communicates growth progress to students and parents

PTG Goal: Standard 1.8- Arranges and manages the classroom environment for student success	**Next Conference/Observation Date:** 8/21 to collect on-task/off-task data	**Focus:** Effective classroom management strategies while students are in cooperative groups

Submit copy to: Mentor and Teacher

Section 2 is labeled Focus. After the discussion of classroom success, the focus of attention is on challenges and concerns that have arisen. As the teacher responds to the question from the mentor regarding challenges or concerns, the mentor can use clarifying questions to reinforce active listening and an accurate understanding of the teacher's statements. An example of a clarifying question is, "What do you mean when you say . . .?" The concerns during a planning conference at the beginning of the year begin to focus around classroom management, lesson plans, or lessons taught. As the conversation proceeds, a mentor might ask the teacher some additional questions to focus on specific issues such as:

- What can you tell me about your classroom management plan?
- What can you tell me about this lesson and its context?
- How does the lesson address academic standards?
- Where does this lesson fit in the curriculum?
- What has led up to this lesson?
- How does this lesson meet your students' needs?

As the conversation proceeds, the teacher identifies an area of focus that will move her practice forward. At this point, the mentor might see the opportunity to assist the teacher by focusing on codeveloping a lesson, collaborating on a problem to be solved, collecting resources, or determining which data collection tool should be used during a classroom observation. The job of the mentor is to collaborate and guide the teacher toward one or two areas of focus. The determined area of focus is recorded in the section.

Section 3 is used to discuss data. It may or may not be used during the planning conference. It depends on the area of focus. This section is used if the purpose of the conversation is data focused. Examples include collecting data during classroom observations, analyzing student formative assessments, or examining student summative assessments. This section can also be left blank. This midsection is to be used as the mentor and teacher deem appropriate for the discussion of any type of data to be collected or a data tool that is to be selected.

The following example is used if the area of focus that emerges during the planning conference is a classroom observation. The mentor will use the midsection of the CDC Journal Record to discuss with the teacher what kind of data is to be collected. It is important that the teacher determines what data will be collected by the mentor during the observation. The terms used during the discussion need to be defined. One example is time on task. What the teacher thinks is time on task may be different from what the mentor thinks, so it is important that the terms and type of data to be collected are clearly understood by both. Some of the questions a mentor might ask would include the following:

- What will we document during the classroom observation?
- What data can I collect during my observation to support your learning and lesson implementation?

- Can we agree on what data will be collected?
- Are there any data terms that need to be defined?

After determining and defining the data to be collected, Section 3: Data to Be Collected is circled (Figure 4.1) in the midsection panel on the CDC Journal Record and the information is recorded. The mentor selects an appropriate tool for the type of classroom data tool that will be collected during the observation, circles Data Tool in the midsection panel, and writes the name of the tool.

Teacher's Action is Section 4. What are the teacher's responsibilities between now and the classroom observation or the next meeting? The basic question to be answered is, "How will you get there?" The main goal in Section 4 is to synthesize the teachers' learning and set the teacher's actions. The teacher's actions are determined and recorded. The teacher's focus may be instructional strategies, student grouping, assessment, curriculum, or methodology. Dependent on the discussion within the previous sections, some questions the mentor may ask include:

- What do you need to do before our next meeting?
- Is there a lesson template that you are to follow?
- How will your students know your expectations?
- How do the instructional strategies and resources support the goals of the lesson?
- How will you promote critical thinking, use technology, or make adjustments for special needs students?
- How will you assess the students' learning?

Section 5 is labeled Mentor's Action. The mentor's responsibilities will be defined through guided questions and suggestions. The main question the mentor asks is, "What can I do to assist you?" How the mentor can support the work of the teacher will be recorded. Some examples might be for the mentor to collect resources for the teacher, to plan collaboratively, or to model a lesson. The roles of the teacher and the mentor are clarified. (Costa & Garmston, 2002)

The mentor will summarize the conversation after recording the conversation through the sections and the data midsection. As part of the closure activity, the mentor will restate the teacher's professional growth goal which is based on one of the specific professional teacher standards. The mentor and the teacher will also set the next meeting date and the mentor will restate the focus of their continued work together for the next conference. The CDC Journal Record is printed on no carbon required (NCR) paper so that the mentor and teacher can each have a copy after every conference.

CDC JOURNAL RECORD TOOL IN ACTION

The following mentor tool is a sample planning conference using the CDC Journal Record. Sue is a first year teacher at Desert Moon School. She is a

37-year-old "midcareer changer" who recently moved to Arizona. In her first meeting with Sally, her mentor, Sue discussed her classroom management plan. Sally began the conference by asking Sue to identify what has been working well in the classroom since their last meeting. Sue is pleased with the success of her classroom management plan (Section 1). As their conversation progressed, Sue expressed concern about her students having a difficult time in reading. Some of them had not completed the assignments and were confused. Others finished early and didn't have anything else to do (Section 2). The conversation led to the need to collect data regarding the students' achievement in reading. Sally knew that the district had a reading assessment that included each student's achievement data. Since Sue did not have any other data assessments, she decided to use the District Reading Assessment (DRA) as the data tool so she could review each student's reading achievement assessments (Section 3). Sue will get a copy of the DRA and review the data for the class as a whole and for the individual student needs in reading (Section 4). Sally will bring a template to organize the reading data (Section 5). The conference is closed by discussing the Professional Teacher Growth (PTG) plan, setting the next conference date, and agreeing on the focus of the next meeting (Figure 4.2).

HOW TO USE THE CDC JOURNAL RECORD DURING THE REFLECTIVE CONFERENCE

The mentor begins a new journal record for the reflective conference using the previous CDC Journal Record as a guide. The types of questions that are asked for Section 1 during a reflective conference are based on the area of focus from the last CDC Journal Record. If the conference is after a classroom observation, the mentor would ask the teacher, "What successes were evident in the lesson you taught?" If the area of focus was classroom management, a question might be, "What success did you have with your classroom management plan this week?" The types of questions a mentor asks during this time will focus on success in the classroom based on the decisions made using the previous CDC Journal Record during the planning conference.

The focus on any concerns the teacher has in regard to what is happening in the classroom is recorded in Section 2. The mentor might ask, "What challenges were evident in the lesson?" or "Can you identify an area of focus based on the data?" if the reflective conference occurs after a classroom observation. If the focus is on classroom management, the question might be, "What part of the classroom management plan is an area of concern for you?" The types of questions a mentor asks during this time will focus on concerns in the classroom based on what was said during Section 1.

Section 3 is used when the discussion centers on data. If there is data to be shared and there is a need to reflect on that data, the mentor will use

Figure 4.2	Sample Planning Conference: Conference Data Conference Journal Record

Teacher: _Sue_   **Mentor:** _Sally_

Grade/Subject Area: _5th Reading_ **School:** _Desert Moon_ **Date:** _9/14_ **Time:** _9 AM_

Professional Teacher Standards	
Professional Teacher Standards **Standard 1: Managing the Learning Environment** O 1. Establishes expectations for student behavior O 2. Establishes and maintains a respectful and nurturing learning environment O 3. Promotes student responsibilities and self-discipline O 4. Recognizes and values differences among individuals O 5. Facilitates collaboration among learners O 6. Establishes an environment for student success O 7. Utilizes active participation strategies O 8. Arranges and manages the classroom environment for student success **Standard 2: Designing and Planning Instruction** O 1. Utilizes academic standards to plan instruction Ɵ 2. Utilizes student assessments to plan instruction O 3. Plans instruction to meet the diverse needs of learners O 4. Links learning to students' prior knowledge and experiences O 5. Plans short term learning objectives and long term curriculum goals O 6. Includes a variety of methods in instructional plans O 7. Includes a variety of technology, materials, and resources in instructional planning O 8. Develops learning experiences that are developmentally appropriate for learners O 9. Develops learning experiences that address the cognitive levels of learners O 10. Plans for experiences that align with learning objectives that accurately represent content. **Standard 3: Facilitating Student Learning** O 1. Utilizes a lesson plan to guide student learning O 2. Communicates high expectations for learning O 3. Demonstrates skills, knowledge, and thinking processes O 4. Uses correct grammar, mechanics, and developmentally appropriate language to communicate with learners O 5. Uses instructional strategies that are appropriate to the developmental levels of learners O 6. Uses strategies to address the diverse needs of learners O 7. Promotes critical thinking O 8. Makes connections between learning and real life situations O 9. Uses a variety of instructional strategies to engage learners O 10. Uses instructional time to maximize learning O 11. Ensures students apply new knowledge and skills O 12. Uses technology and instructional resources **Standard 4: Assessing Student Learning** O 1. Aligns formal and informal assessments to instruction O 2. Designs student assessments to measure progress O 3. Promotes student self assessment O 4. Maintains records of student performance and respects privacy of student records O 5. Communicates growth progress to students and parents	**1 Success:** _Sue says that the classroom management plan is working well. The students follow directions easily and complete most of the assignments._ **2 Focus:** _The students are having a difficult time in reading. Some of them are not completing the assignments and are confused. Others finish early and don't have anything else to do._ --- **3 (Data to Be Collected) or Data Shared:** _District Reading Assessment student achievement data for Sue's classroom_ **(Data Tool) or Data-Based Reflection:** _District Reading Assessment (DRA)_ --- **4 Teacher Action:** **5 Mentor Action:** 1. _Get a copy of the District Reading Assessment for the classroom._ 2. _Review the data for the class and the students._ 1. _Bring to Sue a template for organizing classroom data in reading._

PTG Goal: _Standard 2.2 - Utilizes student assessments to plan instruction_	**Next Conference/Observation Date:** _9/22 to review the data from the DRA_	**Focus:** _Reading instruction based on student assessment._

Submit copy to: Mentor and Beginning Teacher

the data midsection to record the data shared with the teacher before proceeding to Section 4. The mentor circles Data Shared in the midsection panel on the CDC Journal Record and the information is recorded. The mentor might ask the following guided questions that will assist the teacher in recognizing patterns and actions based on the focus of the data collection:

- What do you see in the data?
- What observable student or teacher behaviors do you see that show your lesson was successful?
- How did you determine if you students were successful?
- Did all of your students meet your learning objective?
- How do you know if your learning objective was met?

The mentor reinforces the teacher's conversation by identifying data pieces that support the teacher's impressions.

The teacher's ability to reflect on the data shared after the teacher and mentor analyze it is the key to accelerating the teacher's practice. The mentor circles Data-Based Reflection in the midsection panel and records the teacher's responses. As the teacher reflects on the data shared, the mentor asks the following questions:

- What patterns or trends do you see?
- What conclusions can you draw from the data?
- What decisions will you make based on the data analysis?

During Section 4, the mentor guides the conversation towards what will happen next. It is important to synthesize the learning and clarify the teacher's action. Some questions during the reflective conference include:

- What are some next steps?
- How might you support your students in moving forward in their learning?
- What will your next lesson look like?
- What future data would you like to have collected?

The mentor has the opportunity to receive feedback in regard to the mentoring process as well as defining what support the mentor will provide to the teacher during Section 5. Some questions the mentor might ask include:

- What action can I take to assist you?
- What feedback do you have about this process and our work together?
- What could I do as your mentor to support you in accomplishing your next lesson?
- Is there another tool that would give you a clearer picture of your learning goal?

The mentor summarizes the conversation after recording the conversation through the sections and, if used, the data midsection. As part of the closure activity, the mentor will restate the teacher's professional growth goal that is based on one of the specific professional teacher standards. The mentor and the teacher will also set the next meeting date; and the mentor will restate the focus of their continued work together for the next conference. The CDC Journal Record is printed on NCR paper so that the mentor and teacher can each have a copy after every conference.

CDC JOURNAL RECORD TOOL IN ACTION

The following mentor tool is a sample reflective conference using the CDC Journal Record. In her last meeting with Sue, they discussed her need to review her students' reading achievement data. Sally began the conference by asking Sue to identify what has happened since their last meeting. Sue has the district reading assessment. She is ready to discuss the data and is looking forward to grouping her students based on that data (Section 1). As their conversation progressed, Sue expressed concern about organizing the seatwork for students during reading group time. Sue wants her students to be on task during the time they are in their reading group (Section 2). The conversation led to sharing the data regarding the students' achievement in reading. Sally shared her template for organizing reading instruction. Sue felt confident that she could use the template to group her students according to their reading needs (Section 3). Sue will determine the rotation of groups according to skill and decide how often to meet with each. She will determine independent work while the students are not in groups. Sue will also develop leveled reading extensions (Section 4). Sally will find a veteran teacher for both of them to observe who models the strategies Sue is trying to implement. In the future, Sally will collect data on student time on task during independent work (Section 5). The conference is closed by discussing the PTG plan, setting the next observation of a veteran teacher date, and agreeing on the focus of the next meeting (Figure 4.3).

NOTES FOR IMPLEMENTATION

The CDC Journal Record is a primary tool for mentors and teachers introduced during the role focused transformational learning stage for mentors. It is important for the mentor to establish protocols at the beginning of the year that will be used throughout the year. The mentor uses the CDC Journal Record at the initial meeting with the teacher emphasizing the confidentiality of the process. This action provides the foundation for all future conversations. The mentor continues to use a new CDC Journal Record for each future conversation, referring to the previous CDC Journal Record as a reminder of the past focus. The cyclic nature of the process will provide the mentor and the teacher a running record of their conversations and the ability to review their progress throughout the year.

Figure 4.3	Sample Reflective Conference: Conference Data Conference Journal Record

Teacher: _Sue_   **Mentor:** _Sally_

Grade/Subject Area: _5th Reading_ **School:** _Desert Moon_ **Date:** _9/22_ **Time:** _10 AM_

Professional Teacher Standards

Standard 1: Managing the Learning Environment
- O 1. Establishes expectations for student behavior
- O 2. Establishes and maintains a respectful and nurturing learning environment
- O 3. Promotes student responsibilities and self-discipline
- O 4. Recognizes and values differences among individuals
- O 5. Facilitates collaboration among learners
- O 6. Establishes an environment for student success
- O 7. Utilizes active participation strate4gies
- O 8. Arranges and manages the classroom environment for student success

Standard 2: Designing and Planning Instruction
- O 1. Utilizes academic standards to plan instruction
- Ø 2. Utilizes student assessments to plan instruction
- O 3. Plans instruction to meet the diverse needs of learners
- O 4. Links learning to students' prior knowledge and experiences
- O 5. Plans short term learning objectives and long term curriculum goals
- O 6. Includes a variety of methods in instructional plans
- O 7. Includes a variety of technology, materials, and resources in instructional planning
- O 8. Develops learning experiences that are developmentally appropriate for learners
- O 9. Develops learning experiences that address the cognitive needs of learners
- O 10. Plans for experiences that align with learning objectives that accurately represent content

Standard 3: Facilitating Student Learning
- O 1. Utilizes a lesson plan to guide student learning
- O 2. Communicates high expectations for learning
- O 3. Demonstrates skills, knowledge, and thinking processes
- O 4. Uses correct grammar, mechanics, and developmentally appropriate language to communicate with learners
- O 5. Uses instructional strategies that are appropriate to the developmental levels of learners
- O 6. Uses strategies to address the diverse needs of learners
- O 7. Promotes critical thinking
- O 8. Makes connections between learning and real life situations
- O 9. Uses a variety of instructional strategies to engage learners
- O 10. Uses instructional time to maximize learning
- O 11. Ensures students apply new knowledge and skills
- O 12. Uses technology and instructional resources

Standard 4: Assessing Student Learning
- O 1. Aligns formal and informal assessments to instruction
- O 2. Designs student assessments to measure progress
- O 3. Promotes student self assessment
- O 4. Maintains records of student performance and respects privacy of student records
- O 5. Communicates growth progress to students and parents

1 Success:

Sue is ready to use the district reading assessment to assign students to groups based on reading level and reading needs.

2 Focus:

Organizing the seatwork for students during reading group time.
On-task time during reading groups of students.

3 Data to Be Collected or Data Shared:
District Reading Assessment class and individual student data

Data Tool or Data-Based Reflection:

Sue feels confident that she can group her students according to reading needs.

4 Teacher Action:

1. Determine rotation of groups.
2. Determine how often to meet with each.
3. Determine independent work while not in reading groups based on reading needs.
4. Develop leveled reading extensions.

5 Mentor Action:

Assist with:
1. Find a veteran teacher for us to observe that models this strategy.
2. Collect data on student time on task during independent work.

PTG Goal: Standard 2.2 - Utilizes student assessments to plan instruction

Next Conference/Observation Date:
9/27 to observe veteran teacher
Future date: To observe classroom

Focus:
Reading instruction based on student assessment.

Submit copy to: Mentor and Teacher

The mentors have shared several points for consideration:

- My teachers got so familiar with me using the journal record to help guide our conversations that we were able to focus immediately on what worked and get to the root of making change.
- It was very easy for me to see what data had already been collected for my teachers by just looking at my CDC Journal Records.
- The journal records became such a useful tool for me. I could go back through and see what strategies had worked for which teachers and then have a great idea bank for other teachers who were facing similar issues.
- One thing the CDC Journal Record did for me was to help me keep track of how many conferences I had with my teachers. It was also a help during conferences with those reluctant teachers who always came up with excuses for not meeting. I could definitely go back to the journal record and use it to show what we had said our next steps were going to be and when we were going to meet.
- Several times throughout the year, I would pull out my journal records and really see how much I had grown as a mentor. I could see how my use of data tools and my conversations really grew. I could also see how my teachers grew or did not grow. Then I could strategize with my peers to help meet their needs while keeping the name of the teacher confidential.

We have found that mentors who use the CDC Journal Record as a collaborative tool for the purposes given previously in this chapter are able to see transformational growth occur at a more consistent and quicker rate than those mentors who do not utilize this tool. Regardless of program constraints, this tool should be utilized by all mentors each time a mentor meets with a teacher.

Figure 4.4	Conference Data Conference Journal Record

Teacher:_____ **Mentor:**_____

Grade/Subject Area: _____ **School:** _____ **Date:** _____ **Time:** _____

Professional Teacher Standards

Standard 1: Managing the Learning Environment
- O 1. Establishes expectations for student behavior
- O 2. Establishes and maintains a respectful and nurturing learning environment
- O 3. Promotes student responsibilities and self-discipline
- O 4. Recognizes and values differences among individuals
- O 5. Facilitates collaboration among learners
- O 6. Establishes an environment for student success
- O 7 . Utilizes active participation strategies
- O 8. Arranges and manages the classroom environment for student success

Standard 2: Designing and Planning Instruction
- O 1. Utilizes academic standards to plan instruction
- O 2. Utilizes student assessments to plan instruction
- O 3. Plans instruction to meet the diverse needs of learners
- O 4. Links learning to students' prior knowledge and experiences
- O 5. Plans short term learning objectives and long term curriculum goals
- O 6. Includes a variety of methods in instructional plans
- O 7. Includes a variety of technology, materials, and resources in instructional planning
- O 8. Develops learning experiences that are developmentally appropriate for learners
- O 9. Develops learning experiences that address the cognitive levels of learners
- O 10. Plans for experiences that align with learning objectives that accurately represent content.

Standard 3: Facilitating Student Learning
- O 1. Utilizes a lesson plan to guide student learning
- O 2. Communicates high expectations for learning
- O 3. Demonstrates skills, knowledge, and thinking processes
- O 4. Uses correct grammar, mechanics, and developmentally appropriate language to communicate with learners
- O 5. Uses instructional strategies that are appropriate to the developmental levels of learners
- O 6. Uses strategies to address the diverse needs of learners
- O 7. Promotes critical thinking
- O 8. Makes connections between learning and real life situations
- O 9. Uses a variety of instructional strategies to engage learners
- O 10. Uses instructional time to maximize learning
- O 11. Ensures students apply new knowledge and skills
- O 12. Uses technology and instructional resources

Standard 4: Assessing Student Learning
- O 1. Aligns formal and informal assessments to instruction
- O 2. Designs student assessments to measure progress
- O 3. Promotes student self assessment
- O 4. Maintains records of student performance and respects privacy of student records
- O 5. Communicates growth progress to students and parents

Success:

Focus:

Data to Be Collected or Data Shared:

Data Tool Selected or Data-Based Reflection:

Teacher's Action:

Mentor's Support:

PTG Goal:

Next Conference/Observation Date:

Focus:

Submit copy to: Mentor and Teacher

5

Beginning
Conversations

This chapter discusses the importance of building a trusting relationship when mentoring teachers through the Transformational Learning stages. Two sets of tools will be introduced including those designed to help the mentor establish rapport with teachers and develop the relationship necessary to transform practice: *tools for building trust* and *tools for understanding context.*

PURPOSE FOR TOOLS FOR BUILDING TRUST

Confidentiality is the key component to an effective relationship between mentors and the teachers with whom they are assigned. Confidentiality ensures that teachers can share their doubts, struggles, and concerns with their mentors without fear that mentors will repeat what has been said. This helps to create a safe environment where teachers feel comfortable to try new ideas or strategies. In order to establish this bond of trust at the beginning of the mentor and teacher relationship, the mentor introduces two tools: The *Mentor-Teacher Agreement* and the *Breaking Confidentiality Protocol.*

These tools help the teacher, mentor, and teacher supervisor establish a protocol of conversation. Sweeny (2003) has identified a flow of communication that needs to exist between all parties in order to maintain a trusting relationship. Conversations between the mentor and teacher should be open and remain confidential. Conversations between the teacher and teacher supervisor should be open and ongoing. Conversations between the mentor and teacher supervisor must be one way. The supervisor can share information about the teacher, but the mentor must never specifically discuss the mentoring work of their teachers.

DESCRIPTION OF THE TOOLS FOR BUILDING TRUST

The mentor-teacher agreement is a one page document that illustrates the confidentiality expectations between mentor and teacher (Figure 5.1). The agreement indicates that any conversation and documentation that occur are only to be utilized by the mentor and teacher for nonevaluative purposes. It also points out that both the mentor and teacher need to behave in a professional manner. At the bottom of the document is a place for the mentor, teacher, and teacher supervisor to sign, indicating each will honor the confidentiality between teacher and mentor.

The breaking confidentiality protocol (Figure 5.2) is a tool for mentors to use that utilizes the procedures for what to do when a teacher has acted in an unprofessional way and confidentiality needs to be broken. It lists the steps a mentor takes when necessary to inform the teacher supervisor of a teacher's inappropriate actions.

Figure 5.1	Mentor–Teacher Confidentiality Agreement

Mentor-Teacher Confidentiality Agreement

Any anecdotal notes stored in the Mentor's Notebook and personal conversations between Mentor and Teacher are to be used exclusively to support the professional growth of the Teacher. No portion of this notebook is intended for use in the district evaluation program. Any written documentation of discussions is not to be duplicated in any format and is to be destroyed by the Program at the end of three years. The purpose of all documents used in the induction process is to direct Mentor and Teacher discussions. Discussions occur weekly.

This agreement is a binding contract between the Mentor and the Teacher. All conversations and documentation are held in confidence with the exception of unprofessional behavior on the part of either party. Unprofessional behavior can be inappropriate actions or language, danger to self or others, failure to keep scheduled appointments, and/or failure to participate. If unprofessional behavior occurs, the Mentor or the Teacher should report incident to the immediate supervisor.

I support and will honor the terms as stated in this agreement. Mentors are to submit this signed form to the Program Coordinator. Each signee should maintain a copy of this signed agreement for reference.

Mentor's Printed Name	Mentor's Signature	Date
Teacher's Printed Name	Teacher's Signature	Date
Teacher Supervisor's Printed Name	Teacher Supervisor's Signature	Date

Submit copies to: Mentor
Teacher
Teacher Supervisor
Program Coordinator

Figure 5.2 Breaking Confidentiality Protocol

Breaking Confidentiality Protocol

The signing of the Mentor–Teacher Agreement establishes confidentiality throughout the professional relationship. However, if the teacher demonstrates unprofessional behavior, then the confidentiality may be broken. In such cases, this protocol will be followed.

1. Verbal Warning
    Discuss the issue with the teacher that initiated a reason for breaking confidentiality (i.e., unprofessional behavior towards mentor, not attending pre-scheduled meetings, danger to students, danger to self, etc.). Be sure to revisit the Mentor–Teacher Agreement that was signed at beginning of year. Share that as a result of unprofessional behavior, it is your responsibility to notify the administrator. Be sure to document this conversation in your logs and on a CDC Journal Record.

2. Teacher improves behavior. Confidentiality is maintained.

3. Teacher continues acting in an unprofessional manner. Notify the teacher that you are reporting the behavior to the appropriate administrator. Request a meeting with the administrator and share the issue that has resulted in breaking confidentiality.

4. Request from the administrator that a meeting be set up between the teacher, the mentor, and the teacher supervisor to resolve whatever the issue is. Together, create a plan of how the behavior or issue will be overcome.

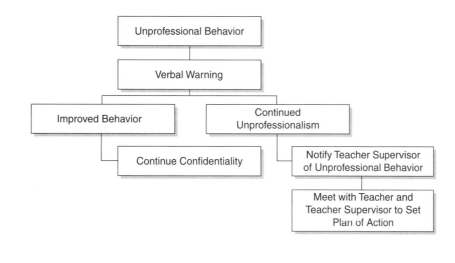

HOW TO USE TOOLS FOR BUILDING TRUST

The initial meetings between the mentor and teacher are essential for building the trusting relationship. During one of the first meetings, mentors share the Mentor-Teacher Agreement to establish how the protocol for dialogue will contribute to their relationship. The tool should be introduced in a positive manner, and emphasis should be placed on how this will benefit and support the teacher throughout the year. Once the teacher has signed, then the mentor signs.

The first mentor meeting with the teacher supervisor is just as important as the teacher meeting. The teacher supervisor must support the confidentiality agreement and trust that the mentor will initiate transformational learning for their teachers. During that first meeting, mentors introduce the Mentor-Teacher Confidentiality Agreement and ask the teacher supervisor to sign for all teachers.

The Breaking Confidentiality Protocol is intended to be utilized only when necessary. Mentors introduce the protocol only when instances of unprofessional behavior are exhibited from teachers.

PURPOSE FOR TOOLS FOR UNDERSTANDING CONTEXT

Another set of tools important in the development of teacher practice is the tools for understanding context. These tools help mentors and teachers establish background information and create an understanding of each other and the surrounding environment. Context for the surrounding environment is critical in helping teachers understand who their students are, where their students come from, as well as what resources are available in the community that can help support student learning. Information can be learned from these tools to help teachers also identify what resources are available within their school contexts. They can identify school personnel and educational materials that will assist in their instructional practices.

Discovering what resources are available in the school and community that would help the teacher is important to building an extended support system beyond the mentor. According to the New Teacher Center at University of California, Santa Cruz (2003), "Identifying resource personnel within the district and community sets the stage for future collaboration with colleagues, parents, and other support agencies."

There are three types of tools that mentors use at the beginning of the year with their teachers to help develop the teachers' contextual situation: *teacher profiles, mentor profiles,* and *community and school profiles.*

DESCRIPTION OF TOOLS FOR UNDERSTANDING CONTEXT

The *teacher* and *mentor profiles* are divided into two sections (Figure 5.3 and Figure 5.4). Both tools have a General Information Section. This section captures background information as well as information pertinent to the current teaching or mentoring position. The teacher profile contains a schedule section as well. This space is for teachers to describe what a typical school day looks like. The mentor profiles contains a teacher information section. This space is for mentors to describe the teachers they have been assigned.

The community and school profiles can provide teachers and mentors with specific information about the school, school personnel, students who attend the school, and the community that surrounds the school. This tool has space for important people, numbers, programs, and information regarding the community and school (Figure 5.5).

Figure 5.3 Teacher Profile

Teacher Profile

Name: *Manuel*		Home Phone: *555-5555*
Mentor: *Tenesha*		Contact Phone: *555-5555*
E-mail: *p@mentorschool.moc*		School Phone: *555-5555*
School: *Mentor School*		Evaluating Administrator: *Marie*

General Information

Education History:	**Teaching Assignment:**	**Regular School Hours:**
University/College Attended: *U of USA*	Grade(s): *7th & 8th*	Start Time: *7:45*
Graduation Date: *6/2010*	Content: *History*	Lunch: *11:25*
Major: *Secondary Education*	Room: *101*	Dismissal: *2:00*
Minor: *Social Studies*	☒ English as a Second Language ☒ Gifted ☒ Special Education	Recess(es): *N/A*
Student Teaching Assignment(s): *Cleveland High School*	Prep Day & Time: *Everyday 5th Period*	**Early Release Day:** Day: *N/A* Start Time:
Certification(s) & Endorsement(s): *Secondary Education Social Studies SEI*	Special Area Assignment(s): *N/A*	Lunch:
	Grade Level Meetings: *Thursday Prep*	Dismissal:
Highly Qualified: ⟨Yes⟩ or No Area: *Social Studies*	Committees and Extra Duties: *Softball Coach*	Bus Information:
Current Education Program: (e.g., TFA, Intern) *N/A*		

Schedule (including prep time)

Room	Period	Time	Subject (including planning)
101	1	7:45-8:35	First Hour American History
101	2	8:40-9:30	Second Hour American History
101	3	9:35-10:25	Third Hour World History
101	4	10:30-11:20	Fourth Hour World History
Café		11:25-12:10	Lunch
101	HR	12:15-1:05	Homeroom
101	5	1:10-2:00	Prep

Additional Information:

Figure 5.4 Mentor Profile

Mentor Profile

Name: *Ron*   Contact Phone: *789-3400*

Schools Served: *Spring High School*

General Information	Educational Background
Current Certification(s): *Secondary grades 7-12*	Degree(s) Earned: *B.S. Secondary Education* *M.A. History*
Endorsement(s): *English as a Second Language*	University/College(s): *University of Oklahoma*
Classroom Experience(s): *15 years grades 8, 10, 11, 12*	Graduation Date(s): *1990*
Grade Level/ Subject Expertise: *Grades 7-12/History*	Major(s): *Secondary Education and History*
Professional Development Expertise: *Engagement Strategies in Teaching American History*	Minor(s): *English*

Teacher Information

	Name	School	Years of Experience	Grade/ Subject	Highly Qualified Information	
					Yes or No	Area of Qualification
1.	Samuel	Same	1	10	Yes	
2.	Jane	Same	1	9	Yes	
3.	Jennifer	Same	1	11	Yes	
4.	Tom	Same	1	11	Yes	
5.	Alicia	Same	1	10	Yes	
6.	Barbara	Same	1	10	Yes	
7.	Butch	Same	1	11	Yes	
8.	Julio	Same	1	10	Yes	
9.	Sherry	Same	1	9	Yes	
10.	Sandy	Same	1	9	Yes	
11.	Timothy	Same	1	9	Yes	
12.	Dalia	Same	1	10	Yes	
13.	Lorin	Same	1	9	Yes	
14.	Dave	Same	1	12	No	*Content Area: Math*
15.	Renee	Same	1	12	No	*Content Area: Science*

Submit copies to: Mentor Program Coordinator, Principal, and Teacher

Figure 5.5 Community and School Profile

Community and School Profile
Important School or District Personnel:

Sue 555-5555	Bilingual Resource Teacher	Kathy ext. 4567	Parent/Teacher Org. Representative
Barb 555-5555	School Psychologist	Terri 555-5555	Payroll
N/A	Technology Specialist	Vicki ext. 7654	School Nurse
Phil 555-5555	Computer Lab(s)	Shelia 555-5555	Community Liaisons
Math Kim ext. 1234	Content Area Coach	Phyllis ext. 5678	School Secretary
Language Arts Ben ext. 4321	Content Area Coach	Meg ext. 8765	Counselor
4th – 8th grade Ann ext. 2345	Special Education Resource	N/A	Counselor
K – 3rd grade Janeel ext. 5432	Special Education Resource	N/A	Counselor
N/A	Special Education Resource	N/A	Custodian
Jane 555-5555	Curriculum Materials	Viola ext. 7890	Cafeteria Manager
Betty 555-5555	Speech/Language Specialist	Peggy 555-5555	Insurance
Julia ext. 3456	ELL Coordinator	LeeAnn 555-5555	Union Representative
Karen ext. 6543	Gifted Education Resource		(Other)
Kate 555-5555	Title I Resources		(Other)

Important Programs for Your Students:

RTI → Laura ext. 0987	After School Intervention	YMCA→ Becky 555-5555	(Other)
Kids at Hope→Lee ext.7586	Conflict Resolution		(Other)
N/A	Homework Club		(Other)
Cindy ext. 3776	After School Tutoring		(Other)

Ethnic Composition of the Students:

Native American or Native Alaskan: 4%	Asian or Pacific Islander: 15%	Hispanic origin: 37%
African American, not Hispanic origin: 25%		White, not Hispanic origin: 19%

Percentage of Students in the Following Categories:

Students who qualify for free/reduced lunches: 76%	Students receiving special education services: 13%
Limited English proficient students: 25%	Number of different languages: 8

Specify Languages: *Spanish, Korean, Vietnamese, Russian, German, Angolian, Egyptian, Arabic*

(Continued)

Figure 5.5 (Continued)

Lesson Planning Form and Expectations:

EEI Structure – District Lesson Plan Format – Need to have daily lesson plans for each day.

School Goal(s)/School Improvement Focus/Special Programs:

The school goal is to raise reading comprehension to 85% of students reading at or above grade level.

Reading First is a School Improvement Focus for the school.

Community Resources Available to You, Your Students, and their Families (e.g., Business Partners, Field Trip Locations within Community, Health Services, Social Services, etc.):

Local Lumber Yard – has donated materials for class projects in the past
Local Craft Store – has donated materials for class projects in the past

Dairy and Hog Farm within walking distance is available for field trips.

Boys and Girls Club within walking distance from school provides activities after school for students.

Contributions Your Students Could Make to the Community:

Students could collect cans of food for the local food bank.
Students could display artwork at the local hospital.

Other Historical Topics with the Community:

Traditionally this community has been very self-contained and small. They have been a very small rural community that has recently experienced growth from several housing developments and a new manufacturing company that has moved nearby.

Submit copies to: Mentor Program Coordinator, Mentor, and Teacher

HOW TO USE THE TOOLS FOR UNDERSTANDING CONTEXT

The teacher profile is completed by the teacher to provide the mentor with specific information regarding background information and daily schedule. The mentors then use this tool from all of their teachers to build their daily working schedules. Mentors strive to schedule meeting time during the teacher's preparation period, before, or after school.

The mentor profile is used to help build and establish a trusting relationship with all program stakeholders. This tool is completed by the mentor and then given to the mentor program coordinator, the principals and teachers with whom they are working. The mentor profile gives all stakeholders the mentor's qualifications and the teachers they are mentoring.

The community and school profile is completed by both the mentor and teacher together. The tool is meant to help create dialogue between the pair and initiate a conversation around students and learning. Together the mentor and teacher can research the information pertinent to the teacher's situation and how the information is relevant.

BEGINNING CONVERSATION TOOLS IN ACTION

In this scenario, Jane, the mentor, is meeting Julia, the beginning teacher, for their first collaborative conference. The pair was introduced during new teacher orientation where they scheduled a first meeting time and date; however, they have not seen each other since. It is the week before school starts and Jane wants to find out as much about Julia as possible in order to plan how to best meet her needs.

Jane initiates the conversation by asking, "What has been the most successful idea you have encountered or tried this week?"

Julia responds by sharing, "Well I found out that I have access to a mobile computer lab in my school. I am so excited about that! I want to use computers with my students as much as possible. I have so many ideas for lessons. I have already scheduled to have the lab for several weeks in September."

"How exciting! Students really value teachers who utilize technology embedded in the learning. What do you know about the students in your community? Do they have computers at home?" Jane questions.

"I don't know much about them. They took us on a field trip around the district, but it was so hot that I couldn't concentrate on what the guide was saying." Julia states.

"Well we have about 45 minutes left in our meeting time. One of the things we could do together right now is to research the school and surrounding community to see what we can find out about your students. Is that something you might be interested in doing?"

"Sure, I would like to know who my students are."

Jane suggests, "I have a tool that might help guide us in our exploration. It is called a community and school profile. This tool has a place to record information about the students who will be in your class, the school, and the community around the school. Why don't we take a look at it to see what information we might want to investigate?"

Together, the duo looks at the community and school profile and determines that some of the information is available on the faculty phone list. They decide to make a photo copy of that list so both have a copy readily available. For information about the student population, the pair decides that a trip to the front office to talk to the school secretaries is needed.

Jane suggests that Julia and the other three beginning teachers she is mentoring meet with the school secretary and principal together. She recommends that she make an appointment for all of them before the end of the week. Julia thought that was a fantastic idea. Jane recorded, "Make an appointment with . . ." on her CDC log in the mentor support section.

Once Jane and Julia have completed as much information from the community and school profile as they can, Jane introduces the mentor profile and teacher profile. Jane shares a copy of her completed mentor profile with Julia. "Just like the community and school profile can help give us information about your students, we have two more tools that will help facilitate our partnership. Here is a copy of my mentor profile. This should help give you some information about who I am and what my experiences are. Please think of me as an open book! Ask me any questions you might have that will help you in our working together.

"I also wanted to give you your teacher profile. This will help me in planning strategies for how to best support you. It will also help me schedule my time so that I can best meet your needs. If you don't mind, we have about 10 minutes left of our meeting time. Can we talk about what your daily schedule looks like?"

"Sure," Julia says. "My principal and team met this morning to go over our schedules."

Together Jane and Julia discuss Julia's daily schedule and determine when the best time for another meeting would be. Julia agrees to finish the remaining sections of the teacher profile before their next meeting.

NOTES FOR IMPLEMENTATION

Each of the tools listed in this chapter were designed with the idea of fostering a trusting relationship and helping all stakeholders gain a picture of each other. We encourage mentors, teachers, and others to share additional information that will enable the collaborative process further, such as describing how each other learns best and how each likes to work.

The mentor-teacher agreement, the teacher profile, the mentor profile, and the community and school profiles are all printed on NCR paper for convenience of all parties who utilize them. We suggest that mentors compile all confidentiality agreements and present them to teacher supervisors at one time. That way there is no misunderstanding as to what they are signing. It is also a time saver for the teacher supervisors.

Figure 5.6 Mentor–Teacher Confidentiality Agreement

Mentor–Teacher Confidentiality Agreement

Any anecdotal notes stored in the Mentor's Notebook and personal conversations between Mentor and Teacher are to be used exclusively to support the professional growth of the Teacher. No portion of this notebook is intended for use in the district evaluation program. Any written documentation of discussions is not to be duplicated in any format and is to be destroyed by the Program at the end of three years. The purpose of all documents used in the induction process is to direct Mentor and Teacher discussions. Discussions occur weekly.

This agreement is a binding contract between the Mentor and the Teacher. All conversations and documentation are held in confidence with the exception of unprofessional behavior on the part of either party. Unprofessional behavior can be inappropriate actions or language, danger to self or others, failure to keep scheduled appointments, and/or failure to participate. If unprofessional behavior occurs, the Mentor or the Teacher should report incident to the immediate supervisor.

I support and will honor the terms as stated in this agreement. Mentors are to submit this signed form to the Program Coordinator. Each signee should maintain a copy of this signed agreement for reference.

_____   _____   _____
Mentor's Printed Name   Mentor's Signature   Date

_____   _____   _____
Teacher's Printed Name   Teacher's Signature   Date

_____   _____   _____
Teacher Supervisor's Printed Name   Teacher Supervisor's Signature   Date

Submit copies to: Mentor
                      Teacher
                      Teacher Supervisor
                      Program Coordinator

Figure 5.7	Teacher Profile

Teacher Profile

Name: _____	Home Phone: _____
Mentor: _____	Contact Phone: _____
E-mail: _____	School Phone: _____
School: _____	Evaluating Administrator: _____

General Information

Education History:	**Teaching Assignment:**	**Regular School Hours:**
University/College Attended:	Grade(s):	Start Time:
	Content:	Lunch:
Graduation Date:	Room:	Dismissal:
Major:		Recess(es):
Minor:	☐ English as a Second Language ☐ Gifted ☐ Special Education	
Student Teaching Assignment(s):		**Early Release Day:**
	Prep Day & Time:	Day:
		Start Time:
Certification(s) & Endorsement(s):	Special Area Assignment(s): *N/A*	Lunch:
	Grade Level Meetings:	Dismissal:
	Committees and Extra Duties:	Bus Information:
Highly Qualified: Yes or No Area:		
Current Education Program: (e.g., TFA, Intern)		

Schedule (including prep time)

Room	Period	Time	Subject (including planning)

Additional Information:

Figure 5.8 Mentor Profile

Mentor Profile

Name: _____   Contact Phone: _____

Schools Served:

General Information	Educational Background
Current Certification(s):	Degree(s) Earned:
Endorsement(s):	University/College(s):
Classroom Experience(s):	Graduation Date(s):
Grade Level/ Subject Expertise:	Major(s):
Professional Development Expertise:	Minor(s):

Teacher Information

Name	School	Years of Experience	Grade/ Subject	Highly Qualified Information	
				Yes or No	Area of Qualification
1.					
2.					
3.					
4.					
5.					
6.					
7.					
8.					
9.					
10.					
11.					
12.					
13.					
14.					
15.					

Submit copies to: Mentor Program Coordinator, Principal, and Teacher

Figure 5.9   Community and School Profile

Community and School Profile

Important School or District Personnel:

_____ Bilingual Resource Teacher	_____ Parent/Teacher Org. Rep	
_____ School Psychologist	_____ Payroll	
_____ Technology Specialist	_____ School Nurse	
_____ Computer Lab(s)	_____ Community Liaisons	
_____ Content Area Coach	_____ School Secretary	
_____ Content Area Coach	_____ Counselor	
_____ Special Education Resource	_____ Counselor	
_____ Special Education Resource	_____ Counselor	
_____ Special Education Resource	_____ Custodian	
_____ Curriculum Materials	_____ Cafeteria Manager	
_____ Speech/Language Specialist	_____ Insurance	
_____ ELL Coordinator	_____ Union Representative	
_____ Gifted Education Resource	_____ (Other)	
_____ Title I Resources	_____ (Other)	

Important Programs for Your Students:

_____ After School Intervention	_____ (Other) _____	
_____ Conflict Resolution	_____ (Other) _____	
_____ Homework Club	_____ (Other) _____	
_____ After School Tutoring	_____ (Other)	

Ethnic Composition of the Students:

Native American or Native Alaskan:	Asian or Pacific Islander:	Hispanic origin:
African American, not Hispanic origin:	White, not Hispanic origin:	

Percentage of Students in the Following Categories:

Students who qualify for free/reduced lunches:	Students receiving special education services:
Limited English proficient students:	Number of different languages:

Specify Languages:

Lesson Planning Form and Expectations:

School Goal(s)/School Improvement Focus/Special Programs:

Community Resources Available to You, Your Students, and their Families (e.g., Business Partners, Field Trip Locations within Community, Health Services, Social Services, etc.):

Contributions Your Students Could Make to the Community:

Other Historical Topics with the Community:

Submit copies to: Mentor Program Coordinator, Mentor, and Teacher

6

The Administrator and Mentor Conversations

PURPOSE FOR ADMINISTRATOR AND MENTOR CONVERSATIONS

Communication with the site administrator is vital to the success of an induction program. One of the responsibilities of the mentor is to keep the communication with the site administrator open and ongoing. Building trusting relationships with site administrators is just as important as establishing trusting relationships between mentors and beginning teachers. Establishing partner relationships with administrators provides allies for the program, the mentors, and the beginning teachers. Continued conversations throughout the year will reinforce the working relationships.

The administrator can support the beginning teacher in a number of ways that have been documented through research (Horn, Sterling, & Blair, 2004). The administrator implements policies that support beginning teachers such as (a) allowing time to attend seminars and observe veteran teachers during the work day, (b) reducing the number of students in their classrooms, assigning the most challenging students to veteran teachers, and providing the needed supplies for the classroom, (c) minimizing extracurricular and committee assignments, and (d) providing opportunities for a collegial culture. As the mentor and administrator develop a working relationship, other strategies of support can be implemented for the purpose of transforming the beginning teacher's practice.

Just as there are six basic reasons for the mentor to use the CDC Journal Record, there are six basic reasons to use the *Administrator and Mentor Journal Record:*

1. To facilitate and document the conversation

2. To identify the school goals or initiatives

3. To reinforce confidentiality

4. To discuss the general focus of the topics between the mentor and the beginning teachers

5. To discuss support and resources

6. To advocate for beginning teachers

DESCRIPTION OF THE ADMINISTRATOR AND MENTOR JOURNAL RECORD

The administrator and mentor journal record parallels the CDC Journal Record. The administrator and mentor journal record is used each time the mentor meets with the site administrator to facilitate and document the conversation. The goal(s) of the school is the focus for site educators and therefore is intended to be the center of the conversation. Since the mentor is providing assistance to the teachers for the purpose of transforming practice and impacting student learning, knowing the goal(s) of the school is one of the responsibilities of the mentor (Figure 6.1).

Sometimes mentors are assigned to a single site while other times mentors are assigned to multiple sites. The mentor meets with each site administrator at least once a month. The previous administrator and mentor journal record is referred to in order to assure the continuity of the conversation. The site administrator may be the principal, the assistant principal, or a teacher on assignment depending on the structure and role responsibilities of the school site.

The professional teacher standards are listed on the side of the journal record to remind the mentor and the administrator of the standards they are using while working with teachers. The journal record that follows uses professional teacher standards (Horn & Metler-Armijo, 2010) as an example: (1) managing the learning environment, (2) designing and planning instruction, (3) facilitating student learning, and (4) assessing student learning. Any state standards or professional teacher standards that are the foundation of a program can be used.

| Figure 6.1 | Administrator and Mentor Journal Record |

Administrator: *Brandi*   **Mentor:** *Rob*

School: *Chandler HS*   **Date:** *8/25*   **Time:** *11 AM*

Professional Teacher Standards

Standard 1: Managing the Learning Environment
- O 1. Establishes expectations for student behavior
- O 2. Establishes and maintains a respectful and nurturing learning environment
- O 3. Promotes student responsibilities and self-discipline
- O 4. Recognizes and values differences among individuals
- O 5. Facilitates collaboration among learners
- O 6. Establishes an environment for student success
- O 7. Utilizes active participation strategies
- O 8. Arranges and manages the classroom environment for student success

Standard 2: Designing and Planning Instruction
- O 1. Utilizes academic standards to plan instruction
- O 2. Utilizes student assessments to plan instruction
- O 3. Plans instruction to meet the diverse needs of learners
- O 4. Links learning to students' prior knowledge and experiences
- O 5. Plans short term learning objectives and long term curriculum goals
- O 6. Includes a variety of methods in instructional plans
- O 7. Includes a variety of technology, materials, and resources in instructional planning
- O 8. Develops learning experiences that are developmentally appropriate for learners
- O 9. Develops learning experiences that address the cognitive levels of learners
- O 10. Plans for experiences that align with learning objectives that accurately represent content

Standard 3: Facilitating Student Learning
- O 1. Utilizes a lesson plan to guide student learning
- O 2. Communicates high expectations for learning
- O 3. Demonstrates skills, knowledge, and thinking processes
- O 4. Uses correct grammar, mechanics, and developmentally appropriate language to communicate with learners
- O 5. Uses instructional strategies that are appropriate to the developmental levels of learners
- O 6. Uses strategies to address the diverse needs of learners
- O 7. Promotes critical thinking
- O 8. Makes connections between learning and real life situations
- O 9. Uses a variety of instructional strategies to engage learners
- O 10. Uses instructional time to maximize learning
- O 11. Ensures students apply new knowledge and skills
- O 12. Uses technology and instructional resources

Standard 4: Assessing Student Learning
- O 1. Aligns formal and informal assessments to instruction
- O 2. Designs student assessments to measure progress
- O 3. Promotes student self assessment
- O 4. Maintains records of student performance and respects privacy of student records
- O 5. Communicates growth progress to students and parents

1 School Goal(s) or Initiative(s):

All students will be able to learn and meet 85% of the expectations in each course benchmark.

2 Mentor Topics:

I am working with each of the beginning teachers in setting their benchmark goals for each student.
They each completed their syllabi which included their classroom management plan.

3 Administrator Topics:

The benchmark goals are important for each teacher. One of the areas of concern for me is the alignment between the benchmarks and classroom instruction.

4 Desired Action(s):

- *Address the alignment of instruction and the benchmark goals with all of the beginning teachers.*
- *Remind all teachers of the school goal. During our staff meeting, we will discuss alignment between instruction and the benchmark goals. I will also discuss the available district assessments for some course benchmarks.*

5 Person Responsible:

- *Rob*

- *Brandi*

Next Meeting Date:
9/20

Focus:
District course benchmark assessments

Submit copy to: Administrator
                 Mentor

HOW TO USE THE ADMINISTRATOR AND MENTOR JOURNAL RECORD

There are five sections of the administrator and mentor journal record that need to be addressed each time a scheduled conference occurs: *mentor topics, administrator topics, school goal(s) or initiative(s), desired action(s)*, and *person responsible*. The mentor records what is being said in each section during the conversation with the administrator.

It is important to begin the conversation with the opportunity for the administrator to update the mentor regarding the goal(s) or initiative(s) of the school (Section 1). This information is recorded in the center of the administrator and mentor journal record.

The upper left box is Section 2, labeled Mentor Topics. The mentor continues the conversation by discussing the current focus of the work between the mentor and the beginning teachers. It is imperative that the mentor honors the confidentiality established with the teachers. The mentor may have to remind the administrator of the confidentiality agreement that is signed by the administrator, the beginning teacher, and the mentor. The discussion is centered on the current focus of work between the mentor and all of the beginning teachers, i.e., classroom management, lesson planning. This is also an opportunity to discuss instructional resources available to the teachers, the responsibilities and expectations of the teachers as well as advocate for the teachers' needs, such as lowering the number of class preparations, staff development, or release time.

The upper right box, labeled Administrator Topics, is Section 3. This is an opportunity for the administrator to give feedback, share concerns, or mention an area of focus about beginning teachers' practice. Some questions to ask include the following:

- What are some of the successes of the beginning teachers from the administrator's viewpoint?
- What are some concerns or areas of focus?

Certain areas of concern might be discussed at this point such as the lack of classroom management. It is the responsibility of the mentor to assure the administrator that all of the beginning teachers are focusing on classroom management. If the administrator singles out one teacher, it is the mentor's responsibility not to break confidentiality, yet assure the administrator that the concern will be addressed with all beginning teachers.

Section 4, Desired Actions(s), is the lower left box. The actions for meeting are discussed and recorded. This might be a commitment to work with all teachers on classroom management to make sure they are following the school's rules and regulations on a consistent basis, provide a lesson plan template, or create strategies to engage parents.

The lower right box, labeled Person Responsible, is Section 5. The opportunity for the mentor and administrator to determine who will be responsible for the action(s) prior to the next meeting is discussed at this point. The administrator might commit to visit one of the teacher's classrooms or to provide the mentor with additional resources.

The mentor summarizes the conversation after recording the key points throughout each section during closure. The mentor and the administrator also set the next meeting date, and the mentor restates the focus of their continued work together for the next conversation. The administrator and mentor journal record is printed on no carbon required (NCR) paper so that the mentor and administrator can each have a copy after every meeting.

ADMINISTRATOR AND MENTOR JOURNAL RECORD TOOL IN ACTION

The following mentor tool is a sample administrator and mentor journal record (Figure 6.2). Sam is a second-year vice principal at Highland High School. One of his responsibilities is to monitor the mentoring program. Beth, the mentor, met with Sam for the first meeting. She begins the conversation by asking Sam to identify the school goal (Section 1). Beth focuses the conversation on her work with the beginning teachers and their classroom management plans. She shares with Sam some of the strategies that she is discussing with each of them (Section 2). As their conversation progresses, Beth asks Sam to share his thoughts about the beginning teachers (Section 3). Sam expresses concern that some of the teachers are not following their own management plans nor do they have their rules and consequences posted. He specifically mentions that Robin needs a lot of assistance and asks Beth whether she could provide that assistance. Beth states that she will focus her conversations with all beginning teachers on their management plans and suggests that all rules and consequences be posted.

She did not enter into a reciprocal conversation regarding Robin (Section 3). Beth writes what she will do with all beginning teachers in Section 4. She indicates what Sam agrees to do in Section 5. Sam will continue to conduct walk-throughs in each beginning teacher's classroom and reinforce the idea of posting rules and consequences. Beth closes the conference by setting the next meeting date with the administrator documenting agreement on the focus of their next meeting.

Figure 6.2	Administrator and Mentor Journal Record

Administrator: *Sam*   **Mentor:** *Beth*

School: *Highland*   **Date:** *9/25*   **Time:** *9 AM*

Professional Teacher Standards

Standard 1: Managing the Learning Environment
O 1. Establishes expectations for student behavior
O 2. Establishes and maintains a respectful and nurturing learning environment
O 3. Promotes student responsibilities and self-discipline
O 4. Recognizes and values differences among individuals
O 5. Facilitates collaboration among learners
O 6. Establishes an environment for student success
O 7. Utilizes active participation strate4gies
O 8. Arranges and manages the classroom environment for student success

Standard 2: Designing and Planning Instruction
O 1. Utilizes academic standards to plan instruction
O 2. Utilizes student assessments to plan instruction
O 3. Plans instruction to meet the diverse needs of learners
O 4. Links learning to students' prior knowledge and experiences
O 5. Plans short term learning objectives and long term curriculum goals
O 6. Includes a variety of methods in instructional plans
O 7. Includes a variety of technology, materials, and resources in instructional planning
O 8. Develops learning experiences that are developmentally appropriate for learners
O 9. Develops learning experiences that address the cognitive levels of learners
O 10. Plans for experiences that align with learning objectives that accurately represent content

Standard 3: Facilitating Student Learning
O 1. Utilizes a lesson plan to guide student learning
O 2. Communicates high expectations for learning
O 3. Demonstrates skills, knowledge, and thinking processes
O 4. Uses correct grammar, mechanics, and developmentally appropriate language to communicate with learners
O 5. Uses instructional strategies that are appropriate to the developmental levels of learners
O 6. Uses strategies to address the diverse needs of learners
O 7. Promotes critical thinking
O 8. Makes connections between learning and real life situations
O 9. Uses a variety of instructional strategies to engage learners
O 10. Uses instructional time to maximize learning
O 11. Ensures students apply new knowledge and skills
O 12. Uses technology and instructional resources

Standard 4: Assessing Student Learning
O 1. Aligns formal and informal assessments to instruction
O 2. Designs student assessments to measure progress
O 3. Promotes student self assessment
O 4. Maintains records of student performance and respects privacy of student records
O 5. Communicates growth progress to students and parents

1 School Goal(s) or Initiative(s):

Reading – All grade levels will achieve 70% on the state achievement test. If not, the teachers will not receive the additional monies at the end of the year.

2 Mentor Topics:

We will be working on strategies to implement each beginning teacher's classroom management plan. We can do that through looking at the rules and consequences posted in the classroom as well as collecting classroom data on the consistency of applying the classroom rules.

3 Administrator Topics:

What I have seen in the classroom is that the beginning teachers are not following their own plans. Some of them don't even have their rules and consequences posted especially Robin. She needs a lot of assistance. Can you provide that kind of assistance?

4 Desired Action(s):

- *Will continue to work with each beginning teacher on the implementation of their classroom management plan.*
- *Will state that the expectation of the school administration is to have the rules and consequences posted in the classroom.*
- *Will conduct "walk-throughs" in each beginning teachers' classroom.*
- *Will reinforce the idea of posting rules and consequences.*

5 Person Responsible:

- *Beth*

- *Beth*

- *Sam*

- *Sam*

Next Meeting Date:
10/11

Focus:
Classroom Management rules and consequences posted in the classroom.

NOTES FOR IMPLEMENTATION

Communication is a key component between the site administrator and the mentor. Establishing a trusting relationship with the administrator enhances the work of the mentor and increases administrators' involvement and support for induction through consistent communication. It is often a different dynamic for the mentors and principals to have the mentors leading the conversation rather than still being a participant. The novice mentors are in the process of transforming their role from one of teacher to one of teacher leader. The experienced mentor is refining her communication skills. As with most change, this may be challenging at first. Using the administrator and mentor journal record tool for conversation with administrators reinforces the process and roles that allow the mentor to establish a new relationship. Each time a mentor enters a new site, the foundation for establishing a relationship with the administrator begins again and forces the mentor back into the *role focused stage.*

Mentors have the opportunity to use the administrator and mentor journal record during the Stage 2: Practice Focused of introducing tools in the field. This tool allows the mentor to keep track of the conversations and monitor the progress of the communication between himself and the administrator.

Here are two quotes from mentors who experienced meeting with school administrators:

> *It was easier than I thought to speak with the site administrator. He was welcoming and appreciated our work with the beginning teachers. It was hard not to talk about specific teachers when he brought up a problem. I did have the opportunity to share with him that we both had signed a confidentiality agreement with the beginning teachers but assured him that I would work with all of the beginning teachers on his concern.*

> *It is hard to schedule an appointment with one of the principals. Something comes up even when he does schedule an appointment. I finally kept making appointments every week so I finally was able to have a conference with him. It went exceedingly well. I found out how much he appreciated the program and our work with beginning teachers.*

Figure 6.3 Administrator and Mentor Journal Record

Administrator: _____   **Mentor:** _____

School: _____   **Date:** _____   **Time:** _____

Professional Teacher Standards **Standard 1: Managing the Learning Environment** O 1. Establishes expectations for student behavior O 2. Establishes and maintains a respectful and nurturing learning environment O 3. Promotes student responsibilities and self-discipline O 4. Recognizes and values differences among individuals O 5. Facilitates collaboration among learners O 6. Establishes an environment for student success O 7. Utilizes active participation strategies O 8. Arranges and manages the classroom environment for student success	**1 School Goal(s) or Initiative(s):**

| **Standard 2: Designing and Planning Instruction**
O 1. Utilizes academic standards to plan instruction
O 2. Utilizes student assessments to plan instruction
O 3. Plans instruction to meet the diverse needs of learners
O 4. Links learning to students' prior knowledge and experiences
O 5. Plans short term learning objectives and long term curriculum goals
O 6. Includes a variety of methods in instructional plans
O 7. Includes a variety of technology, materials, and resources in instructional planning
O 8. Develops learning experiences that are developmentally appropriate for learners
O 9. Develops learning experiences that address the cognitive levels of learners
O 10. Plans for experiences that align with learning objectives that accurately represent content |

2 Mentor Topics: | **3 Administrator Topics:**

Standard 3: Facilitating Student Learning
O 1. Utilizes a lesson plan to guide student learning
O 2. Communicates high expectations for learning
O 3. Demonstrates skills, knowledge, and thinking processes
O 4. Uses correct grammar, mechanics, and developmentally appropriate language to communicate with learners
O 5. Uses instructional strategies that are appropriate to the developmental levels of learners
O 6. Uses strategies to address the diverse needs of learners
O 7. Promotes critical thinking
O 8. Makes connections between learning and real life situations
O 9. Uses a variety of instructional strategies to engage learners
O 10. Uses instructional time to maximize learning
O 11. Ensures students apply new knowledge and skills
O 12. Uses technology and instructional resources

4 Desired Action(s): | **5 Person Responsible:**

Standard 4: Assessing Student Learning
O 1. Aligns formal and informal assessments to instruction
O 2. Designs student assessments to measure progress
O 3. Promotes student self assessment
O 4. Maintains records of student performance and respects privacy of student records
O 5. Communicates growth progress to students and parents

Next Meeting Date: | **Focus:**

Submit copy to: Administrator
Mentor

7

Professional Teacher Growth Process

PURPOSE FOR PROFESSIONAL TEACHER GROWTH PROCESS

The *Professional Teacher Growth (PTG) process* involves a series of tools to assist in the development of a teacher's instructional practice through continual self-reflection, analysis, goal setting, and artifact collection. This process of guided self-assessment leads teachers to identify their assets of practice (strengths) and recognize opportunities for growth (challenges). Honest self-assessment in the unfamiliar and multidimensional context of their classroom can be tricky and confusing. A mentor serves as an invaluable guide through this process.

It is essential that teachers make the connection between what is occurring in the classroom and the expectations of performance set forth in the applicable professional teacher standards. To be meaningful the self-assessment must involve comparing one's instructional practice to performance criteria within the standards. The role of the mentor is to encourage and guide the teacher to establish realistic professional goals based on an honest self-assessment of instructional practice. Mentors encourage this by assisting in the process of goal setting and identification of artifacts, for example lesson plans, classroom management plan, and student work, that serve as evidence of the desired behaviors named in the goals.

Research reveals that setting specific, challenging goals leads to higher levels of performance when those goals are planned, focused, and specific (Stronge, Tucker, & Hindman, 2004). Five basic components of goal setting are identified:

1. Identification of need

2. Description of baseline data relevant to the need

3. Articulation of a goal

4. Strategies for achieving the goal

5. Documentation of results (pp. 18, 20)

The process for developing the *Professional Teacher Growth (PTG) Plan* described below incorporates the teacher self-assessment process, the development of professional goals based on the assessment, identification of evidential artifacts, and reflection on growth.

DESCRIPTION OF THE PROFESSIONAL TEACHER GROWTH (PTG) PROCESS

There are four steps in the teacher self-assessment process for developing a PTG plan. In brief these steps are *self-assessing practice, establishing professional growth priorities, developing a professional growth plan*, and *reflecting on professional growth*. On the following pages each step of the process and the tools used will be described in detail. A completed sample of each tool is included for the reader to see the tool in context.

Step 1: Self-Assessing Practice

Teachers first self-assess their current level of practice using two tools: (a) *Framework of Professional Growth Teacher Practice* and (b) *Professional Practice Teacher Self-Assessment Checklist*. Both of these tools were designed using professional teacher standards. The examples in this book are based on professional teacher standards (Horn & Metler-Armijo, 2010). The sample included in this chapter is one of the four standards. All of the four standards can be found in Resource C, and the checklist for all four standards can be found in Resource D.

The Framework of Professional Growth Teacher Practice is a continuum of professional teaching standards based on different levels of mastery as described by performance criteria. The framework is based on the work of Patty J. Horn, Heidi C. Blair, Kristin Metler-Armijo, Rick Vanosdall (2005); the New Teacher Center at University of California, Santa Cruz (2004); Pendergast School District mentors Kristin Metler-Armijo, Tammy House, Misty Arthur, Carrie Carlisle, Michelle Pogue, Shahla Nye, Jamie Bolster

(2002); Moir, Freeman, Petrock, and Baron (2001); Charlotte Danielson (1996); and David Berliner (1994). The Framework of Professional Growth Teacher Practice was established in 2007 by the authors and revised in 2010 to reflect the diversity of students and to meet the changing needs of teachers.

The Framework of Professional Growth Teacher Practice is divided into five developmental levels, which include:

1. Novice: Seeks rules and regulations, duplicates lessons in textbook, and tries to use previous learned formats, dependent on surviving the role of teacher

2. Emergent: Moves toward understanding basic classroom procedures, begins to apply new strategies while still dependent on textbook, rules, and regulations

3. Proficient: Implements strategies and classroom procedures to meet the academic needs of students, assessment drives instruction, decisions are made during the lesson that impact student learning

4. Accomplished: Organizes multiple levels of classroom procedures simultaneously, meets the various developmental and academic needs of students through multifarious strategies, groups and regroups students based on skill levels

5. Master: Moves smoothly throughout the day utilizing a knowledge of teaching to the extent that all students' learning needs are met, instruction is at a high level of proficiency in all areas of teaching, promotes independence within student responsibilities, data is analyzed and used in daily teaching decisions formally and informally

Each framework level addresses what a teacher should know and be able to do relative to each of the professional teacher standards. They represent developmental levels of a teacher's performance.

The concept of documenting the different levels of teacher's work first began in 1975 under the direction of Fuller and Bown followed by Berliner in 1994 as he labeled a teacher's developmental performance from novice to expert. A teacher's developmental level of performance changes, as she moves into the profession for the first time, moves from one grade level to another, or moves into a new content area. The framework was designed to accommodate these various levels of teacher development throughout a teachers' career (Figure 7.1).

The Professional Practice Teacher Self-Assessment Checklist (Figure 7.2) is used in conjunction with the Framework of Professional Growth Teacher Practice to provide teachers a means of keeping a written record of their determined level of current practice. Teachers use this tool by placing an N (novice), E (emergent), P (proficient), A (accomplished), or M (master) by the performance criteria to indicate how they self-assessed their practice (Figure 7.2).

Figure 7.1 Framework of Professional Growth Teacher Practice*

	The teacher:	NOVICE	EMERGENT	PROFICIENT	ACCOMPLISHED	MASTER
PERFORMANCE CRITERIA	1. Establishes expectations for student behavior	Communicates rules and consequences. Establishes basic routines and procedures.	Establishes clear high expectations for student behavior. Creates specific routines and procedures. Responds appropriately to disruptive behaviors and uses some strategies for maintaining students' productive behavior.	Monitors and uses strategies that reinforce behavior expectations, routines, and procedures. Uses strategies that prevent or lessen disruptive behavior and reinforce expectations for behavior. Transitions are seamless and without disruptions.	Maintains a positive environment through use of consistent routines and procedures, engagement, and behavior reinforcement. Encourages students to develop self-monitoring and reflective skills. The classroom is consistently conducive to learning.	Fosters an environment in which students show ownership of routines and procedures, are continually engaged, and reflect on learning and behavior. The classroom is exceptionally focused on learning.
	2. Establishes and maintains a respectful and nurturing learning environment	Establishes mutual respect with individual students. Acknowledges some incidents of unfairness and disrespect.	Establishes standards of respect. Models equitable and respectful relationships. Uses some strategies to respond to unfairness and disrespect.	Promotes caring and respectful interactions between all students. Responds to all incidents of unfairness and disrespect equitably. Encourages students to respect differences.	Reflects adherence to established standards of mutual respect. Frequently recognizes students' efforts with positive, constructive remarks. Responds to students' disrespect and implements consequences.	Provides opportunity for the students' to monitor their own behavior and offers suggestions for maintaining a positive, caring environment conducive to learning. Students demonstrate caring attitudes for one another.
	3. Promotes student responsibilities and self-discipline	Promotes student responsibility for self. Creates opportunities for individual students to have classroom responsibilities. The teacher acts as a professional role model and demonstrates integrity and ethical behavior.	Uses some strategies and activities to develop students' self discipline and responsibility to others recognizing their rights and needs. Students share in classroom responsibilities.	Promotes positive student interactions as members of large and small groups. Provides some opportunities for student leadership within the classroom.	Engages students in individual and group work that promotes responsibility to the classroom community. Supports students to take initiative in classroom leadership recognizing individual and others' rights.	Facilitates an environment in which students take initiative socially and academically. Promotes and supports student leadership beyond the classroom.
	4. Recognizes and values differences among individuals	Acknowledges individual differences among students.	Develops some strategies to address individual differences among students.	Uses a variety of strategies to address individual differences among students.	Promotes caring, respectful, and equitable relationships among students with individual differences.	Fosters a safe, inclusive, and equitable learning community. Students actively participate in maintaining a climate of equity, caring, and respect.

*Refer to Resource C for Framework Standards 1–4.

Figure 7.2 Professional Practice Teacher Self-Assessment Checklist*

Use the ***Framework of Professional Growth Teacher Practice*** to determine your level of performance. Use this tool by placing an **N** (Novice), **E** (Emergent), **P** (Proficient), **A** (Accomplished), or **M** (Master) by the performance criteria to indicate how you self-assessed your practice in the framework. Think about the evidence you have to document that level of practice.

☐ Fall
☐ Winter
☐ Spring

Standard 1: Managing the Learning Environment		Standard 2: Designing and Planning Instruction	Standard 3: Facilitating Student Learning
P	1. Establishes expectations for student behavior	1. Utilizes academic standards to plan instruction	1. Utilizes a lesson plan to guide student learning
P	2. Establishes and maintains a respectful and nurturing learning environment	2. Utilizes student assessments to plan instruction	2. Communicates high expectations for learning
P	3. Promotes student responsibilities and self-discipline	3. Plans instruction to meet the diverse needs of learners	3. Demonstrates skill, knowledge, and thinking processes
N	4. Recognizes and values differences among individuals	4. Links learning to students' prior knowledge and experiences	4. Uses correct grammar, mechanics, and developmentally appropriate language to communicate with learners
N	5. Facilitates collaboration among learners	5. Plans short term learning objectives and long term curriculum goals	5. Uses instructional strategies that are appropriate to the developmental levels of learners
E	6. Establishes an environment for student success	6. Includes a variety of methods in instructional plans	6. Uses strategies to address the diverse needs of learners
E	7. Utilizes active participation strategies	7. Includes a variety of technology, materials, and resources in instructional plans	7. Promotes critical thinking
P	8. Arranges and manages the classroom environment for student success	8. Develops learning experiences that are developmentally appropriate for learners	8. Makes connections between learning and real life situations
		9. Develops learning experiences that address the cognitive levels of learners	9. Uses a variety of instructional strategies to engage learners
			10. Uses instructional time to maximize learning
		10. Plans for experiences that align with learning objectives that accurately represent content.	11. Ensures students apply new knowledge and skills
Name:		**Date:**	12. Uses technology and instructional resources

*Refer to Resource D for complete Self-Assessment Checklist 1–4.

Step 2: Establishing PTG Priorities

Teachers identify areas for growth based on their self-assessment using the Establishing PTG Priorities tool. This tool is designed to assist teachers as they focus on their own performance and identify their professional development growth needs. The top priority is determined and becomes the focus of the professional growth goal. The priority goal should be in alignment with the school's goal (Figure 7.3).

Figure 7.3	Establishing Professional Teacher Growth Priorities

Name: _Amy_   **Mentor:** _Brooklyn_   **Date:** _10/1_   X Fall

School: _Coyote Hills_   **Grade:** _3rd_   ☐ Winter

School Goal(s): _To implement a variety of teaching strategies to increase test per grade Reading achievement by 80% on the state achievement level._   ☐ Spring

First: Identify the standard performance criteria that are marked with an N (Novice), E (Emergent), or P (Proficient) in the space below.

N = Novice	E = Emergent	P = Proficient
1.4 Recognizes and values differences among individuals 1.5 Facilitates collaboration among learners	1.6 Establishes an environment for student success 1.7 Utilizes active participation strategies	1.1 Establishes expectations for student behavior 1.2 Establishes and maintains a respectful and nurturing learning environment 1.3 Promotes student responsibilities and self-discipline 1.8 Arranges and manages the classroom environment for student success

Next: Identify your top three priorities for professional growth.

1.4 Recognizes and values differences among individuals
1.5 Facilitates collaboration among learners
1.6 Establishes an environment for student success

Finally: Identify your number one priority for growth and determine the next level of practice you wish to accomplish. Write the level descriptor for each. This becomes your professional growth goal.

Current Level of Practice	Desired Level of Practice
Standard and Performance Criteria: 1.4 Recognizes and values differences among individuals **Performance Level and Descriptor:** N 1.4 Acknowledges individual differences among students	**Performance Level and Descriptor:** P 1.4 Uses a variety of strategies to address individual differences among students

Step 3: Developing a PTG Plan

Based on the professional growth goal identified in Step 2, the teacher develops a plan of action for meeting the goal. Using the tool, PTG plan, helps teachers to focus on a specific professional growth goal that is relevant to both the individual teacher and to the school as a whole. The mentor assists the teacher toward developing goals in each standard that are achievable and measurable in this process. The action plan provides the teacher and the mentor a focus for support and a pathway towards achievement throughout the mentoring process (Figure 7.4).

This process of conferences, decision making, and data collection observations will give the teacher a sense of gratification in transforming their own classroom practice as well as a sense of professional success. Research (Darling-Hammond & Bransford, 2005) supports the statement that quality teaching increases student achievement.

Figure 7.4 Professional Teacher Growth (PTG) Plan

Name: _Amy_   **Mentor:** _Brooklyn_   **Date:** _10/1_   **X Fall**

School: _Coyote Hills_   **Grade:** _3^rd_   ☐ **Winter**

School Goal(s):   _To implement a variety of teaching strategies to increase test per_   ☐ **Spring**
          grade Reading achievement by 80% on the state achievement level.

Professional Teacher Standard Number and performance Criteria: _1.4_ Level Practice selected for Professional Growth Goal: _Proficiency_ **Professional Growth Goal:** _Uses a variety of strategies to address individual differences among students_	Next steps and strategies toward achieving goal: • _To work with mentor and generate a list of strategies that I will be able to use. I will keep this list in my lesson plan book to use when I am planning. I also want to go to a workshop that will help me with new strategies_ • _Submit a plan to my mentor_
Resources needed including people, materials, and staff development: • _Mentor_ • _Staff Development Workshop on Teaching Strategies_	**Evidence of goal achievement that reflects changes in teaching, student action, or learning progression:** • _Strategy list_ • _Use of a variety of strategies in my lesson plan book_ • _Students are engaged_ • _Students are on task_ • _Less behavior problems_
Observable and/or concrete documentation of the data to be collected: • _90% of students are engaged throughout lesson as evidenced in data that mentor collected_ • _Students are on task as evidenced in data that mentor collected_ • _Three to five different teaching strategies are evident in my lesson plan and in my instruction_	**Timeline for completion:** _10/20 – Find Staff Development Workshop on teaching strategies_ _10/22 – Generate list of strategies with mentor_ _10/29 – Attend workshop if possible_ _11/4 – Generate lesson plan_ _11/11 – Present Lesson for mentor to observe and collect data_

Copies to: Beginning Teacher
          Mentor

Step 4: Reflecting on Professional Growth

Using the *PTG Plan Data Summary* (Figure 7.5) and the *PTG Plan Reflection* (Figure 7.6) tools as a scaffold, teachers document evidence of actions taken toward meeting a professional goal, then analyze this data, and reflect on the progress made toward the goal.

Once one goal is achieved through a series of selected strategies and documented evidence of results, the teacher reviews the PTG Plan Data Summary. At this point, a decision needs to be made:

- Modify the current PTG plan, or
- Determine the next professional growth goal and create another PTG plan. If the decision is to create another PTG plan, the teacher completes the PTG Plan Reflection.

Figure 7.5	Professional Teacher Growth Plan Data Summary

Name: *Amy*   **Mentor:** *Brooklyn*   **Date:** *10/1*   X **Fall**

School: *Coyote Hills*   **Grade:** *3rd*   □ **Winter**

School Goal(s): *To implement a variety of teaching strategies to increase test per grade Reading achievement by 80% on the state achievement level.*   □ **Spring**

Specific data collected to document growth:
Data collected by my Mentor:

11/11 Logging Student Behavior Tool

11/19 On-Task/Off-Task Seating Chart Tool

11/30 Selective Scripting Tool focused on teaching strategies used during instruction

Observed Teacher Behaviors:	**Observed Student(s) Behaviors:**
11/30 Three to five different teaching strategies are evident in my lesson plan and in my instruction	*11/11 90% of students are engaged throughout lesson as evidenced in data that mentor collected* *11/19 Students are on task as evidenced in data that mentor collected*

Summary of growth or lack of growth:

I have met my goals as documented by the tools used by my mentor during observing in my classroom.

Next steps to move forward or modifications to current plan:

I will start working on my next goal using Standard 1: Designs and Plans Instruction.

Copies to: Beginning Teacher
Mentor

| Figure 7.6 | Professional Teacher Growth Plan Reflection |

Name: _Amy_   **Mentor:** _Brooklyn_   **Date:** _10/1_   X Fall

School: _Coyote Hills_   **Grade:** _3rd_   ☐ Winter

School Goal(s): _To implement a variety of teaching strategies to increase test per grade Reading achievement by 80% on the state achievement level._   ☐ Spring

Description: The description explains the "what".	**Describe the Professional Teacher Growth (PTG) goal you selected for yourself based on your *Professional Practice Teacher Self-Assessment Checklist* of the Professional Teacher Standards? What specific areas of growth towards that goal(s) have you made? How did you achieve that growth?** *I selected using a variety of strategies to address individual differences among students as I recognized that not all of my students were learning. I have learned how to group my students according to what they know and what they need to know. Just by grouping my students I recognized that I needed to have a variety of teaching strategies to meet their various needs. I used to web to find different strategies for different kids and found a variety of strategies on differentiated instruction.*
Analysis: Analysis deals with reasons, motives, and interpretation. Any analysis that you provide should be supported by concrete examples.	**What were the results of what you described? What went well in advancing student learning? What specific area of your goal(s) still needs to be improved upon? Why do you believe that you were (or not) able to achieve the growth you desired in this area?** *My students were all learning and were becoming more successful as I designed each group according to their academic needs. I used a different strategy with each group and found out what worked and what didn't work.* *Inquiry worked with some of my students and did not work with others. I think that I need to work on my skills in implementing inquiry learning and use that strategy with one group at a time until all students are familiar with those procedures.* *I need to search for additional resources in determining other needs of my students such as learning styles and developmentally appropriate activities.* *My mentor was supportive and helped me find the resources that I needed. Our grade level meetings also focused on strategies to meet the needs of students.*
Reflection: Your reflection provides the basis for starting the professional growth cycle over or making modifications on your current professional growth goal. Give specific details and concrete examples.	**Based on your analysis, what did you learn about your students and your practice? Identify specific areas of growth your students have made. What did you do to promote this growth? What would you change in your instruction? What would you do differently for your students? Do you need to modify your current professional growth goal or select a new professional growth goal? What goal(s) will you select for yourself next? Why?** *I learned that each of my students has individual needs, and I am becoming more proficient in not only determining what those needs are but how to instructionally meet them. My student success rate went from 50% to 85% as they met in groups based on needs.* *I will continue to grow in this area but I feel that I am prepared to create a new PTG Plan. I will review my Professional Practice Teacher Self-Assessment Checklist to determine my next level of growth.*

Reflection on one's practice is an important component in the process of becoming a professional teacher. This entire protocol is revisited throughout the year as each standard is introduced. Transformation of practice is evidenced through the ability of the teacher to describe, analyze, and reflect. The teacher begins to visibly see the transformation that occurs between comparing the fall, winter, and spring professional growth goals. As the mentor sees what has occurred in the teacher's practice, he also sees what has occurred in his own practice, and he recognizes the part he played in assisting the transformation of the teacher's practice. The partnership that exists between the two will become a cause for celebration.

HOW TO USE THE PROFESSIONAL TEACHER GROWTH PROCESS TOOLS

Step 1: Self-Assessing Teacher Practice

The Professional Teacher Growth Process begins with the teacher selecting a professional teaching standard to focus on during the process. In this sample the teacher standards are embedded within the tools. The teachers read across the Framework of Professional Growth Teacher Practice for each performance criteria and thinks about her performance in the classroom. Each level is cumulative from left to right even though not explicitly stated.

They think about the question, "What evidence do you have to document your level of practice?" Teachers determine which descriptor best describes their practice for each performance criteria (N for novice, E for emergent, P for proficient, A for accomplished, or M for master). They place the correct abbreviation next to the corresponding descriptor on the Professional Practice Teacher Self-Assessment checklist. This process is repeated for each of the standards and all of the performance criteria.

Step 2: Establishing PTG Priorities

Once the teachers have self-assessed their practice on each standard, they now use the Establishing PTG Priorities tool to compile their performance criteria level into a one page document. In the first section the standard performance criteria that is marked with an N for novice, E for emergent, or P for proficient is listed. In the next section the top three priorities are identified for growth. Finally, the number one priority for growth is selected. Teachers refer back to the Framework of Professional Growth Teacher Practice and determine their current level of performance as well as their desired level. This becomes the professional growth goal (Figure 7.7).

Figure 7.7	Establishing Professional Teacher Growth Priorities

Name: _Rod_   **Mentor:** _Molly_   **Date:** _11/1_   X Fall

School: _Cactus HS_   **Grade:** _9th_ _Math_   ☐ Winter

☐ Spring

School Goal(s): _100% of the 2013 Cactus High School cohort will meet or exceed the standards in the state math exam_

First: Identify the standard performance criteria that are marked with an N (novice), E (Emergent), or P (Proficient) in the space below.

N= Novice	E= Emergent	P=Proficient
3.6 Uses strategies to address the diverse needs of learners 3.7 Promotes critical thinking 3.8 Makes connections between learning and real life situations 3.10 Uses instructional time to maximize learning	3.5 Uses instructional strategies that are appropriate to the developmental levels of learners 3.6 Uses a variety of instructional strategies to engage learners 3.11 Ensures students apply new knowledge and skills 3.12 Uses technology and instructional resources	3.1 Utilizes a lesson plan to guide student learning 3.2 Communicates high expectations for learning 3.3 Demonstrates skill, knowledge, and thinking processes 3.4 Uses correct grammar, mechanics, and developmentally appropriate language to communicate with learners

Next: Identify your top three priorities for professional growth.

3.6 Uses strategies to address the diverse needs of learners
3.8 Makes connections between learning and real life situations
3.10 Uses instructional time to maximize learning

Finally: Identify your number one priority for growth and determine the next level of practice you wish to accomplish. Write the level descriptor for each. This becomes your professional growth goal.

Current Level of Practice	Desired Level of Practice
Standard and Performance Criteria: 3.8 Makes connections between learning and real life situations **Performance Level and Descriptor:** N 3.8 Recognizes the value of students' life experiences during lessons.	 **Performance Level and Descriptor:** P 3.8 Implements activities that help students make connections between real life experiences, learning objectives, and goals.

Step 3: Developing a PTG Plan

Teachers begin developing their plan by writing the school's academic goal at the top of the PTG plan tool. The professional growth goal is written using the standard and the performance criteria identified as the number one priority in Step 2. A professional growth goal is specific, measureable, and realistic. The teacher brainstorms strategies for achieving that goal in the form of next steps with the mentor. Resources needed to accomplish the goal are identified as people, materials, and professional development activities. Evidence of goal achievement to determine the impact of the activities on student learning is identified in the next section. Determining the data that will be collected to document professional growth follows. Finally, a timeline is established for accomplishing the goal. The PTG goal is flexible and ongoing in nature. The goal may be initiated as a yearlong goal or as a six-week goal depending on the teacher's needs. A goal is established in the first three to five weeks of the academic year (Figure 7.8).

Step 4: Reflecting on Professional Growth

Using the PTG Plan Data Summary and the PTG Plan Reflection tools as scaffolding, the teacher documents evidence of actions taken toward meeting a professional goal then analyzes this data and reflects on the progress made toward the goal.

In the PTG Plan Data Summary the teacher documents the specific data collected to indicate growth. He writes a summary of both the growth made and areas for growth that may still remain. Finally, he identifies whether he will move on to another goal and PTG plan, or whether he will make modifications to the existing plan. If the decision is to create another PTG plan, the teacher completes the PTG Plan Reflection. Reflection gives the teacher the opportunity to analyze their practice, thinking about what went well and what they need to do differently in the future.

PROFESSIONAL TEACHER GROWTH PROCESS TOOLS IN ACTION

The following mentor example is based on *Establishing PTG Priorities* tool. Rod, a first year ninth grade math teacher at Cactus High School, has self-assessed his performance focusing on Standard 3: Implements and Manages Instruction using the Framework of Professional Growth Teacher Practice and the Professional Practice Teacher Self-Assessment checklist. Molly, his mentor, begins the conference by asking Rod what has happened since their last meeting. When they begin discussing some of Rod's concerns, Rod refers to his students as not being very successful on the math concept he is trying to teach. Molly asks Rod if he has completed his self-assessment for Standard 3 and Rod shares with her his completed Professional Practice Teacher Self-Assessment checklist. Molly asks to see his Establishing PTG Priorities. She asks Rod to complete the first section of the tool. Molly then asks Rod to think about his classroom and his concern. Molly asks Rod to identify his top three priorities for professional growth based on his entry in section one.

Molly asks Rod what he thinks of each of those priorities. She asks, "Which one would have the greatest impact on your practice and your students' learning?" Rod identifies 3.4 and completes his current level of practice. Molly asks Rod, "At what level in the future would you like to see your practice?" Rod states he would prefer to be at the proficient level and he completes the section for his desired level of practice. Since this is the second Establishing PTG Priorities tool that Rod has completed, Molly thinks that he is ready to complete a PTG plan. They proceed to complete the PTG plan together starting with the statement of the school goal for math. The priority goal in the first section is completed. This is the same professional growth goal establish on the priorities tool. Molly asks Rod to think about the different strategies he could use toward achieving his goal. They brainstorm together and decide that Rod will contact the district math director and acquire his students' previous math scores. Molly has a template that she will share with Rod for analyzing the scores.

Rod will determine what his students know and need to know in comparing their scores with the math curriculum. He will design his lesson based on that information. Molly suggests that she will use the scripting tool during the classroom observation to document his instruction and his students' understanding. Molly asks Rod how he will know if his students were successful. Rod responds that he will look at the math assignment and will expect 80% of his students to be successful. They agree to meet after the classroom observation to review the data collected from the lesson and the success rate of the students.

NOTES FOR IMPLEMENTATION

Mentors must become familiar with the instruments and timeline of the school's evaluation system. One of the roles of the mentor is to have a conversation with the site administrator to review the procedures and process for the site evaluation system. Mentors should use this as an opportunity for the administrator to become familiar with the teacher's PTG plan. Teachers and mentors should align the self-assessment process with the school's evaluation system. However, this tool is intended to be used for teacher self-reflection not for evaluation purposes. Teachers may choose to share their growth plans with administrators, but should not be expected to submit them.

At the beginning of the year, this self-assessment process for the teachers is part of the *role focused stage* in transformational learning using the building block of orientation to orient themselves where they are in their role of teacher and their current practice based on the teaching standards. Throughout the year, the self-assessment process will assist the teacher in moving from the role focused stage to the practice focused stage to hopefully arrive at the last stage which is learning focused.

Figure 7.8	Professional Teacher Growth (PTG) Plan

Name: *Rod*　　**Mentor:** *Molly*　　**Date:** *11/1*　　X **Fall**

School: *Cactus HS*　　**Grade:** *9th*　*Math*　　□ **Winter**

□ **Spring**

School Goal(s): *100% of the 2013 Cactus High School cohort will meet or exceed the standards in the state math exam*

Professional Teacher Standard Number and performance Criteria *3.8* **Level Practice selected for Professional Growth Goal:**_ *Proficiency* **Professional Growth Goal:** *3.8 Implements activities that help student make connections between real life experiences, learning objectives, and goals.*	**Next steps and strategies toward achieving goal:** 1. *Rod will acquire his students' previous math scores from the district* 2. *Molly will provide a template for Rod to analyze his students' scores* 3. *Rod will compare what his students know with the math curriculum* 4. *Rod will design one lesson in alignment with students' scores and the math curriculum*
Resources needed including people, materials, and staff development: 1. *District math scores for Rod's students* 2. *Template to analyze scores*	**Evidence of goal achievement that reflects changes in teaching, student action, or learning progression:** 1. *Rod will align his math curriculum based on his students' previous knowledge* 2. *Rod's lesson plan will reflect students previous knowledge and design the lesson accordingly* 3. *Rod will review student work*
Observable and/or concrete documentation of the data to be collected: 1. *Lesson plan will be in alignment with students' previous knowledge* 2. *90% of the students will understand the math instruction as documented by the scripting tool used during classroom observation* 3. *80% of the students will successfully complete the math assignment after instruction*	**Timeline for completion:** *11/3 Acquire district math scores for students* *11/7 Use template to analyze data* *11/9 Generate lesson plan* *11/11 Present lesson for mentor to observe and collect data* *11/13 Analyze % of student success on math Assignment* *11/14 Rod and Molly will review scripting notes and % of student success*

Copies to: Beginning Teacher
　　　　　　Mentor

Figure 7.9 Framework of Professional Growth Teacher Practice*

STANDARD 1: MANAGING THE LEARNING ENVIRONMENT

The teacher:	NOVICE	EMERGENT	PROFICIENT	ACCOMPLISHED	MASTER
1. Establishes expectations for student behavior	Communicates rules and consequences. Establishes basic routines and procedures.	Establishes clear high expectations for student behavior. Creates specific routines and procedures. Responds appropriately to disruptive behaviors and uses some strategies for maintaining students' productive behavior.	Monitors and uses strategies that reinforce behavior expectations, routines, and procedures. Uses strategies that prevent or lessen disruptive behavior and reinforce expectations for behavior. Transitions are seamless and without disruptions.	Maintains a positive environment through use of consistent routines and procedures, engagement, and behavior reinforcement. Encourages students to develop self-monitoring and reflective skills. The classroom is consistently conducive to learning.	Fosters an environment in which students show ownership of routines and procedures, are continually engaged, and reflect on learning and behavior. The classroom is exceptionally focused on learning.
2. Establishes and maintains a respectful and nurturing learning environment	Establishes mutual respect with individual students. Acknowledges some incidents of unfairness and disrespect.	Establishes standards of respect. Models equitable and respectful relationships. Uses some strategies to respond to unfairness and disrespect.	Promotes caring and respectful interactions between all students. Responds to all incidents of unfairness and disrespect equitably. Encourages students to respect differences.	Reflects adherence to established standards of mutual respect. Frequently recognizes students' efforts with positive, constructive remarks. Responds to students' disrespect and implements consequences.	Provides opportunity for the students to monitor their own behavior and offers suggestions for maintaining a positive, caring environment conducive to learning. Students demonstrate caring attitudes for one another.
3. Promotes student responsibilities and self-discipline	Promotes student responsibility for self. Creates opportunities for individual students to have classroom responsibilities. The teacher acts as a professional role model and demonstrates integrity and ethical behavior.	Uses some strategies and activities to develop students' self discipline and responsibility to others recognizing their rights and needs. Students share in classroom responsibilities.	Promotes positive student interactions as members of large and small groups. Provides some opportunities for student leadership within the classroom.	Engages students in individual and group work that promotes responsibility to the classroom community. Supports students to take initiative in classroom leadership recognizing individual and others' rights.	Facilitates an environment in which students take initiative socially and academically. Promotes and supports student leadership beyond the classroom.
4. Recognizes and values differences among individuals	Acknowledges individual differences among students.	Develops some strategies to address individual differences among students.	Uses a variety of strategies to address individual differences among students.	Promotes caring, respectful, and equitable relationships among students with individual differences.	Fosters a safe, inclusive, and equitable learning community. Students actively participate in maintaining a climate of equity, caring, and respect.

(left margin label: PERFORMANCE CRITERIA)

*Refer to Resource C for Framework Standards 1–4.

Figure 7.10 Professional Practice Teacher Self-Assessment Checklist*

Use the ***Framework of Professional Growth Teacher Practice*** to determine your level of performance. Use this tool by placing an **N** (Novice), **E** (Emergent), **P** (Proficient), **A** (Accomplished), or **M** (Master) by the performance criteria to indicate how you self-assessed your practice in the framework. Think about the evidence you have to document that level of practice.

❑ Fall
❑ Winter
❑ Spring

Standard 1: Managing the Learning Environment	Standard 2: Designing and Planning Instruction	Standard 3: Facilitating Student Learning
1. Establishes expectations for student behavior	1. Utilizes academic standards to plan instruction	1. Utilizes a lesson plan to guide student learning
2. Establishes and maintains a respectful and nurturing learning environment	2. Utilizes student assessments to plan instruction	2. Communicates high expectations for learning
3. Promotes student responsibilities and self-discipline	3. Plans instruction to meet the diverse needs of learners	3. Demonstrates skill, knowledge, and thinking processes
4. Recognizes and values differences among individuals	4. Links learning to students' prior knowledge and experiences	4. Uses correct grammar, mechanics, and developmentally appropriate language to communicate with learners
5. Facilitates collaboration among learners	5. Plans short term learning objectives and long term curriculum goals	5. Uses instructional strategies that are appropriate to the developmental levels of learners
6. Establishes an environment for student success	6. Includes a variety of methods in instructional plans	6. Uses strategies to address the diverse needs of learners
7. Utilizes active participation strategies	7. Includes a variety of technology, materials, and resources in instructional plans	7. Promotes critical thinking
8. Arranges and manages the classroom environment for student success	8. Develops learning experiences that are developmentally appropriate for learners	8. Makes connections between learning and real life situations
	9. Develops learning experiences that address the cognitive levels of learners	9. Uses a variety of instructional strategies to engage learners
		10. Uses instructional time to maximize learning
	10. Plans for experiences that align with learning objectives that accurately represent content.	11. Ensures students apply new knowledge and skills
Name:	**Date:**	12. Uses technology and instructional resources

*Refer to Resource D for complete Self-Assessment Checklist 1–4.

Figure 7.11	Establishing Professional Teacher Growth Priorities

Name: _____ **Mentor:** _____ **Date:** _____ ☐ **Fall**

School: _____ **Grade:** _____ ☐ **Winter**

School Goal(s): _____ ☐ **Spring**

First: Identify the standard performance criteria that are marked with an N (Novice), E (Emergent), or P (Proficient) in the space below.

N = Novice	E = Emergent	P = Proficient

Next: Identify your top three priorities for professional growth.

Finally: Identify your number one priority for growth and determine the next level of practice you wish to accomplish. Write the level descriptor for each. This becomes your professional growth goal.

Current Level of Practice	Desired Level of Practice
Standard and Performance Criteria: _____ (i.e., 1.4 Respect the individual differences among learners)	
Performance Level and Descriptor: _____ (i.e., N 1.4 Acknowledges individual differences among students)	**Performance Level and Descriptor:** _____ (i.e., P 1.4 Uses a variety of strategies to address individual differences among students)

| Figure 7.12 | Professional Teacher Growth (PTG) Plan |

Name: _____ **Mentor:** _____ **Date:** _____ ☐ **Fall**

School: _____ **Grade:** _____ ☐ **Winter**

School Goal(s): _____ ☐ **Spring**

Professional Teacher Standard Number and performance Criteria: Level Practice selected for Professional Growth Goal: Professional Growth Goal:	Next steps and strategies toward achieving goal:
Resources needed including people, materials, and staff development:	Evidence of goal achievement that reflects changes in teaching, student action, or learning progression:
Observable and/or concrete documentation of the data to be collected:	Timeline for completion:

Copies to: Beginning Teacher
Mentor

Figure 7.13 Professional Teacher Growth Plan Data Summary

Name: _____ **Mentor:** _____ **Date:** _____ ☐ **Fall**

School: _____ **Grade:** _____ ☐ **Winter**

School Goal(s): _____ ☐ **Spring**

Specific data collected to document growth: **Data collected by my Mentor:**

Observed Teacher Behaviors:	**Observed Student(s) Behaviors:**

Summary of growth or lack of growth:

Next steps to move forward or modifications to current plan:

Copies to: Beginning Teacher
Mentor

Figure 7.14	Professional Teacher Growth Plan Reflection

Name: _____ **Mentor:** _____ **Date:** _____ ☐ **Fall**

School: _____ **Grade:** _____ ☐ **Winter**

School Goal(s): _____ ☐ **Spring**

Description: The description explains the "what."	Describe the Professional Teacher Growth (PTG) goal you selected for yourself based on your *Professional Practice Teacher Self-Assessment Checklist* of the Professional Teacher Standards? What specific areas of growth towards that goal(s) have you made this year? How did you achieve that growth?
Analysis: Analysis deals with reasons, motives and interpretation. Any analysis that you provide should be supported by concrete examples.	What were the results of what you described? What went well in advancing student learning? What specific area of your goal(s) still needs to be improved upon? Why do you believe that you were (or not) able to achieve the growth you desired in this area?
Reflection: Your reflection provides the basis for starting the professional growth cycle over or making modifications on your current professional growth goal. Give specific details and concrete examples.	Based on your analysis, what did you learn about your students and your practice? Identify specific areas of growth your students have made. What did you do to promote this growth? What would you change in your instruction? What would you do differently for your students? Do you need to modify your current professional growth goal or select a new professional growth goal? What goal(s) will you select for yourself next? Why?

8

Professional Mentor Growth Process

PURPOSE FOR THE PROFESSIONAL MENTOR GROWTH PROCESS

The *Professional Mentor Growth Process* involves a series of tools to assist in the development of a mentor's practice through continual self-reflection, analysis, goal setting, and artifact collection. The process of guided self-assessment leads mentors to identify their assets of practice (strengths) and recognize opportunities for growth (challenges). Just as the mentor acts as a support provider to the beginning teacher during the professional growth process, it is important that the mentor supervisor act as a support provider to the mentor. The person can help in goal setting and data collection as well as provide reflective collaboration to help transform mentor practice.

It is essential that mentors make the connection between what is occurring within the interactions of their mentoring and the expectations of performance set forth in the Professional Mentor Standards (Horn & Metler-Armijo, 2010). To be meaningful, the self-assessment must involve comparing one's practice to performance criteria within the standards. There are six mentor standards that were developed in 2004 by the authors and mentors to assess practice and set professional goals and revised in 2010. These include:

1. Establish and maintain mentoring relationships.

2. Demonstrate diverse mentor roles.

3. Use effective communication skills.

4. Implement transformative assessment.

5. Catalyst for instructional practices.

6. Model professional growth.

Research reveals that setting challenging goals leads to higher levels of performance when those goals are planned, focused, and specific (Stronge, Tucker, & Hindman, 2004). The researchers identified five basic components of goal setting:

1. Identification of need

2. Description of baseline data relevant to the need

3. Articulation of a goal

4. Strategies for achieving the goal

5. Documentation of results (pp. 18, 20)

The process for developing the Professional Mentor Growth (PMG) plan described below incorporates the self-assessment process, the development of professional goals based on the assessment, identification of evidential artifacts, and reflection on growth.

DESCRIPTION OF THE PROFESSIONAL MENTOR GROWTH (PMG) PROCESS

The four steps in the professional mentor growth process for developing a Professional Mentor Growth (PMG) plan mirrors the Professional Teacher Growth Process described in Chapter 7. In brief the steps are *self-assessing practice, establishing professional growth priorities, developing a professional growth plan*, and *reflecting on professional growth*. Evidential artifacts are collected in a professional portfolio by the mentor. Each step of the professional growth process and the tools used are described in detail on the following pages. Each step is cumulative and builds on one another.

A completed sample of each tool is included for the reader to see the tool in context.

Step 1: Self-Assessing Practice

Mentors first self-assess their current level of practice using two tools: *Framework of Professional Growth Mentor Practice* and *Professional Practice Mentor Self-Assessment Checklist.* Both of these tools were designed using the Professional Mentor Standards (Horn & Metler-Armijo, 2010).

The Framework of Professional Growth Mentor Practice is a continuum of professional mentoring standards based on different levels of mastery as described by performance criteria. Each level is cumulative from left to right. The mentor starts at the emerging level. If they are proficient at the emerging level, they go to the next level. The mentor continues until he reaches his level of proficiency.

The Framework of Professional Growth Mentor Practice is divided into three developmental levels which includes:

1. Emerging: Moves toward understanding basic mentoring procedures, begins to apply new strategies, and implements tools to be used during classroom observations.

2. Applying: Successfully collaborates with teachers in support of their practice and easily applies mentoring performance criteria.

3. Integrating: A level of development in which the mentor is consistently innovative and creative in all areas of mentoring and professional development and easily integrates what he or she has learned. As a leader in the school, district, and local community, the integrating mentor conducts professional development classes for beginning and continuing teachers and attends conferences and workshops that further develop their professional growth.

Each framework level addresses what a mentor should know and be able to do relative to each of the Professional Mentor Standards. Each developmental level describes the mentor's professional practice (Figure 8.1).

The Professional Practice Mentor Self-Assessment Checklist is used in conjunction with the Framework of Professional Growth Mentor Practice Standards 1–6 to provide mentors a means of keeping a written record of their determined level of current practice. Each level is abbreviated using E for Emergent, A for Applying, or I for Integrating to indicate how they self-assessed their practice (Figure 8.2). The next two examples are just a sample extracted from the complete tools. The Framework of Professional Growth Mentor Practice is in Resource E, and the checklist can be found in Resource F.

Figure 8.1 Framework of Professional Growth Mentor Practice*

Mentor Standard 2: Demonstrate Diverse Mentor Roles Mentors demonstrate diverse roles effectively in mentoring relationships			
Performance Criteria	**Emerging**	**Applying**	**Integrating**
2.1 Work collaboratively with teachers and others.	Mentor meets regularly with teachers as established by the district.	Mentor works together with the teachers to follow the *CDC Cycle and Journal Record* procedures.	Mentor works collaboratively with teachers and other school and district personnel to accomplish district and site-based goals.
2.2 Facilitate discussion with the teacher regarding analyzing classroom observation data and reflecting on teacher and student behaviors in order to accelerate the teacher's practice.	Mentor collects classroom data based on the discussion with the teacher during the *Planning Conference*. During the *Reflective Conference* the mentor allows the teacher to begin to analyze the data.	Mentor leads the discussion with the teacher to identify the impact of instructional practices on student behavior and learning as evidenced by the collected data.	Mentor regularly uses the *CDC Cycle and Journal Record* procedures to assist the teacher in the identification of effective instructional practices, reflection, and determining next steps.
2.3 Model differentiated mentoring stances (instructive, collaborative, and facilitative).	Mentor identifies the three stances of mentoring and begins to use them in practice.	Mentor demonstrates the use of instructive, collaborative, and facilitative stances when conferencing with others.	Mentor demonstrates the use of the instructive, collaborative, and facilitative stances and uses each appropriately.
2.4 Differentiate mentoring based on andragogy to meet the diverse needs of teachers.	Mentor has a basic understanding of adult learning theory and strategies.	Mentor utilizes some differentiated adult learning strategies in working with teachers.	Mentor differentiates adult learning strategies when interacting with the teacher during the *CDC Cycle and Journal Record* procedures.

*Refer to Resource E for Framework Standards 1–6.

Figure 8.2 Professional Practice Mentor Self-Assessment Checklist*

Place an **E** (Emerging), **A** (Applying), or **I** (Integrating) by the performance criteria to indicate how you self-assessed your practice in the Framework for Professional Growth.						*X* Fall ☐ Winter ☐ Spring
Standard 1: Establish and Maintain Mentoring Relationships		**Standard 2: Demonstrate Diverse Mentor Roles**		**Standard 3: Use Effective Communication**		
A	1.1 Work collaboratively to utilize school and community resources.	*E*	2.1 Work collaboratively with teachers and others.	*A*	3.1 Use a variety of communication tools with teachers and school community to respond professionally to verbal and written communication.	
E	1.2 Establish a confidential relationship.	*E*	2.2 Facilitate discussion with the teacher regarding analyzing classroom observation data and reflecting on teacher and student behaviors in order to accelerate the teacher's practice.	*E*	3.2 Use appropriate non-verbal behaviors.	
E	1.3 Use the *Conference Data Conference (CDC) Cycle* to provide a variety of experiences for the teachers through the use of mentor language, tools, and reflection.	*A*	2.3 Model differentiated mentoring stances (instructive, collaborative, and facilitative).	*A*	3.3 Use active listening skills.	
E	1.4 Identify and address the professional needs of the teachers based on teacher standards and expectations.	*A*	2.4 Differentiate mentoring based on andragogy to meet the diverse needs of teachers.	*E*	3.4 Use questioning techniques and strategies that address a variety of cognitive levels.	
				E	3.5 Develop a positive working relationship with school and district personnel.	
Name: *Karen*				**Date:** *8/7*		

*Refer to Resource F for complete Self-Assessment Checklist 1–6.

Step 2: Establishing PMG Priorities

Mentors identify areas for growth based on their self-assessment using the tool Establishing PMG Priorities. The tool is designed to assist mentors as they focus on their own performance and identify their professional development growth needs. The top priority is determined and becomes the focus for a professional growth goal (Figure 8.3).

Figure 8.3	Establishing Professional Mentor Growth Priorities

Name: _Karen_

District: _Desert Hills_

Date: _10/1_   **X Fall**
☐ **Winter**
☐ **Spring**

First: Using the *Professional Mentor Practice Self-Assessment Checklist,* place the standard performance criteria that are marked with an E (Emerging), or A (Applying), or I (Integrating) in the corresponding space below.

E = Emerging	A = Applying	I = Integrating
1.2 Confidential relationships 1.3 Using CDC Cycle 1.4 Needs of teacher 2.1 Collaboration with teachers 2.2 Facilitate discussion 3.2 Use non-verbal behaviors 3.4 Questioning skills 3.5 Positive relationships	1.1 Collaboration with school and community 2.3 Models stances 2.4 Differentiation 3.1 Communication tools 3.3 Listening skills	

Next: Identify your top three priorities for professional growth.

1.2 Establish a confidential relationship.
1.3 Use the Conference Data Conference (CDC) Cycle to provide a variety of experiences for the teachers through the use of mentor language, tools, and reflection.
2.1 Work collaboratively with teachers and others.

Finally: Identify your number one priority for growth and determine the next level of practice you wish to accomplish. Write the level descriptor for each. This will become your professional growth goal.

Current Level of Practice	Desired Level of Practice
Standard: Standard 1:Establish and Maintain Mentoring Relationships **Performance Level and Criteria:** E 1.3 Mentor uses an instructive stance in the Conference Data Conference (CDC) Cycle and CDC Journal Record. Mentor shows an awareness of mentor language.	**Performance Level and Criteria:** A 1.3 Mentor uses a collaborative stance in the CDC Cycle and CDC Journal Record. A variety of data collection tools are used to foster reflection.

Step 3: Developing a PMG Plan

Based on the professional growth goal identified in Step 2, the mentor develops a plan of action for meeting the goal. Using the tool, *Professional Mentor Growth (PMG) plan* helps mentors to focus on a specific professional growth goal that is relevant to both the mentor and to the district he or she serves. A goal is established in the first three to five weeks of the academic year. The PMG goal is flexible and ongoing in nature. The goal may be initiated as a yearlong goal or as a six-week goal depending on the mentor's needs. Mentors meet with their supervisor to discuss their goal and establish the PMG plan. The action plan provides the mentor a focus for support from the supervisor and a pathway towards achievement throughout the mentoring process (Figure 8.4).

Figure 8.4	Professional Mentor Growth (PMG) Plan

Name: _Karen_ **Supervisor:** _Brandi_ **Date:** _10/1_   X **Fall**
☐ **Winter**
District: _Desert Hills_   ☐ **Spring**

Professional Mentor Standard Number and Performance Criteria _1.3_	**Next steps and strategies toward achieving goal:**
Level Practice selected for Professional Growth Goal: _Applying_ **Professional Growth Goal:** *Work with the Beginning Teacher in using the Framework of Professional Growth Teacher Practice to identify areas of growth. Mentor identifies tools to collect data for evidence of growth and provides relevant data. Specific needs are addressed through the Conference Data Conference (CDC) Journal Record.*	• *To work with the beginning teacher to review areas of growth from the Establishing Professional Growth Priorities based on the framework.* • *Identify a set of tools to collect data* • *Use the CDC Journal Record.*
Resources needed including people, materials, and staff development: • *Tools* • *Continued Mentor Staff Development Workshops on Mentoring* • *Get permission from teachers to share the CDC Journal Records*	**Evidence of goal achievement that reflects changes in teaching, student action, or learning progression:** • *Completed Framework of Professional Growth Teacher Practice to identify needs* • *Completed tools based on beginning teachers' needs* • *Needs are documented through the CDC Journal Records* • *Series of CDC Journal Entries to document growth*
Observable and/or concrete documentation of the data to be collected: • *100% of teachers complete the Framework of Professional Growth Teacher Practice to identify needs* • *Tools are aligned with needs of teachers* • *For each tool used, CDC Journal Records are submitted* • *Three to five different CDC Journal Records document growth* • *All teachers' names will be removed before submission.*	**Timeline for completion:** *10/20—Attend Staff Development Workshop on mentoring* *10/22—Generate list of tools to use with teachers* *11/4—Complete tools for each teachers* *11/11—Present three to five CDC Journal Records to the teacher for documentation of growth*

Copies to: Mentor
Supervisor

Step 4: Reflecting on Professional Growth

Using the *PMG Plan Data Summary* (Figure 8.5) and the *PMG Plan Reflection* (Figure 8.6) tools as a scaffold, mentors document evidence of actions taken, analyze the data, and reflect on the progress made.

The PMG Plan Reflection is used once the mentor decides that the PMG plan is accomplished. The mentor may decide that the goal has not been accomplished once the tool is used. If not, the mentor returns to the plan. The reflection is completed once the mentor determines the goal has been accomplished. Reflection on one's practice is an important component in the process of being a professional. Transformation of practice is evidenced through the ability of the mentor to describe, analyze, and reflect. The mentor begins to visibly see the transformation that occurs between comparing numerous professional growth goals.

Figure 8.5 Professional Mentor Growth Plan Data Summary

Name: *Karen*   **Supervisor:** *Brandi*   **Date:** *10/1*   **X** Fall
                                                                      ☐ Winter
District: *Desert Hills*   ☐ Spring

Specific data collected to document growth:

10/20—Attended Staff Development Workshop on mentoring
10/22—Generated list of tools to use with teachers
11/4—Completed tools for each teachers
11/11—Presented three to five CDC Journal Entries aligned to the needs of the teacher for documentation of growth

---

Observed Mentor Behaviors:

11/15 Conversation with the Supervisor to share mentor portfolio documented change in behavior from emerging to applying

---

Summary of growth or lack of growth:

I have as met my goals documented by the CDC Journal Entries, the use of appropriate tools aligned with the needs of my teachers, and my ability to discern what is needed to transform the teachers' practice as well as my own.

Next steps to move forward or modifications to current plan:

I will start working on my next goal using the emerging criteria from Standard 1: Establish and Maintain Mentoring Relationships.

Copies to: Mentor
          Supervisor

Figure 8.6	Professional Mentor Growth Plan Reflection

Name: _Karen_

District: _Desert Hills_

Date: _10/1_   **X** Fall
☐ Winter
☐ Spring

Description: The description explains the "what."	**Describe the Professional Mentor Growth (PMG) goal you selected for yourself based on your *Professional Practice Self-Assessment Checklist* of the *Professional Mentor Standards*. What specific areas of growth towards that goal(s) have you made? How did you achieve that growth?** *I selected to work with the Beginning Teacher in using the Framework of Professional Growth Teacher Practice to identify areas of growth. I identified tools to collect data for evidence of growth and provide relevant data. Specific needs are addressed through the Conference Data Conference (CDC) and CDC Journal Records. I have learned how to use a variety of tools to meet the needs of my beginning teachers based on their own self-assessment using the framework. I have also incorporated the use of the CDC Journal Records every time I meet with my beginning teacher to keep running records of our conversations so that we can look at them and identify areas of growth.*
Analysis: Analysis deals with reasons, motives, and interpretation. Any analysis that you provide should be supported by concrete examples.	**What were the results of what you described? What went well in transforming teacher practice? What specific area of your goal(s) still needs to be improved upon? Why do you believe that you were or were not able to achieve the growth you desired in this area?** *My teachers became more successful as I used the CDC Journal Records and selected appropriate tools to document what was happening in the classroom. I used a different tool with each teacher dependent upon their specific needs. The data collected in the classroom allowed the teacher to see what worked and what didn't work.* *I need to continue my staff development workshops to gain a higher level of knowledge and skills in working collaboratively with my beginning teachers.* *I believe I did accomplish my professional goal.*
Reflection: Your reflection provides the basis for starting the professional growth cycle over or making modifications on your current professional growth goal. Give specific details and concrete examples.	**Based on your analysis, what did you learn about your teachers and your practice? Identify specific areas of growth your teachers have made. What did you do to promote this growth? What would you change in your mentoring? Do you need to modify your current professional growth goal or select a new professional growth goal?** *I learned that each of my teachers has individual needs and I am becoming more proficient in not only determining what those needs are but how to have a collaborative conversation with each teacher to allow her to determine what needs to be accomplished in her classroom. All of my teachers completed the framework and identified areas of growth.* *I will continue to grow in this area but I feel that I am prepared to create a new PMG Plan.*

HOW TO USE THE PROFESSIONAL MENTOR GROWTH PROCESS TOOLS

Step 1: Self-Assessing Mentor Practice

The Professional Mentor Growth Process begins with the mentors individually selecting a mentor standard to focus on during the process. The mentors read across the Framework of Professional Growth Mentor Practice for each performance criteria and think about their interactions with their teachers. They ask the question, "What evidence do you have to document your level of practice?" Each level is cumulative from left to right.

Mentors determine which descriptor best describes their practice for each performance criteria (E for emerging, A for applying, or I for integrating). They place the correct abbreviation next to the corresponding descriptor on the Professional Practice Mentor Self-Assessment Checklist (Figure 8.7). The process is repeated for each of the standards and all of the performance criteria.

Step 2: Establishing PMG Priorities

The mentors use the *Establishing PMG Priorities* tool to compile their performance criteria level into a one-page document. In the first section, the standard performance criteria that are marked with an E for emerging, A for applying, or I for integrating is listed. In the next section, the top three priorities are identified for growth. Finally, the number one priority for growth is selected. Mentors refer back to the Framework of Professional Growth Mentor Practice and determine their current level of performance as well as their desired level. The becomes the mentor's professional growth goal (Figure 8.8).

Step 3: Developing a PMG Plan

The professional growth goal is written using the standard and the performance criteria identified as the number one priority in Step 2. A professional growth goal is specific, measureable, and realistic. The mentor brainstorms strategies for achieving that goal in the form of next steps with their supervisor. Resources needed to accomplish the goal are identified as people, materials, and professional development activities. Evidence of goal achievement to determine the impact of the activities on transforming the teachers' practice is identified in the next section. Determining the data that will be collected to document professional growth follows. Finally, a timeline is established for accomplishing the goal (Figure 8.9).

Step Four: Reflecting on Professional Growth

In the PMG Plan Data Summary the mentor documents specific data collected that indicates growth. He writes a summary of both the growth made and areas for growth that may still remain. Finally, he identifies whether he will move on to another goal and PMG plan or whether he will make modifications to the existing plan. If the decision is to create another PMG plan, the mentor completes the PMG Plan Reflection. Completing the form gives the mentor the opportunity to analyze his practice and think about what went well and what he needs to do differently in the future.

PROFESSIONAL MENTOR GROWTH PROCESS TOOLS IN ACTION

The following example is based on Establishing PMG Priorities tool. Lori, a first-year mentor in the Rolling Hills K–12 District, has self-assessed her performance focusing on Standard 2: Demonstrate Diverse Mentor Roles using the Framework of Professional Growth Mentor Practice and the Professional Practice Mentor Self-Assessment Checklist. Natalie, her supervisor, begins the session by asking Lori, "What has happened since our last meeting?" Lori informs Natalie that she would like assistance in completing her PMG plan. Lori shares with her her completed Professional Practice Mentor Self-Assessment Checklist and her Establishing PMG Priorities. Lori has completed her priorities and selected a growth goal.

They proceed to complete the PMG plan together starting with the priority professional goal established at the end of the priorities tool. Natalie says to Lori, "Think about the different strategies you could use toward achieving her goal." They brainstorm together, and Lori decides that she will contact a veteran mentor and ask permission of the mentor and one of her teachers to observe them during a data collection session and the reflective conference when they analyze the data. Lori will then practice the same protocol with one of her teachers. She will select appropriate student behavior data collection tools as needed. When Lori is ready, she will ask one of her teachers if Natalie could observe them through the data collection sessions. Once permission is given, Natalie will become an observer during the data collection sessions.

Lori determines what observable and concrete data needs to be collected. She decides that she needs to write a reflection herself on the process and provide Natalie with the following documentation: (a) summaries of five reflective conferences, (b) data collection tools that were used will be attached, and (c) CDC journal entries of those five teachers will also be attached. She makes a commitment to delete the names of any of her teachers if she shares data collection tools or reflective conference conversations. Lori will ask five teachers for their permission to share their information with Natalie with their names deleted.

Figure 8.7 Professional Practice Mentor Self-Assessment Checklist*

Place an **E** (Emerging), **A** (Applying), or **I** (Integrating) by the performance criteria to indicate how you self-assessed your practice in the Framework for Professional Growth.	**X** Fall ☐ Winter ☐ Spring

Standard 1: Establish and Maintain Mentoring Relationships		Standard 2: Demonstrate Diverse Mentor Roles		Standard 3: Use Effective Communication	
A	1.1 Work collaboratively to utilize school and community resources.	**E**	2.1 Work collaboratively with teachers and others.	**A**	3.1 Use a variety of communication tools with teachers and school community to respond professionally to verbal and written communication.
E	1.2 Establish a confidential relationship.	**E**	2.2 Facilitate discussion with the teacher regarding analyzing classroom observation data and reflecting on teacher and student behaviors in order to accelerate the teacher's practice.	**E**	3.2 Use appropriate non-verbal behaviors.
E	1.3 Use the *Conference Data Conference (CDC) Cycle* to provide a variety of experiences for the teachers through the use of mentor language, tools, and reflection.	**A**	2.3 Model differentiated mentoring stances (instructive, collaborative, and facilitative).	**A**	3.3 Use active listening skills.
E	1.4 Identify and address the professional needs of the teachers based on teacher standards and expectations.	**A**	2.4 Differentiate mentoring based on andragogy to meet the diverse needs of teachers.	**E**	3.4 Use questioning techniques and strategies that address a variety of cognitive levels.
				E	3.5 Develop a positive working relationship with school and district personnel.

Name: *Lori*   **Date:** *9/15*

*Refer to Resource F for complete Self-Assessment Checklist 1–6.

Figure 8.8 Establishing Professional Mentor Growth Priorities*

Name: _Lori_

District: _Rollingwood_

Date: _11/1_

X **Fall**
☐ **Winter**
☐ **Spring**

First: Identify the standard performance criteria that are marked with an E (Emerging), A (Applying), or I (Integrating) in the space below.

E = Emerging	A = Applying	I = Integrating
2.1 Collaboration with teachers 2.2 Facilitate discussion	2.3 Models stances 2.4 Differentiation	

Next: Identify your top three priorities for professional growth.

2.1 Mentor meets regularly with teachers as established by the district.

2.2 Mentor collects classroom data based on the discussion with the teacher during the Planning Conference. During the Reflective Conference the mentor allows the teacher to begin to analyze the data.

Finally: Identify your number one priority for growth and determine the next level of practice you wish to accomplish. Write the level descriptor for each. This becomes your professional growth goal.

Current Level of Practice	Desired Level of Practice
Standard: Standard 2:Demomstrates Diverse Mentor Roles **Performance Level and Criteria:** E 2.2 Assist the Beginning Teachers in analyzing observation data and identifying teaching behaviors in areas that are strong and need improvement.	**Performance Level and Criteria:** A 2.2 Mentor works with Beginning Teachers to identify the impact of instructional practices on student behavior as evidenced by collected data.

---

*Refer to Resource E for Framework Standards 1–6.

| Figure 8.9 | Professional Mentor Growth (PMG) Plan |

Name: _Lori_   **Supervisor:** _Natalie_   **Date:** _11/1_   X Fall
                                                                                    ☐ Winter
District: _Rollingwood_   ☐ Spring

Professional Mentor Standard Number and Performance Criteria: *Standard 2:Demomstrates Diverse Mentor Roles* ***Level Practice selected for Professional Growth Goal:*** *Applying* **Professional Growth Goal:** *2.2 Mentor leads the discussion with the teacher to identify the impact of instructional practices on student behavior and learning as evidenced by the collected data.*	**Next steps and strategies toward achieving goal:** 1. *Lori will ask permission of a veteran mentor and one of her teachers to shadow walk during the classroom data collection observation and a reflective conference.* 2. *Lori will practice the data collection and reflective conference with her teachers.* 3. *Lori will ask permission of one of her teachers if Natalie can observe him through the data sessions.* 4. *Lori will invite Natalie to sit in on one data collection observation and reflective conference when he is ready.*
Resources needed including people, materials, and staff development: 1. *Veteran mentor and one of her teachers*	**Evidence of goal achievement that reflects changes in teaching, student action, or learning progression:** 1. *Lori will align her protocol with the veteran mentor's protocol regarding data collection.* 2. *Lori will select student behavior data collection tools as appropriate.* 3. *Lori will confidently implement the reflective conference based on a classroom observation data collection session with all of her teachers.*
Observable and/or concrete documentation of the data to be collected: 1. *Lori will summarize her reflective conferences with five of her teachers discussing the appropriateness of her student behavior data collection tools or other tools used with her teachers. This summary will include what went well, what didn't, and her future plans.* 2. *Lori will delete the names of the teachers and share five data collection tools with Natalie.* 3. *Lori will delete the names of the teachers and share five reflective conference CDC journal entries with Natalie to document following the reflective conference protocol when discussing data.*	**Timeline for completion:** *11/3 Seek permission from the veteran mentor and one of the teachers she selects* *11/7 Observe the classroom observation and note any data collection ideas* *11/9 Observe the veteran mentor and teacher during a reflective conference.* *11/11 Begin using appropriate data collection tools during classroom observations with her own teachers and conducting reflective conferences based on data.* *12/13 Ask Natalie to observe.* *1/14 Prepare summary report for Natalie.* *1/21 Meet with Natalie to discuss her PMG Plan.*

Copies to: Mentor
            Supervisor

NOTES FOR IMPLEMENTATION

The professional growth process is used for self-assessment and reflection. The process provides an opportunity for the mentor to create a portfolio of her work based on the mentor standards. At the beginning of the year, the professional growth process for the mentors is part of the *role focused stage* in transformational learning. Mentors identify where they are in their role of mentor based on the mentor standards. Throughout the year the self-assessment process assists the mentors in moving from the role focused stage to the practice focused stage using their organization and analysis skills as building blocks.

Districts might use the process as part of their mentors' evaluation system. Just as teachers' evaluation systems are based on standards, the process allows mentors to be evaluated on standards. The mentors' portfolios could be used as bodies of evidence in a performance-based evaluation.

| Figure 8.10 | Framework of Professional Growth Mentor Practice* |

Mentor Standard 2: Demonstrate Diverse Mentor Roles
Mentors demonstrate diverse roles effectively in mentoring relationships

Performance Criteria	Emerging	Applying	Integrating
2.1 Work collaboratively with teachers and others.	Mentor meets regularly with teachers as established by the district.	Mentor works together with the teachers to follow the *CDC Cycle and Journal Record* procedures.	Mentor works collaboratively with teachers and other school and district personnel to accomplish district and site-based goals.
2.2 Facilitate discussion with the teacher regarding analyzing classroom observation data and reflecting on teacher and student behaviors in order to accelerate the teacher's practice.	Mentor collects classroom data based on the discussion with the teacher during the *Planning Conference*. During the *Reflective Conference* the mentor allows the teacher to begin to analyze the data.	Mentor leads the discussion with the teacher to identify the impact of instructional practices on student behavior and learning as evidenced by the collected data.	Mentor regularly uses the *CDC Cycle and Journal Record* procedures to assist the teacher in the identification of effective instructional practices, reflection, and determining next steps.
2.3 Model differentiated mentoring stances (instructive, collaborative and facilitative).	Mentor identifies the three stances of mentoring and begins to use them in practice.	Mentor demonstrates the use of instructive, collaborative, and facilitative stances when conferencing with others.	Mentor demonstrates the use of the instructive, collaborative, and facilitative stances and uses each appropriately.
2.4 Differentiate mentoring based on andragogy to meet the diverse needs of teachers.	Mentor has a basic understanding of adult learning theory and strategies.	Mentor utilizes some differentiated adult learning strategies in working with teachers.	Mentor differentiates adult learning strategies when interacting with the teacher during the *CDC Cycle and Journal Record* procedures.

*Refer to Resource E for Framework Standards 1–6.

Figure 8.11 Professional Practice Mentor Self-Assessment Checklist*

Place an **E** (Emerging), **A** (Applying), or **I** (Integrating) by the performance criteria to indicate how you self-assessed your practice in the Framework for Professional Growth.			☐ Fall ☐ Winter ☐ Spring

Standard 1: Establish and Maintain Mentoring Relationships		**Standard 2: Demonstrate Diverse Mentor Roles**		**Standard 3: Use Effective Communication**	
	1.1 Work collaboratively to utilize school and community resources.		2.1 Work collaboratively with teachers and others.		3.1 Use a variety of communication tools with teachers and school community to respond professionally to verbal and written communication.
	1.2 Establish a confidential relationship.		2.2 Facilitate discussion with the teacher regarding analyzing classroom observation data and reflecting on teacher and student behaviors in order to accelerate the teacher's practice.		3.2 Use appropriate non-verbal behaviors.
	1.3 Use the *Conference Data Conference (CDC) Cycle* to provide a variety of experiences for the teachers through the use of mentor language, tools, and reflection.		2.3 Model differentiated mentoring stances (instructive, collaborative, and facilitative).		3.3 Use active listening skills.
	1.4 Identify and address the professional needs of the teachers based on teacher standards and expectations.		2.4 Differentiate mentoring based on andragogy to meet the diverse needs of teachers.		3.4 Use questioning techniques and strategies that address a variety of cognitive levels.
					3.5 Develop a positive working relationship with school and district personnel.

Name: **Date:**

*Refer to Resource F for complete Self-Assessment Checklist 1–6.

| Figure 8.12 | Establishing Professional Mentor Growth Priorities |

Name: _____   **Date:** _____ ☐ **Fall**
                                                        ☐ **Winter**
District: _____   ☐ **Spring**

First: Using the *Professional Practice Mentor Self-Assessment Checklist*, place the standard performance criteria that are marked with an E (Emerging), or A (Applying), or I (Integrating) in the corresponding space below.

E = Emerging	A = Applying	I = Integrating

Next: Identify your top three priorities for professional growth.

Finally: Identify your number one priority for growth and determine the next level of practice you wish to accomplish. Write the level descriptor for each. This will become your professional growth goal.

Current Level of Practice	Desired Level of Practice
Standard: **Performance Level and Criteria:**	**Performance Level and Criteria:**

Figure 8.13 Professional Mentor Growth (PMG) Plan

Name: _____ **Supervisor:** _____ **Date:** _____ ☐ Fall
☐ Winter
District: _____ ☐ Spring

Professional Mentor Standard Number and Performance Criteria __ Level Practice selected for Professional Growth Goal: Professional Growth Goal:	Next steps and strategies toward achieving goal:
Resources needed including people, materials, and staff development:	Evidence of goal achievement that reflects changes in teaching, student action, or learning progression:
Observable and/or concrete documentation of the data to be collected:	Timeline for completion:

Copies to: Mentor
Supervisor

| Figure 8.14 | Professional Mentor Growth Plan Data Summary |

Name: _____ **Supervisor:** _____ **Date:** _____ ☐ **Fall**
☐ **Winter**
District: _____ ☐ **Spring**

Specific data collected to document growth:
Observed mentor behaviors:
Summary of growth or lack of growth:
Next steps to move forward or modifications to current plan:

Copies to: Mentor
Supervisor

Figure 8.15 Professional Mentor Growth Plan Reflection

Name: _____

District: _____

Date: _____

☐ **Fall**
☐ **Winter**
☐ **Spring**

Description: The description explains the "what."	Describe the Professional Mentor Growth (PMG) goal you selected for yourself based on your *Professional Practice Self-Assessment Checklist* of the *Professional Mentor Standards.* What specific areas of growth towards that goal(s) have you made? How did you achieve that growth?
Analysis: Analysis deals with reasons, motives, and interpretation. Any analysis that you provide should be supported by concrete examples.	What were the results of what you described? What went well in transforming teacher practice? What specific area of your goal(s) still needs to be improved upon? Why do you believe that you were or were not able to achieve the growth you desired in this area?
Reflection: Your reflection provides the basis for starting the professional growth cycle over or making modifications on your current professional growth goal. Give specific details and concrete examples.	Based on your analysis, what did you learn about your teachers and your practice? Identify specific areas of growth your teachers have made. What did you do to promote this growth? What would you change in your mentoring? Do you need to modify your current professional growth goal or select a new professional growth goal?

Section II

Practice Focused Transformational Learning Stage

The second stage we identified as being *practice focused*. During this stage, individuals spend the greatest part of their time enhancing their practice and skill. They become more familiar with the tools and resources that are available to them in their role as mentor or teacher. Novice mentors increase their organizational skills, develop the expertise necessary for capturing evidence during observations, and hone their data analysis skills to expand beyond student work to teacher development. Novice teachers focus their energy on examining student data in order to get to know their students better. They spend time developing effective lesson plans, organizing their time more efficiently, and implementing instructional strategies that engage students. The experienced mentor refines their practice each time they begin working with a new teacher.

Each chapter in this stage becomes the transition for the mentor role or the teacher role as each focuses on the practice of the teacher within the classroom. Chapters 9–17 present collaborative opportunities for how to look at the work of the classroom teacher through conversation and the collection of classroom data. These chapters answer the questions: What behaviors are occurring in the classroom between the teacher and the student? What interactions are occurring in the classroom between the teacher and the student? What happens in a master teacher's classroom that is different from what happens in a beginning teacher's classroom? How do you use student data to plan for instruction? How do you plan for instruction? What lesson design format do you select for instruction? How does reviewing a video tape of the beginning teacher's instruction in the classroom strengthen the success of his students? How does the beginning teacher engage all of the students in the lesson most of the time? Does the teacher give the students the opportunity to think at a higher level?

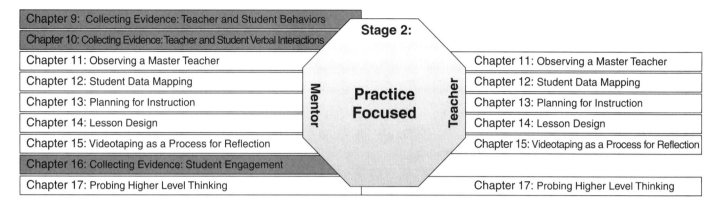

Chapter Introduced	Practices and Tools
Chapter 9	1. General Seating Chart – NCR
	2. On Task/Off Task Seating Chart – NCR
	3. Lesson Pacing Seating Chart – NCR
Chapter 10	4. General Scripting – NCR
	5. Focused Scripting – NCR
	6. Question-Response-Question Scripting – NCR
Chapter 11	7. Veteran Teacher Observation Planning and Reflection – NCR
	8. Veteran Teacher Observation Data Collection – NCR
Chapter 12	9. Student Data Map Characteristics
	10. Student Data Map Standardized Assessment: Multiple Content
	11. Student Data Map Standardized Assessment: Single Content
	12. Student Data Map Teacher Created Assessment
Chapter 13	13. Learning Objectives Worksheet
	14. Task Analysis Part I
	15. Task Analysis Part II
	16. Lesson Element Alignment
Chapter 14	17. Basic Lesson Plan
	18. Inquiry Lesson Plan
	19. Essential Elements Lesson Plan
Chapter 15	20. Video Preparation Checklist
	21. Videotaping Guidelines
	22. Videotaping Reflection
Chapter 16	23. Logging Student Engagement
	24. Logging Engaging Behavior
Chapter 17	25. Questioning Skills: Levels of Knowledge
	26. Questioning Skills: Levels of Knowledge Totals
	27. Questioning Skills: Student Response
	28. Word Bank for Questions Used to Gather Information
	29. Word Bank for Questions Used to Analyze Data
	30. Word Bank for Questions Used to Promote Action
NCR = No carbon required paper. NCR copies are made for the mentor and the beginning teacher to provide each with a copy of the tool.	

9

Collecting Evidence

Teacher and Student Behaviors

PURPOSE FOR COLLECTING EVIDENCE: TEACHER AND STUDENT BEHAVIORS

Transforming instructional practice often requires educators to think of conventional tools in a different way. Seating charts are traditionally used by teachers to show how students are arranged in the classroom. Seating charts used by mentors as transformational data collection tools are designed to capture and record specific behaviors and interactions between the teacher and students. Educators who use seating charts for this purpose go beyond simply putting students' names on paper. They use seating charts for capturing observable teacher and student behaviors, such as

- Students' actions during instruction
- Students and groups of students participating
- Students talking and time of occurrence
- Students interacting with other students
- Students moving around the room and for what purposes
- Students engaging in the content and activities
- The teacher directing questions
- The teacher moving around the room
- The teacher making contact with students

The seating charts described in this chapter provide mentors with a tool to collect data on the complex issues and challenges teachers may encounter.

DESCRIPTION OF SEATING CHARTS

The seating chart tools shared in this book are comprised of two sections designed to focus instruction and transform practice. The top section is intended for the mentor and teacher to identify the context in which the data collection will occur. The teacher identifies the grade level, content, and instructional objectives students should achieve during the lesson. A professional teacher standard is also recorded in this section to emphasize what skills and standards the teacher has selected as an area for growth (see Self-Assessing Teacher Practice, Chapter 7). Collaboratively, the mentor and teacher determine the focus for the observation, why the data is being collected, and what data codes will be used.

The bottom section of the seating chart tools is designed for mentors to capture observable classroom data that reflects the context described in the top section. This section is divided into quadrants to help define the shape of the instructional space. Here the mentor draws the physical layout and student arrangement prior to observation. Data codes, movement patterns, or words are then utilized by the mentor to show evidence of the desired observation focus.

Both sections of the seating chart tools were developed with the intention of focusing reflective conference conversations on what was intended to occur during the lesson and actual observed student and teacher behaviors. Mentors should help teachers analyze the illustrated behaviors in order to make a plan transforming practice, thereby impacting student learning.

There are three basic types of seating charts that mentors can use to help teachers transform their practice: the *general seating chart*, the *on-task/off-task seating chart*, and the *lesson pacing seating chart*.

The *general seating chart* is designed for a variety of data collection responses (Figure 9.1). The data collection area is nondescriptive of the types of actions and focus mentors might capture during an observation. It is intentionally open and meant to reflect the wide range of behaviors that occur in classrooms. Mentors might use this tool to collect data for the teacher to determine how the classroom layout impacts teacher interaction with students. Other possible uses for this tool are recording numbers of students called upon, drawing teacher movement, and capturing student-to-student interactions.

The *on-task/off-task seating chart* is designed for mentors to collect evidence of specific student actions that reflect on- and off-task behaviors (Figure 9.2). The teacher and the mentor define on-task behavior and determine what codes will be used. Data collection codes are listed on this tool to indicate which student behaviors are present during instructional time. Mentors use the codes to illustrate such behavior as students who are engaged in the task, students who are not engaged in the task, students talking, or students who are out of seat.

Figure 9.1 General Seating Chart

Beginning Teacher: _Bryce_   **Mentor:** _Jack_

Observation Date: _9/21_   **Grade Level:** _12th_   **Content:** _Physics_

Lesson Objective(s): _SW analyze the relationships among position, velocity, acceleration, and time mathematically._

Professional Teacher Standard: _Create a motivating and engaging classroom environment._

Observation Focus: _How many students do I call on? Which students do I call on?_

Data Focus: ○ Classroom Design   ◉ Students Called On   ○ Teacher Movement   ○ Student Movement

       ○ Teacher/Student Interaction   ○ Interactions between Students   ○ Other _____

Suggestion: Use the quadrants to help draw the classroom design and the student arrangement prior to observation.

Front of Room

Overhead and lecture area

XX X 0		0 0 0
0 X 0	XXX XX XX XXX X XX	XXX 0 A XXX XX
0 0 0	XX X X	0 0 0
0 X 0	0 A 0	X XX A

Figure 9.2	On-Task/Off-Task Seating Chart

Beginning Teacher: _Angie_   **Mentor:** _Kaden_

Observation Date: _9/27_   **Grade Level:** _2ⁿᵈ grade_   **Content:** _Reading_

Lesson Objective(s): _____

Professional Teacher Standard: _Ensuring all students are learning at a high level of engagement._

Observation Focus: _Which students are on and which are off task during reading instruction._

Data Collection Codes: √ = On Task   **T** = Talkers   ↓ = Off Task   **O** = Out of Seat

A = Absent   Other = _Data was collected at 3 minute intervals._

Suggestion: Use the quadrants to help draw the classroom design and the student arrangement prior to observation.

Front of Room

Teacher's Desk

Back of Room

Figure 9.3	Lesson Pacing Seating Chart

Beginning Teacher: _Barbara_   **Mentor:** _Gina_

Observation Date: 10/2   **Grade Level:** _10th_   **Content:** _English_

Lesson Objective(s): _SW use a prewriting plan to develop the main idea(s) with supporting details._

Professional Teacher Standard: _Promotes appropriate classroom participation._

Observation Focus: _How often do students interact with each other during independent work?_

Data Focus: O Interaction between Teacher and Students   O Teacher Talk   O Student Talk

            O Students Called On   ⊙ Interactions between Students   O Other

Time	Lesson Element(s)	Suggestion: Use the grid to help capture observable behaviors.	
10:10 – 10:20	Teacher giving directions		
10:20 – 10:45	Independent Work		
10:45 – 10:55	Whole Group Discussion		

The *lesson pacing seating chart* is designed to show specific evidence of the speed at which observable teacher and student behaviors occur during a lesson (Figure 9.3, page 123). The data collection section of this tool is divided into three segments: time, lesson elements, and data grid. In the *time* column, mentors track specific time intervals during which they collect data. In the *lesson elements* column, mentors record what instructionally is occurring during the lesson. For example, direct instruction, modeling, small group work, or independent work. In the *data grid* column, mentors capture data on the entire class or on individual students. This grid is divided into four quadrants to represent an entire classroom. In the following example, the data shows students interacting with each other during each of the lesson elements. Students are not indicated by individual desks, but by quadrants of the behavior.

HOW TO USE SEATING CHARTS TO COLLECT DATA

During a planning conference early in the year, seating charts can prompt conversations with beginning teachers concerning the physical environment of the classroom and why students are seated in a particular location. For example, a mentor could sit with a beginning teacher and capture the layout and design of the classroom on a general seating chart. During this conversation, the mentor might ask why the teacher chose to place their desk in the back of the room or why all students' desks face each other in rows. Hearing the reasoning behind why the classroom is arranged in the manner it is can help the mentor craft leading questions when issues and concerns arise as a result of the physical arrangement of the classroom.

Building the general seating chart with the beginning teacher allows the mentor to become familiar with the students in the teacher's classroom. Discussions about how students are arranged in the classroom can open a door for the mentor to gain an understanding of how much or how little the beginning teacher knows about her students. For example, if the teacher does not know if the students seated in her classroom have special needs or services, the mentor can direct the teacher to accommodate these needs.

During the planning conference, the beginning teacher and mentor determine which type of seating chart they wish to use based on which form would capture the desired evidence. For example, if a beginning teacher is having concerns about whether he or she was calling on more girls than boys the mentor might suggest the use of a general seating chart. If the beginning teacher is having concerns about how often he or she asks questions to girls vs. boys, the mentor might suggest the lesson pacing seating chart.

During the data collection, the mentor captures the specific data as determined during the planning conference. When using seating charts for a specific purpose, it is important for the mentor to only collect the predetermined teacher and student behaviors. Symbols listed on the chart would be used to notate any teacher or student behaviors. Mentors and teachers can also create their own symbols to reflect a desired behavior.

The conversation during the reflective conference should revolve around what behaviors can or cannot be seen in the collected data. The mentor should begin with questions to help the beginning teacher see what student and teacher behaviors are evident. Listed below are some questions used to gather information evident from seating charts:

- What do you notice about the students' behaviors?
- What insight do you have about your movement patterns around your room?
- Could you list which behaviors were most common in the class?
- On the whole, were your students on task or off task?
- What do you notice about student interactions and their proximity to other students?
- When looking at the timing of your lesson, does the data show similar students responding to your questions?
- Can you articulate parallels between Student A's and Student B's behaviors?

Once the beginning teacher has identified behaviors that relate to the identified data focus, the mentor can help the teacher begin an analysis of the data. Listed below are some questions used to analyze data from seating charts:

- Suppose you had moved into this area of the room more often; what kind of impact might that have had on these four students?
- Did you expect that Student A might be more focused and on task because you moved his seat?
- How often did you include the students in the back of the room when redirecting?
- When you compare the behavior of the students in this half of the room to the other half, what conclusions can you make?
- Can we break down what student behaviors occurred during the last five minutes of your lesson?

Once the teacher determines connections between student behaviors and teacher behaviors, an action plan to transform practice should be created. A sample list of questions used to promote action is listed below:

- If you want to promote change in on-task time, what goal could we create that could cause that change?
- Based on what we've seen, what options do we have to meet the engagement requirements your principal has set?
- Would you like to role-play some possible questions you could ask when dealing with the challenging students?
- In anticipation of your questioning strategies, what student behaviors do you expect to see?

- Which of the steps we have just brainstormed do you need to take first to produce success?

SEATING CHART TOOLS IN ACTION

Sue, the beginning teacher, was preparing to implement small-group instruction. She was concerned about how many of her students would stay on task during independent work while she was teaching mini lessons to small groups. During a planning conference, Sally, her mentor, suggested that data be collected during a time when most of the class was given independent work and Sue worked at the small-group table with students. Sue determined that a small-group mini lesson would last about fifteen minutes. Both agreed that an on-task/off-task seating chart would give them the evidence they needed to determine which students were prepared to work independently. Together, they determined what behaviors would indicate students were on task.

Before the lesson observation occurred, Sally rechecked the room and seating arrangement with Sue. She also reconfirmed the lesson objectives and observation focus and recorded those on the on-task/off-task seating chart form. Every three minutes during the data collection, Sally used the identified symbols to note what each of the students was doing. She also indicated those students that were absent and which desks were empty.

That afternoon, during the prearranged time, Sally met with Sue to discuss the data that was collected. Sally began the conversation with, "So, what went well during this time?"

Sue shrugged her shoulders and stated, "Well it looks like most of my kids were doing what I asked them to do. I had a really hard time not looking at them while they were doing the independent work, but I knew that you would see what was going on. What did you see during the time?"

Sally pulled out the data from her files and laid it on the table in front of Sue. "Let's look at what I recorded. Can you identify which students were generally on task during the independent work?" (Figure 9.4).

"Yes, it looks like most of the students were on task, but there is a group of students who were not."

Sally pointed to the data and asked, "What can we assume about these students in the middle toward the back?"

"Well I just changed where those students sit because they talk all of the time. I felt that if they were in the back, they wouldn't bother the rest of the students as much. Since I put them all together, now those six are really not doing what I expected. I am just not sure where to put them."

"One of the strategies I have seen other teachers use is to put challenging students in places where the teacher has easy access. That way when the students needed redirection, the teacher can easily reach them without drawing the attention of the other students. Can you move those students nearer to the table where you will be doing your small-group instruction without disrupting those students who were on task?"

Sue replied pointing to the seating chart data, "Yes, I can definitely rearrange my seating chart again. This time I will use the empty seats to help buffer the talkers. Can you come in and do this again? I really want to have my management down before I have to be observed doing small groups."

Nodding her head, Sally responded, "Sure! Let's jot this down as a plan of action. You are going to rearrange your seating charts, and I will come in to observe you again during an independent assignment, right?"

"Yes, I can have the students rearranged tomorrow, can you come in Thursday?"

"Definitely!"

NOTES FOR IMPLEMENTATION

During the *practice focused stage,* novice mentors are developing their role as mentor and transitioning from the role of observed to the practice of observer. Experienced mentors, who may want to refine their practice, can use these tools or create additional tools. Seating charts are the easiest set of data collection tools to manipulate and allow mentors the opportunity to connect with familiar classroom behaviors. They assist mentors in building trusting relationships with teachers by providing concrete evidence that can be discussed during reflective conferences rather than having judgmental conversations.

Teachers, during the practiced focused stage, are transitioning from the role of teacher into the practice of classroom and instructional leader. They are building their teaching habits and developing classroom management skills. Seating charts can provide teachers with a visual picture necessary to transform their practice into a more productive and beneficial routine.

The use of seating charts assists mentors and teachers as they transition into the practice of their new roles and build relationships to foster student learning.

Figure 9.4 On-Task/Off-Task Seating Chart

Beginning Teacher: _Sue_   **Mentor:** _Sally_

Observation Date: _9/27/06_   **Grade Level:** _6th grade_   **Content:** _Math_

Lesson Objective(s): _Students will identify how to divide fractions._

Professional Teacher Standard: _APTS #2: Establishing a Learning Climate_

Observation Focus: _Identifying which students are on task and which are off task during a mini lesson._

Data Collection Codes: √ = On Task   **T** = Talkers   ↓ = Off Task   **O** = Out of Seat

A = Absent   Other = _Data was collected at 3 minute intervals._

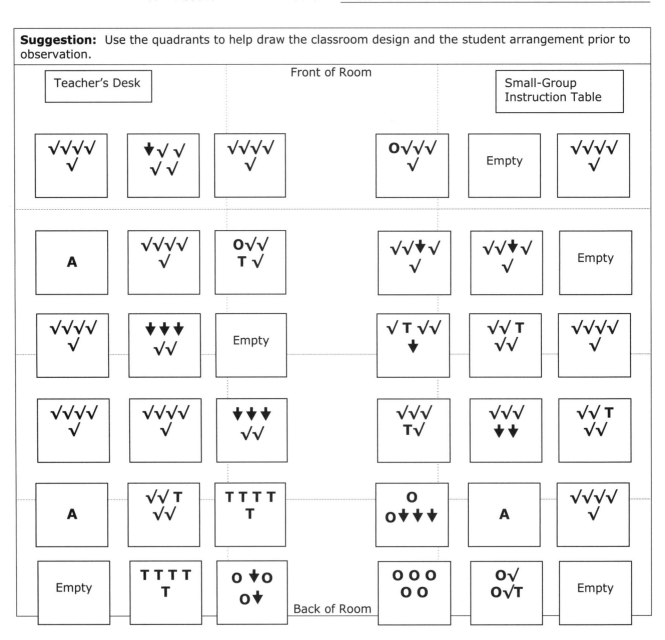

Figure 9.5	General Seating Chart

Beginning Teacher:_____ **Mentor:**_____

Observation Date:_____ **Grade Level:**_____ **Content:**_____

Lesson Objective(s):_____

Professional Teacher Standard: _____

Observation Focus: _____

Data Focus: ○Classroom Design ○Students Called On ○Teacher Movement ○Student Movement
   ○Teacher/Student Interaction ○Interactions between Students ○Other _____

Suggestion: Use the quadrants to help draw the classroom design and the student arrangement prior to observation.

Figure 9.6	On-Task/Off-Task Seating Chart

Beginning Teacher:_____ **Mentor:** _____

Observation Date:_____ **Grade Level:**_____ **Content:**_____

Lesson Objective(s):_____

Professional Teacher Standard: _____

Observation Focus: _____

Data Collection Codes: √ = On Task   **T** = Talkers   ✔ = Off Task   **O** = Out of Seat

A = Absent   Other = _____

Suggestion: Use the quadrants to help draw the classroom design and the student arrangement prior to observation.

| Figure 9.7 | Lesson Pacing Seating Chart |

Beginning Teacher: _____ **Mentor:** _____

Observation Date: _____ **Grade Level:** _____ **Content:** _____

Lesson Objective(s): _____

Professional Teacher Standard: _____

Observation Focus: _____

Data Focus: O Interaction between Teacher and Students   O Teacher Talk   O Student Talk

O Students Called On   O Interactions between Students   O Other _____

Time	Lesson Element(s)	Suggestion: Use the grid to help capture observable behaviors.	

10

Collecting Evidence

Teacher and Student Verbal Interaction

PURPOSE FOR COLLECTING EVIDENCE: TEACHER AND STUDENT VERBAL INTERACTION

The practice of scripting has been used in education for decades as a method to collect data to provide teachers the opportunity to view what they are saying and doing in their classroom and what their students are saying and doing. Scripting is useful for gathering data on most areas of instructional practice and provides an opportunity for the mentor to assist the teacher in analyzing what is happening in the classroom based on facts, not judgments or interpretations. Because the practice is commonly used and a plethora of variations of process and forms exist, it is important that a mentor and beginning teacher have a common understanding of what is meant by scripting. For this reason we present three scripting tools: *general scripting*, *focused scripting*, and *question-response-question* tools along with the process for using each.

DESCRIPTION OF COLLECTING EVIDENCE: TEACHER AND STUDENT VERBAL INTERACTION TOOLS

The mentor uses the *general scripting* tool to script what is generally happening in the classroom (Figure 10.1). The mentor scripts what the teacher says and how students respond. Periodically recording time allows the mentor to ask specific questions such as, "How long did it take you to start the content of the lesson?"

The *focused scripting* tool (Figure 10.2) is used in a process which narrows the focus of what is scripted. The tool itself is similar to the general scripting tool with two additional features: an observation focus and three specific columns for scripting the time, the teacher behavior, and the students' behavior. The three columns are labeled *time, teacher,* and *student.* Periodically the mentor notes the time in the *time* column then records what is being said and done in the appropriate column. The mentor only scripts what is related to the focus of the observation as he uses this tool. The tool includes two copies that are on NCR paper so the mentor and the teacher have a copy of the scripting. It is duplicated to accommodate the majority of the scripting notes. Some areas of focus are expectations, content, rules and procedures, and instructions.

The *question-response-question* tool is used to selectively script a beginning teacher's question, the students' response, and the beginning teacher's follow-up question (Figure 10.3). While analyzing the data, conversations may focus on: Bloom's Taxonomy, higher level versus lower level questioning, open-ended versus closed questions, why the students are giving short one answer response vs. elaborate or thought provoking responses, why the same number of students are always being called on, which students are called on according to gender, or why the same students always share the same kinds of answers.

Figure 10.1	General Scripting

Date: _3/18_   Page 1 of 5

Name: _Fredrick_   **Mentor:** _Kaden_

Grade Level/Subject Area: _Kindergarten – Math_

Lesson Topic: _Patterns_

Academic Standard: **Math Strand 3 PO1:** _Recognize, describe, extend, create, and record simple repeating patterns._

Professional Teacher Standard: _3.5. Use strategies that are appropriate to students' developmental levels_

Time	Scripting
10:05	TD - Everyone come to the group area and sit in our learning circle.
	TD - Hurry up everyone come to the group area.
	TD - James, you need to come too.
	TD – Good job class. You all made it to the group area in less than two minutes!
10:10	TI - Look at what is in the middle of the floor.
	TI - If someone could not see them, how would you describe what is in the middle of the circle?
	I hear lots of different words being used to describe what you see.
	TD - Sam, how would you describe them?
	SR – They are shoes.
10:13	TR - Please describe the shoes.
	SR – They are different colors; white, and red.
	TD - James, what else do you notice?
	SR – They are white then red then white then red.
	TD – That is a pattern; white, red, white, red.
10:15	TD – I have two more shoes, if we wanted to make the row of shoes longer and keep the pattern, which color would go next?

Key: TD=Teacher Directions; TI=Teacher Information; TR=Teacher Response; SR=Student Response

Figure 10.2	Focused Scripting

Date: _9/01_ Page 1 of 3

Name: _Sue_ **Mentor:** _Sally_

Grade Level/Subject Area: _6th Grade Reading_

Lesson Topic: _Reading Comprehension_

Academic Standard: _Reading: Strand 1, Concept 6, PO 5_

Observation Focus: _Teacher stated behavior expectations and student response_

Professional Teacher Standard: _3.2: Communicates high expectations for learning_

Time	Teacher	Students
10:15	• We are continuing our story from yesterday. What story were we reading? • Today we will finish the story and answer some questions.	• The Pufflings
	• We will be operating today as a 3 ring circus. What does that mean? • Some will read by yourself, some with a buddy, and some in small groups with me.	• 5 Students shout out guesses incorrectly.
	• Everyone will answer the same questions.	• Will we answer all of the questions?
	• Yes, everyone will answer all of the questions. • When I look around, all reading books should be open to page 19, and all practice books on page 4.	
	• All will start by reading on your own.	
	• If I don't come around and say anything to you, what does that mean?	• You are reading by yourself.
10:25	• You can start reading.	
	• Teacher walks around room and places some students into reading groups and partners.	• Students begin reading.

| Figure 10.3 | Question-Response-Question Scripting |

Date: _12/3rd_   _Page 1 of 3_

Name: _Sarah_   **Mentor:** _Kent_

Grade Level/Subject Area: _Third/ Reading_

Lesson Topic: _Interpreting/Predicting_

Academic Standard: _(3-R1-C6) PO Make relevant inferences by synthesizing concepts and ideas from a single reading selection._

Professional Teacher Standard: _3.7 Promotes critical thinking_

Teacher Question	Student Response	Teacher Question/Response
We have read most of "The True Story of the 3 Little Pigs." What do you think will happen next in the story?	It's like the other three little pigs story we read. The wolf will go crazy.	Yes, but for now, what do you think will happen next in this story?
What do you mean "the wolf will go crazy?"	He'll get really angry like he did before with he other pigs. He will blow the house down and eat him.	Hmmm. Do you really think the wolf will eat the third pig?
Does some someone else think differently?	I think the third little pig will be okay and the wolf won't be able to hurt him. Well, the third pig was smart, so he'll trick the wolf.	What makes you say the third little pig will be okay?
Where does it say that in the story...that the third little pig was smart?	Student reads the sentence, "He must have been the brains in the family."	Does someone have another example?
What is an example of a way you think the pig will trick the wolf?	Well, this pig had a brick house, so the wolf won't be able to blow it down. Yeah, and if he does, there will be a big mess and the pig will be able to run away. All students respond "yes."	If this is true, do you think the story will have a happy ending?
How do you think the story will end?	The wolf will give up and the third pig will live happily ever after.	Well, let's read on and see what happens, and then we'll compare this story with the first one we read, "The Three Little Pigs."

HOW TO USE THE COLLECTING EVIDENCE: TEACHER AND STUDENT VERBAL INTERACTION TOOLS

While scripting, it is often difficult to record in prose everything being said and the related events. Use shorthand notations to help with the difficulty in recording everything and do not worry about connecting events. Remember to write down only facts, not judgments. Shorthand notations can be helpful when using any of the three scripting tools. Figure 10.4 shows a few shorthand suggestions.

| Figure 10.4 | Scripting Shorthand Notations |

Categories of Teacher Talk = T	Categories of Student Talk = S
T? = Questions	S? = Questions
TR? = Responses to questions	SR? = Responses to questions
TR = Responses to statements	SR = Responses to statements
TI = Information statements	SS = Student initiated statements
TM = Management statements	SMR – Student response to management
TP = Reward and praise statements	
TC = Criticisms and constructive feedback	
TD = Directions or assignments	

Creating a seating map of the classroom and number the students is helpful when noting who is speaking. Use the numbers to refer to which student is speaking. Use quotation marks or capital letters to denote specific actual statements. You may draw a diagram of what is happening in the classroom, such as teacher and student movement (see Chapter 9).

The mentor uses his own shorthand version to recall what was said using the exact words as spoken. When mentors cannot keep up with the pace, it is important not to paraphrase but rather indicate the pause with an ellipsis or a series of three dots (. . .) until they can once again write down exactly what was said. Teachers usually will recall what occurred if the mentor uses their exact words and the exact words of the student. The focus of analysis will depend upon the individual lesson, the chosen focus, and what stands out as relevant or important since as much of the conversation as possible is noted.

How to Use the General Scripting Tool

The *general scripting* tool includes an initial page and second page that is duplicated to accommodate the majority of the scripting notes. The mentor records general information about the beginning teacher and the lesson being taught on the top section of the initial page. This information can be recorded from the lesson plan provided by the beginning teacher. The mentor completes the sections on this tool as he periodically notes the time in the *time* column and records what is being said and done in the class in the *scripting* section. This tool is used to script the overall happenings in the classroom. The mentor scripts the teacher and student behaviors.

How to Use the Focused Scripting Tool

The mentor records not only general information about the beginning teacher and the lesson being taught but also the focus behavior(s) for this scripting session in the top section of the initial page. This information can be copied from the lesson plan provided by the beginning teacher and the focus area(s) determined during the *Planning Conference.* The other additional feature is a third column in the data collection area. The columns are labeled time, teacher, and student. Periodically the mentor notes the time in the *time* column then records what is being said and done by the teacher and student in the appropriate column.

How to Use the Question-Response-Question Tool

This tool is used for scripting what questions the teacher asks, the students' response, and the teacher's follow-up questions. There are three columns: teacher questions, student responses, and teacher questions/responses. The beginning teacher may ask the mentor to observe what types of questions she is asking, or the mentor may suggest that he will come in and script the types of questions the teacher is asking. This occurs during a planning conference. After the observation, the mentor will guide the conversation during the reflective conference so the teacher can identify what types of questions she is asking and how she is responding to her students' responses. The mentor leads the teacher to realize that the type of question she asks depends on the type of response the student gives. The teacher may ask an analysis question, but if the student responds with a factual answer, the question is labeled as a comprehension question. It is the student's response that identifies the type of question asked.

COLLECTING EVIDENCE: TEACHER AND STUDENT VERBAL INTERACTION TOOLS IN ACTION

Christina is an energetic sixth grade science teacher in her first full year of teaching. Jennifer, her mentor, has taught middle school science for 15 years. In their last planning conference, Christina expressed frustration that her students did not seem to be thinking on a systems level about the frog they had dissected virtually. She was planning on having them dissect a real frog next but was worried that they would not take the activity seriously and look at the systems involved. She explained that she had tried several different strategies during the first lessons of the unit, but the students were not responding to her questions at the systems level she was hoping for. She asked Jennifer for ideas. Instead of providing solutions and ideas, Jennifer offered to come in and script what Christina was asking the students and how the students responded. Together they selected the question-response-question scripting tool and set the date and time for the scripting session.

In the reflection conference, Jennifer shares the scripting she did of Christina's lesson (Figure 10.5). Christina takes a few minutes to read over the pages of scripting provided by Jennifer. Pointing to the first page she says, "Why did I ask the first two questions? I know better than that." Together they went through the remaining scripting data. Christina identified questions that she wanted to avoid asking in the future and questions those that she thought were effective to lead the students to think about the systems. Christina plans to use what she learned about questioning during the next dissection she had the class perform.

NOTES FOR IMPLEMENTATION

As discussed in previous chapters, a trusting relationship between the beginning teacher and mentor is key when using the various data collection tools in the classroom. The beginning teacher must have confidence that the scripting data is private. The general scripting tool is used when an immediate concern or focus is not prevalent. Focused scripting narrows what will be scripted because there is a specific focus identified for the observation. The mentor scripts what the teacher says and does as well as scripts the students' behavior. Question-response-question scripting tool is used when the teacher needs to identify the types of questions she is asking and how the students respond. All three tools can be used for classroom observations throughout the year and are printed on NCR paper for immediate feedback.

| Figure 10.5 | Question-Response-Question Scripting |

Date: _10/28_ _Page 1 of 5_

Name: _Christina_ **Mentor:** _Jennifer_

Grade Level/Subject Area: _Sixth Grade Science_

Lesson Topic: _Body systems of a frog_

Academic Standard: _6-S4-C1- PO 7 Describe how the various systems of living organisms work together to perform a vital function_

Professional Teacher Standard: _3.7 Promotes critical thinking_

Teacher Question	Student Response	Teacher Question/Response
Good morning. T? - Are you ready to get started?	SR? No SR? ugh SR? I am so tired,…	Let's start over, Let's get started this morning by reviewing the various systems of living organisms we looked for in the virtual frog dissection we did last week.
T?- Wasn't it cool dissecting the frog on the computer?	SR? (Yelling out) No blood SR? I want to see the guts. SR? When do we get to do the real thing?	TR - Well, I think it was neat to see them on the computer before we dissect a real frog.
TI- The reason we are dissecting frogs is to look at the parts of a living creature that are a part of the various systems of living organisms. T? - Who can name one of the systems we discussed when we did the virtual discussion?	(Students yell out) SR?1 - Lungs SR?2 – Bones SR?3 - Stomach	TR - Many of you have named structures that we saw in the virtual frog; lungs, bones, stomach. We did see these in the dissection. TC -These are parts of systems, not the systems themselves. T? One of you said lungs. Are lungs a system themselves? No, right, what system are they a part of? TP- Yes, the respiratory system
T? What other structures of the frog are in the respiratory system?	SR?1 – Trachea S?2 – Nostrils	TP – Yes T? How do these structures work together?

Figure 10.6	General Scripting

Date: _____ **Page** ____ of _____

Name: _____ **Mentor:** _____

Grade Level/Subject Area: _____

Lesson Topic: _____

Academic Standard: _____

Professional Teacher Standard: _____

Time	Scripting

Figure 10.7	Focused Scripting

Date: _____ **Page** _____ of _____

Name: _____ **Mentor:** _____

Grade Level/Subject Area: _____

Lesson Topic: _____

Academic Standard: _____

Observation Focus: _____

Professional Teacher Standard: _____

Time	Teacher	Students

Figure 10.8 Question-Response-Question Scripting

Date: _____ **Page** ___ **of** ___

Name: _____ **Mentor:** _____

Grade Level/Subject Area: _____

Lesson Topic: _____

Academic Standard: _____

Professional Teacher Standard: _____

Teacher Question	Student Response	Teacher Question/Response

11

Observing a Master Teacher

PURPOSE FOR OBSERVING A MASTER TEACHER

One important component of the mentoring program is the observation of veteran teachers. The purpose for the observation is to allow beginning teachers to watch master teachers demonstrate skills and knowledge sets that match the beginning teacher's individual professional needs.

DESCRIPTION OF OBSERVING A MASTER TEACHER TOOLS

The veteran teacher observation is based on a specific focus arising from a specific need of the beginning teacher. Perhaps the beginning teacher knows reading strategies but has not yet mastered when to use the various strategies with specific groups of students. Observing a master reading teacher in action will expose the beginning teacher new insights into implementing reading strategies with different groups of students.

There are two different tools used for these observations: the *Veteran Teacher Observation Planning and Reflection* tool and the *Veteran Teacher Observation Data Collection* tool. These tools are used in conjunction and follow the CDC Cycle. Both are printed on NCR paper so that both mentor and teacher have instantaneous documentation of the observation process.

The Veteran Teacher Observation Planning and Reflection tool (Figure 11.1) is used before and after the observation. During the planning conference, the tool is used collaboratively to assist the teacher in defining a focus for the observation. Once data has been collected, this tool is used during the reflective conference to capture what the teacher saw and heard related to the observation focus. It also helps establish how the observation will improve the teacher's practice. The Veteran Teacher Observation Data Collection tool (Figure 11.2) is used to record observable student and teacher behaviors that are related to the beginning teacher's identified focus.

HOW TO USE THE OBSERVING A MASTER TEACHER TOOLS

The mentor guides the conversation for clarity between the professional growth goal and the purpose of the observation. Once there is a focus for the observation, that focus is recorded. The mentor will make arrangements with the veteran teacher for the beginning teacher to observe the classroom in action once an area of focus has been determined. Prior to arranging the observation, the mentor asks the beginning teacher the following questions during the planning conference:

- What is your professional growth goal?
- What will assist you with your goal if you were to observe a veteran teacher's classroom?
- What is the focus of the observation?
- How will this increase student learning in your classroom?
- Does the focus of the observation relate to your Professional Teacher Growth (PTG) Goal (see Chapter 7). If it does, how does it relate? If not, why not?
- What questions do you want to ask the veteran teacher?

The mentor then discusses the Veteran Teacher Observation Data Collection tool. The mentor can model for the beginning teacher specific data to collect such as writing down a specific question the teacher asked or a statement the teacher made. It is important for the beginning teacher and the mentor to write down specifically what the teacher is asking or saying rather than paraphrasing what she thinks the teacher asked or said. The mentor can also suggest teachers make a diagram or use descriptive words of what she saw. The mentor emphasizes that the teacher behaviors and the student behaviors that will be recorded correlate to the focus of the

| Figure 11.1 | Veteran Teacher Observation Planning and Reflection |

To be used during the *Planning Conference* and the *Reflective Conference* only

Beginning Teacher: _Kaden_   **Visiting Veteran Teacher:** _Phyllis_

Mentor: _Susan_   **Content/Grade Level:** _Geometry/9th_

Date of Visit: _10/14_   **Professional Growth Goal:** _Standard 3.5_

Determine the following during the *Planning Conference*:

Focus of Observation:

To observe hands-on math strategies in a beginning Geometry class.

How will this observation help increase student learning in my classroom?

I will be able to know which math strategies to use in my classroom without always lecturing.

How does the focus of observation relate to your *Professional Teacher Growth (PTG) Goal or does it*?

My PTG was focused on Standard 3.5: Facilitating Student Learning: Uses strategies that are appropriate to students' developmental levels – Even though my students are in high school, they do not understand the relationships of using geometry in real life situations. This observation will allow me the opportunity to watch Phyllis using hands-on strategies in a geometry classroom.

Questions I want to ask the veteran teacher:

How do you implement hands-on strategies with students who are used to sitting in rows and still manage the classroom?

Data to be Collected: *Teacher directions/hands-on activities/Student actions*

Discuss the following during the *Reflective Conference*:

I saw:	**I heard:**
• *Hands-on Math Strategies* • *Use of technology* • *Students working independently as well as collaboratively* • *Students preparing group presentations* • *Teacher moving around room* • *Teacher writing anecdotal records* • *Teacher was prepared.*	• *Specific teacher directions* • *Students interacting with one another* • *Students preparing to give presentation* • *Teacher redirecting students to task* • *Purposeful noise*
Application to My Practice/What I Learned: *Ways to use hands-on strategies with high school students and meet their developmental levels.*	**Questions I Still Have:** *Do you use hands-on strategies with your algebra students?*

Next Steps:

I will implement the lesson Phyllis used when I have the same objective to teach. I will implement one hands-on strategy with one math group next week.

Figure 11.2	Veteran Teacher Observation Data Collection

Beginning Teacher: _Kaden_ **Visiting Veteran Teacher:** _Phyllis_

Mentor: _Susan_ **Content/Grade Level:** _Geometry/9th_

Date of Visit: _10/14_ **Professional Growth Goal:** _Standard 3.9_

Observed Teacher Behaviors

- _Divided students into two groups_
- _"Today we will be solving problems by applying the relationship between circles, angles, and intercepted arcs."_
- _She then reviewed circles, angles, and intercepted arcs. "Group 1 will look at magazines to identify and circle the circles, angles, and intercepted arcs. Group 2 will use the list of architectural websites to identify the relationship between circles, angles, and intercepted arcs. Both groups will prepare a short presentation. Each member of the group will be held responsible for their own work."_
- _Teacher had materials and activities ready_
- _Anecdotal records were kept during group time_
- _Teacher redirected students_

Beginning Teacher Professional Growth Goal: _3.9: Uses a variety of instructional strategies to engage learners._

Focus of Observation: _How to use math strategies without always lecturing._

Observed Students' Behaviors

- _Group 1: Looking at architectural magazines to identify circles, angles, and intercepted arcs. They were using markers to record the circles, angles, and intercepted arcs._
- _Group 2: Looking up the websites on the list and making pictures of what they saw by identifying circles, angles, and intercepted arcs._
- _By the end of the block period, both groups were preparing their presentation to explain the relationship between circles, angles, and intercepted arcs._
- _Students working independently._
- _Students working collaboratively._

visit. Collecting this data captures classroom evidence for further discussion between the beginning teacher and the mentor.

The Veteran Teacher Observation Data Collection tool is then used during the observation. The beginning teacher and the mentor observe the veteran teacher together and watch for behaviors, conversations, or activities that meet the teacher's stated focus. Both student and teacher behaviors are recorded. The mentor and the beginning teacher both record what they see and hear throughout the observation. Because both are recording the information gathered, they will have the opportunity to share their data during the reflective conference.

The Veteran Teacher Observation Data Collection tool is utilized as a reference during the reflective conference. This conference occurs at the end of the observation while the events are still fresh in the mentor's and teacher's mind. The mentor guides the conversation with the beginning teacher to determine what was learned, and how it can be applied to the instruction in the classroom. The mentor also asks the teacher what questions she has that have not been addressed. The Conference Data Conference (CDC) Cycle is designed so that the reflective conference leads into the next planning conference where the next steps are determined to implement what was observed.

OBSERVING A MASTER TEACHER TOOLS IN ACTION

Ron, a mentor, begins the conversation with his fourth grade teacher Samantha by asking, "How are things going?" Samantha shares her concerns. She has a difficult time with the various reading levels of her students. She does not know what to do if she groups her students according to their academic reading levels. Ron suggests that perhaps they could visit another teacher's classroom and observe what happens when that teacher instructs the various academic reading levels of students. Samantha states that she would really like to observe a teacher who uses different strategies with the various reading levels. Ron shares that he will arrange for the pair of them to go on a veteran teacher observation. Samantha is excited about the opportunity to observe a master reading teacher.

Ron says, "Let's plan what we hope to see and accomplish." He shares the Veteran Teacher Observation Planning and Reflection tool and suggests that it will provide clarity and focus during the planning conversation. Together they use the form during their planning conference (Figure 11.3). Samantha clarifies the focus of the observation by stating, "I really want to observe someone using reading strategies for different levels of students in reading, so I will know which reading strategy to use with each specific group of students based on their reading levels." Ron shares with Samantha that he will ask Aleda, a master reading teacher, if they can come observe as she uses a wide range of strategies in her reading classroom.

| Figure 11.3 | Veteran Teacher Observation Planning and Reflection |

To be used during the *Planning Conference* and the *Reflective Conference* only

Beginning Teacher: *Samantha*   **Visiting Veteran Teacher:** *Aleda*

Mentor: *Ron*   **Content/Grade Level:** *Reading/4th*

Date of Visit: *10/24*   **Professional Growth Goal:** *Standard 2.6*

Determine the following during the *Planning Conference*:

Focus of Observation:
To observe reading strategies for the different student levels in reading

How will this observation help increase student learning in my classroom?
I will be able to know which reading strategy to use with each specific group of students based on reading levels.

How does the focus of observation relate to your *Professional Teacher Growth (PTG) Goal*?
My PTG was focused on Standard 2.6: Designing and Planning Instruction: includes a variety of methods in instructional plans. This observation will allow me the opportunity to watch Aleda using a variety of methods with her different reading groups.

Questions I want to ask the veteran teacher:
How do you know which strategies to use with which group of students? How did you determine those strategies?

Data to be Collected: *Teacher and student behaviors that focus on reading strategies for different student levels in reading.*

Discuss the following during the *Reflective Conference*:

I saw:	**I heard:**
• *Two groups of students based on reading levels*	• *Specific teacher instruction and definitions*
• *Different reading activities for groups but same objective*	• *Students interacting in their groups*
• *Students working independently*	• *Quiet time as well as productive noise*
• *Students on task*	• *Teacher redirecting students.*

Application to My Practice/What I Learned:	**Questions I Still Have:**
How to use two different strategies with two of my reading groups based on the needs of the students and their level of development.	*How do you learn about additional strategies to use with different groups of students?*

Next Steps:
I will seek professional development opportunities to learn additional reading strategies based on the developmental needs of students. By January, I will implement two additional strategies.

Ron and Samantha continue to follow the Veteran Teacher Observation Planning and Reflection tool as they plan for the observation. It is important to Samantha that she not only learn new strategies but that this observation relates to her TPG goal which states that, "A teacher recognizes and values differences among individuals." With this observation, Samantha will have the opportunity to watch Aleda using a variety of methods with her different level reading groups. Ron prompts Samantha's thinking by asking, "What questions do you want to ask Aleda about her teaching?" Samantha responds by stating, "I want to make sure that I ask Aleda how she knows which strategies to use with which group of students. I also want to know how she determined that those strategies would work!" Ron records those questions on the tool as a reminder for later.

Ron talks with Samantha about the importance of recording exactly what Aleda says during the observation. Ron also suggests that they use drawings and any other descriptors to record what they saw.

After the observation, Ron and Samantha compare notes and observations based on the Veteran Teacher Observation Planning and Reflection tool (Figure 11.4). Samantha determines that she will use two different strategies with two of her reading groups based on what she saw in Aleda's classroom. Samantha still has a question for Aleda. She wants to know, "How did you learn about additional strategies to use with different groups of students?" Samantha will seek professional development opportunities to learn about additional reading strategies based on the developmental needs of students. Samantha wants to implement at least two additional reading strategies in her class by January.

NOTES FOR IMPLEMENTATION

Veteran teacher observations should be made after the beginning teachers have an opportunity to create the context of their own classrooms. Once their context is established, they see the need for observing someone else's classroom. This time usually occurs toward the end of the second month of school. Observing at least once each semester ensures that the beginning teacher observes different viewpoints at different times of the year. The mentors are in the *practice focused stage* of their transformational learning using the Veteran Teacher Observation Planning and Reflection and Veteran Teacher Observation Data Collection tools as a building block for their beginning teachers to experience a master teacher at work.

Figure 11.4 Veteran Teacher Observation Data Collection

Beginning Teacher: _Samantha_   **Visiting Veteran Teacher:** _Aleda_

Mentor: _Ron_   **Content/Grade Level:** _Reading/4th_

Date of Visit: _10/24_   **Professional Growth Goal:** _Standard 2.6_

Observed Teacher Behaviors

Aleda, "Today we will be using graphic organizers to sequence the events in our story. A graphic organizer uses geometric shapes to make connections between information. It can help us show relationships, cause and effect, or the sequence of events."

The second group of students was instructed by Aleda.

She said, "Today we will be using story mapping to tell our story. This is a technique that is used after we have read. A story map identifies the main elements of a story and categorizes the main events in sequence."

Walking around the room
Redirecting students individually
Prepared

Beginning Teacher Professional Growth Goal:
Standard 2.6 - Includes a variety of methods in instructional plans.

Focus of Observation:
To observe reading strategies for the different student levels in reading.

Observed Students' Behaviors
Group 1:

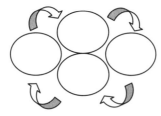

Group 2:

1. Setting	2. Main
3. Problem	4. Solution

The students worked on their sequencing of events after they read the story.
Students working independently
Individually asking questions for clarification
Talking about their story
Most on task

Figure 11.5 Veteran Teacher Observation Focus

Beginning Teacher: _____   **Visiting Veteran Teacher:** _____

Mentor: _____   **Content/Grade Level:** _____

Date of Visit: _____   **Professional Growth Goal:** _____

Determine the following during the *Planning Conference*:
Focus of Observation:
How will this observation help increase student learning in my classroom?
How does the focus of observation relate to your *Professional Teacher Growth (PTG) Goal or does it*?
Questions I want to ask the veteran teacher:
Data to be Collected:

Discuss the following during the *Reflective Conference*:	
I saw:	**I heard:**
Application to My Practice/What I Learned:	**Questions I Still Have:**
Next Steps:	

Figure 11.6	Veteran Teacher Observation Data Collection

Beginning Teacher: _____ **Visiting Veteran Teacher:** _____

Mentor: _____ **Content/Grade Level:** _____

Date of Visit: _____ **Professional Growth Goal:** _____

Observed Teacher Behaviors

Beginning Teacher Professional Growth Goal:

Focus of Observation:

Observed Students' Behaviors

12

Student Data Mapping

PURPOSE FOR STUDENT DATA MAPPING

Planning for instruction requires knowledge of content and knowledge of students. Teachers know the content when they enter the classroom. However, teachers do not always know their students at the beginning of the year. While most teachers recognize the uniqueness of each student, they often do not know how to adjust their instruction based on that uniqueness. Reviewing all aspects of each learner is complex. The purpose of this chapter is to explore ways to acquire knowledge of the students in the classroom.

Most teacher standards take into account several aspects of knowing students in the classroom:

- Knowing the physical, mental, social, cultural, and community differences among learners
- Providing developmentally appropriate learning experiences for learners
- Engaging students actively in learning by using a variety of effective teaching strategies
- Providing learning experiences that address a variety of cognitive levels
- Using prior knowledge of individual and group performance
- Creating appropriate assessments of student progress
- Maintaining records of student work and performance to use as a guide in making instructional decisions

Effective teachers take into account all of the above in order to link teaching, learning, and assessing. Teachers use appropriate language to communicate with learners clearly and accurately. They use strategies that incorporate the uniqueness of each student such as interest, multiple intelligences, learning style, and strengths. For a beginning teacher, this can be overwhelming as they attempt to transform their practice from role focused to practice focused.

Gagne (1985), an American educational psychologist who pioneered the "conditions of learning" during World War II, emphasizes that it is the learner's activity that results in the learning. It is the function of the instructor to provide conditions that will increase the probability that the student will acquire the particular performance (Joyce, Weil, & Calhoun, 2009, p. 428). Identifying significant information available about a student will increase the teacher's ability to provide conditions of learning for all students. Maintaining various records becomes a map of student data that provides the teacher with multiple pathways to assess student needs that will be used to guide instruction.

We have created the student data map tools to help teachers organize student information. The student data maps are continual and updated every quarter as circumstances change over time. All data maps containing information regarding students are to be kept in a safe, locked place as the information is confidential.

DESCRIPTION OF STUDENT DATA MAPPING

The *Student Data Map Characteristics* is a record of the students' physical, cognitive, social, cultural, and community differences. This map also includes the community demographics and the students' interest, multiple intelligences, learning style, and strengths. Often this information is contained in a district-provided software program. The tools provided in this chapter are provided to help gather that information into one concise document (Figure 12.1).

Figure 12.1	Student Data Map Characteristics

Beginning Teacher: _Samuel Huff_   **Mentor:** _Harleigh_

School: _Willow Spring Elementary_   **Subject:** _All Grade 3_   **Period:** _All_

# of Boys: _11_   **# of Girls:** _15_   **Date:** _11/4_

Community Demographics: _80% Hispanic, 10% Black; 10% White; low economic' 75% free and reduced lunch; 14% unemployment_

Directions: Use available resources from your school and district, including your mentor, to compile a student data map for each student in your classroom which delineates demographics, special needs, language, and assessment information of your students. Instead of entering data, you may opt to include any district or school data that is provided. Learning Profile, such as interests, intelligences, learning styles and strengths, may be listed, or if there is other information that you deem important, include an extra column or change the column headings.

	Student Name Last Name, First Initial	**Student Characteristics** Physical, cultural, mental, and/or social				**Learning Profile**			
		Age in Year and Month	**Home Language** e.g., E=English S=Spanish, use other notations for others	**Special Services** e.g., AD=attention deficient, G=Gifted, use other notations for others	**Attendance** Number of Days Present/ Number of School Days	* Interest	◇ Multiple Intelligences	□ Learning Style	O Strengths
1	Arron, A	8.3	E		37/40	BB	BK,S	R	Ach
2	Branson, B	7.9	S & E		30/40	AT	S,BK	P	Ach
3	Brook, S	8.6	E		40/40	B	INE,L	T	Rel
4	Bright, M	7.8	S		25/40	AT	S,N	A	Har
5	Horn, H	7.3	E	Gifted	40/40	H	L,M	P	Str
6	Juarez, B	8.1	E		38/40	C	INA	A	Dev
7	Kadhouse, P	7.5	E		37/40	A	LO	R	Act
8	Kristal, L	8.3	E	ADD	38/40	M	BK,M	A	Com
9	Monman, J	8.5	E		37/40	H	BK	T	Pos
10	Phylos, S	7.4	S	ELL	25/40	FB	S,BK	A	Arc
11	Ronstat, C	7.3	E		38/40	C	LO	R	Con
12	Samual, J	8.1	E		40/40	AT	LO	R	Res
13	Simomez, S	8.5	S	ELL	40/40	FB	S, BK	A	Rel
14	Shark, T	7.8	S	ELL	40/40	AT	M	R	Rel
15	Toby, K	7.9	S	ELL	40/40	B	N	A	Com

Copies to: Teacher Mentor

Learning Profile Key:
* A=animals; AT= art; BB=baseball; B=books; C=construction; FB=football; H=horses; M=music
◇ Gardner Multiple Intelligences- L=Linguistic; LO=Logical mathematical; S=Spatial; BK=Bodily-kinesthetic; M=Musical; INE=Interpersonal; INA=Intrapersonal; N=Naturalist
□ Kolb – A=Activist; R=Reflector; T=Theorist; P=Pragmatist
O See web-based Strengthsfinder

Note: This information is regulated by FERPA.

Academic student information is data that a teacher can also use for instructional purposes. The teacher can use this data to focus on the student's strengths in order to give the student a sense of confidence, competence, and self-worth. A student's deficiencies will be remediated as students gain knowledge and confidence in their ability to succeed. Understanding that there is more than one way to learn may suggest ways of helping children learn. Teachers can assist students in their learning by supporting their strengths and working with their weaknesses (Bransford, Brown, & Cocking, 2000). We have developed three basic tools to help teachers organize student academic information: *characteristics, standardized assessments,* and *teacher created assessments.*

The student data map academic assessment tools are designed to be flexible to accommodate various formats of assessment. The academic assessment map can use data from the district standardized assessments of multiple content areas or a single content area. The student data map for teacher-created assessments tool is designed for the teacher who creates specialized assessments to track the progress of each student instead of standardized assessments. This information provides the teacher with basic information throughout the year. Using data from the prior academic year to the current informs the teacher of student performance. Determining which students have mastered the material and which students need additional instruction impact instructional decisions. Each of the following student data maps can be used in the format presented or adapted to meet the criteria of the assessments as reported through the various software programs used by the district. There are three basic academic maps:

1. Student Data Map Standardized Assessment: Multiple Contents (Figure 12.2)

2. Student Data Map Standardized Assessment: Single Content (Figure 12.3)

3. Student Data Map Teacher-Created Assessment (Figure 12.4)

HOW TO USE THE STUDENT DATA MAP CHARACTERISTICS

Mentors can support teachers by helping them identify the location of the information for the student data maps. Some of the student information may be found at the district level because it is confidential. The community demographics are usually available at the school site. The teacher lists each student's name on the form in the first column. The information found at the district level or school site is entered in the last three columns. If any information is missing, the data may be obtained through conversations with the parent or guardian.

Figure 12.2	Student Data Map Standardized Assessment: Multiple Contents

Beginning Teacher: _Samuel Huff_   **Mentor:** _Harleigh_

School: _Willow Spring Elementary_   **Subject:** _All Grade 3_   **Period:** _All_

# of Boys: _11_   **# of Girls:** _15_   **Date:** _11/4_

Community Demographics: _80% Hispanic, 10% Black; 10% White; low economic' 75% free and reduced lunch; 14% unemployment_

Directions: Use available resources from your school and district, including your mentor, to compile a student data map for each student in your classroom which delineates demographics, special needs, language, and assessment information of your students. Instead of entering data, you may opt to include any district or school data that is provided. If there is other information that you deem important, include an extra column or change the column headings.

	Student Name Last Name, First Initial	**Previous year scores**			**1st Quarter**			**2nd Quarter**			**3rd Quarter**			**4th Quarter**		
		R	M	L	R	M	L	R	M	L	R	M	L	R	M	L
1	Arron, A	23	35	41	26	38	47									
2	Branson, B	25	40	25	26	41	31									
3	Brook, S	36	37	48	33	38	52									
4	Bright, M	25	37	35	27	39	41									
5	Horn, H	25	25	22	28	27	27									
6	Juarez, B	22	12	31	25	16	35									
7	Kadhouse, P	11	13	19	16	18	19									
8	Kristal, L	22	22	36	24	26	36									
9	Monman, J	22	27	48	26	29	49									
10	Phylos, S	44	54	62	48	59	70									
11	Ronstat, C	22	32	45	26	37	46									
12	Samual, J	36	33	26	40	47	26									
13	Simomez, S	24	19	11	27	28	13									
14	Shark, T	21	15	22	26	26	24									
15	Toby, K	28	29	31	34	38	33									

Copies to: Teacher
Mentor

Multiple Content Key:
R=Reading; M=Math; L=Language Arts

Note: This information is regulated by FERPA.

| Figure 12.3 | Student Data Map Standardized Assessment: Single Content |

Beginning Teacher: Samuel Huff **Mentor:** Harleigh

School: Willow Spring Elementary **Subject:** All Grade 3 **Period:** All

# of Boys: 11 **# of Girls:** 15 **Date:** 11/4

Community Demographics: 80% Hispanic, 10% Black; 10% White; low economic' 75% free and reduced lunch; 14% unemployment

Directions: Use available resources from your school and district, including your mentor, to compile a student data map for each student in your classroom which delineates demographics, special needs, language, and assessment information of your students. Instead of entering data, you may opt to include any district or school data that is provided. If there is other information that you deem important, include an extra column or change the column headings.

	Student Name Last Name, First Initial	**Previous year scores**	**1st Quarter**	**2nd Quarter**	**3rd Quarter**	**4th Quarter**
		M	M	M	M	M
1	Arron, A	35	38			
2	Branson, B	40	41			
3	Brook, S	37	38			
4	Bright, M	37	39			
5	Horn, H	25	27			
6	Juarez, B	12	16			
7	Kadhouse, P	13	18			
8	Kristal, L	22	26			
9	Monman, J	27	29			
10	Phylos, S	54	59			
11	Ronstat, C	32	37			
12	Samual, J	33	47			
13	Simomez, S	19	28			
14	Shark, T	15	26			
15	Toby, K	29	38			

Copies to: Teacher
Mentor

Content Key:
M= Math

Note: This information is regulated by FERPA.

| Figure 12.4 | Student Data Map Teacher-Created Assessment |

Beginning Teacher: _Samuel Huff_   **Mentor:** _Harleigh_

School: _Willow Spring Elementary_   **Subject:** _All Grade 3_   **Period:** _All_

# of Boys: _11_   **# of Girls:** _15_   **Date:** _11/4_

Community Demographics: _80% Hispanic, 10% Black; 10% White; low economic' 75% free and reduced lunch; 14% unemployment_

Directions: Use available resources from your school and district, including your mentor, to compile a student data map for each student in your classroom which delineates demographics, special needs, language, and assessment information of your students. Instead of entering data, you may opt to include any district or school data that is provided. If there is other information that you deem important, include an extra column or change the column headings.

	Student Name Last Name, First Initial	Assessment: Laboratory Subject: Science Date: Nov.4	Assessment: Subject: Date:	Assessment: Subject: Date:	Assessment: Subject: Date:
1	Arron, A	E			
2	Branson, B	E			
3	Brook, S	E			
4	Bright, M	E			
5	Horn, H	M			
6	Juarez, B	A			
7	Kadhouse, P	A			
8	Kristal, L	M			
9	Monman, J	A			
10	Phylos, S	E			
11	Ronstat, C	M			
12	Samual, J	E			
13	Simomez, S	A			
14	Shark, T	A			
15	Toby, K	M			

Copies to: Teacher Mentor

Assessment Key:
E=Exceeds Standards; M=Meets Standards; A= Approaches Standards; F=Falls far below

Note: This information is regulated by FERPA.

Mentors can support their teachers by helping them identify or create data collection tools to find students' interests, multiple intelligences, learning styles, and strengths. A variety of inventories, surveys, or other data collection tools are available using a web-based search. Four are listed below:

1. Interest inventories

2. Multiple intelligences

3. Learning styles

4. Strengths survey

HOW TO USE STUDENT DATA MAP STANDARDIZED ASSESSMENTS

The teacher and the mentor can review both of the standardized assessments. The mentor can assist the teacher through collaborative conversations in making a decision regarding which assessment map best fits the teacher's needs. The Multiple Contents map is used to enter data from three academic content areas. The Single Content map is used to enter data from one academic content area. Mentors can support teachers by exploring the district student data systems with them. As the data from the district is accessed, the teacher enters the data of the standardized assessment from the previous year. The teacher uses the other quarterly columns to enter data if the district uses end of the quarter assessments or quarterly benchmarks.

HOW TO USE THE STUDENT DATA MAP TEACHER-CREATED ASSESSMENT

Teachers enter the data from each assessment they created. State the type of the assessment, the content area, and the date administered. The types of assessments can be essay, open-ended questions, problem-solving scenarios, multiple choice, and laboratories.

STUDENT DATA MAPPING TOOLS IN ACTION

In this scenario, Karen is a second grade beginning teacher in the second school quarter who is working with her mentor, Ashley, to complete the Student Data Map: Academic Assessment Multiple Contents. Ashley utilized her role of instructor to teach Karen how to access the district assessments online. Collaboratively they looked at the student academic data from the previous year and the first quarter district benchmarks. As they worked, Ashley began to ask meditational questions to help Karen make connections to the process of collecting and analyzing data, such as "When you think about who your students are, what do their assessment scores tell you?" By the end of their session Karen felt confident that she could complete the rest of the data map. It took Karen several hours to complete the academic assessment map (Figure 12.5).

Karen began to think of her students in four categories: exceeds standards, meets standards, approaches standards, and falls far below. Karen was tempted to put the data away as she did not know how to design instruction around four groups much less in three content areas. Karen decided to at least list the students in the four groups in reading (Figure 12.6).

When Ashley entered Karen's classroom the next week, she asked Karen, "How are things going?" Karen shared her frustration with Ashley regarding the four groups. Ashley encouraged Karen to start with one content area at a time using two groups for instruction until she felt confident to move into instruction for four groups. Ashley told Karen, "Once you can design instruction for two groups in one content area, you will begin to see ways to design instruction using four groups. Once you accomplish designing instruction for four groups, you can continue to add one area of content at a time." Karen felt relieved that she was not expected to design instruction for four groups in three content areas at one time. Karen shared her list of the four groups in reading with Ashley.

They decided to use Karen's list to begin designing instruction by using only two groups. Karen and Ashley spent the next month focusing on strategies to meet the needs of the students in each of the two groups in reading (Figure 12.7).

| Figure 12.5 | Student Data Map Standardized Assessment: Multiple Contents |

Beginning Teacher: Karen Shell   **Mentor:** Ashley

School: Cooper King Elementary   **Subject:** Reading Grade 2   **Period:** All

# of Boys: 9   **# of Girls:** 23   **Date:** 11/10

Community Demographics: 40% Hispanic; 30% Black; 30% White; 55% Free and reduced lunch; 5% Unemployment

Directions: Use available resources from your school and district, including your mentor, to compile a student data map for each student in your classroom which delineates demographics, special needs, language, and assessment information of your students. Instead of entering data, you may opt to include any district or school data that is provided. If there is other information that you deem important, include an extra column or change the column headings.

	Student Name Last Name, First Initial	**Previous year scores**			**1st Quarter**			**2nd Quarter**			**3rd Quarter**			**4th Quarter**		
		R	M	L	R	M	L	R	M	L	R	M	L	R	M	L
1	Ackron, A	19	22	35	26	28	40									
2	Bradford, B	11	20	33	14	22	32									
3	Book, S	16	17	24	17	21	26									
4	Broust, M	8	23	22	11	23	23									
5	Harmon, H	25	25	27	25	28	28									
6	Juarez, K	21	27	30	22	26	31									
7	Krokitt, P	35	47	45	37	50	47									
8	Krow, L	24	31	33	26	33	35									
9	Moon, J	19	22	25	22	22	26									
10	Phylos, M	18	35	26	18	33	27									
11	Ridell, C	20	29	22	29	32	27									
12	Simon, J	25	22	28	29	25	22									
13	Stilwater, S	22	15	32	26	16	33									
14	Stoll, T	18	23	22	20	22	24									
15	Tradby, K	10	22	17	15	23	18									

Copies to: Teacher
        Mentor

Multiple Content Key:
R=Reading; M=Math; L=Language Arts

Note: This information is regulated by FERPA.

Figure 12.6 Reading 1st Quarter Scores

Exceeds Standards	Meets Standards	Approaches Standards	Falls far below Standards
Ackron (29)	Juarez (22)	Phylos (18)	Bradford (14)
Harmon (25)	Moon (22)	Book (17)	Broust (11)
Krokitt (37)	Stoll (20)		Tradby (15)
Krow (26)			
Ridell (29)			
Simon (29)			
Stilwater (26)			

Figure 12.7 Reading 1st Quarter Scores

Exceeds Standards/ Meets Standards		Approaches Standards/ Falls far below Standards
Ackron (29)	Ridell (29)	Phylos (18)
Juarez (22)	Simon (29)	Bradford (14)
Harmon (25)	Stilwater (26)	Book (17)
Krokitt (37)	Moon (22)	Broust (11)
Stoll (20)	Krow (26)	Tradby (15)

NOTES FOR IMPLEMENTATION

Using student data maps in the classroom in the second quarter of school will provide the mentor the opportunity to discuss the teachers' abilities to design instruction around the individual needs of the students. Starting with one characteristic or one content area at a time will make the task easier. As the mentor encourages the teacher to take one step at a time, it instills confidence within the teacher to make instructional decisions regarding the individual needs of the students. The teachers begin to transform their practice as they take the first step toward practice focused.

As the students become more successful, the teacher becomes more successful. Meeting individual student needs is difficult but an important aspect of student success. Focusing on the strengths of the student will give the student an advantageous beginning. Students enhance their ability to move forward in their own learning when given the opportunity to work in groups according to their interests, multiple intelligences, or academics. Student maps will change throughout the year as the students enhance and change their own knowledge, skills, and interests.

Figure 12.8	Student Data Map Characteristics

Beginning Teacher: _____ **Mentor:** _____

School: _____ **Subject:** _____ **Period:** _____

# of Boys: _____ **# of Girls:** _____ **Date:** _____

Community Demographics: _____

Directions: Use available resources from your school and district, including your mentor, to compile a student data map for each student in your classroom which delineates demographics, special needs, language, and assessment information of your students. Instead of entering data, you may opt to include any district or school data that is provided. Learning Profile, such as interests, intelligences, learning styles, and strengths, may be listed or if there is other information that you deem important, include an extra column or change the column headings.

	Student Name Last Name, First Initial	**Student Characteristics** Physical, cultural, mental, and/or social				**Learning Profile**			
		Age in Year and Month	**Home Language** e.g., E=English S=Spanish, use other notations for others	**Special Services** e.g., AD=attention deficient, G=Gifted, use other notations for others	**Attendance** Number of Days Present/ Number of School Days	*	◇	□	O
1									
2									
3									
4									
5									
6									
7									
8									
9									
10									
11									
12									
13									
14									
15									
Copies to: Teacher Mentor	**Learning Profile Key:** * ◇ □ O								

Note: This information is regulated by FERPA.

| Figure 12.9 | Student Data Map Standardized Assessment: Multiple Contents |

Beginning Teacher: _____ **Mentor:** _____

School: _____ **Subject:** _____ **Period:** _____

# of Boys: _____ **# of Girls:** _____ **Date:** _____

Community Demographics: _____

Directions: Use available resources from your school and district, including your mentor, to compile a student data map for each student in your classroom which delineates demographics, special needs, language, and assessment information of your students. Instead of entering data, you may opt to include any district or school data that is provided. If there is other information that you deem important, include an extra column or change the column headings.

	Student Name Last Name, First Initial	**Previous year scores**			**1st Quarter**			**2nd Quarter**			**3rd Quarter**			**4th Quarter**		
1																
2																
3																
4																
5																
6																
7																
8																
9																
10																
11																
12																
13																
14																
15																
Copies to: Teacher Mentor	**Multiple Content Key:**															

Note: This information is regulated by FERPA.

| Figure 12.10 | Student Data Map Standardized Assessment: Single Content |

Beginning Teacher: _____ **Mentor:** _____

School: _____ **Subject:** _____ **Period:** _____

# of Boys: _____ **# of Girls:** _____ **Date:** _____

Community Demographics: _____

Directions: Use available resources from your school and district, including your mentor, to compile a student data map for each student in your classroom which delineates demographics, special needs, language, and assessment information of your students. Instead of entering data, you may opt to include any district or school data that is provided. If there is other information that you deem important, include an extra column or change the column headings.

	Student Name Last Name, First Initial	**Previous year scores**	**1st Quarter**	**2nd Quarter**	**3rd Quarter**	**4th Quarter**
1						
2						
3						
4						
5						
6						
7						
8						
9						
10						
11						
12						
13						
14						
15						

| Copies to: Teacher
Mentor | **Content Key:** |

Note: This information is regulated by FERPA.

| Figure 12.11 | Student Data Map Teacher-Created Assessment |

Beginning Teacher: _____ **Mentor:** _____

School: _____ **Subject:** _____ **Period:** _____

# of Boys: _____ **# of Girls:** _____ **Date:** _____

Community Demographics: _____

Directions: Use available resources from your school and district, including your mentor, to compile a student data map for each student in your classroom which delineates demographics, special needs, language, and assessment information of your students. Instead of entering data, you may opt to include any district or school data that is provided. If there is other information that you deem important, include an extra column or change the column headings.

	Student Name Last Name, First Initial	**Assessment:** Subject: Date:	**Assessment:** Subject: Date:	**Assessment:** Subject: Date:	**Assessment:** Subject: Date:
1					
2					
3					
4					
5					
6					
7					
8					
9					
10					
11					
12					
13					
14					
15					
Copies to: Teacher Mentor	**Assessment Key:**				

Note: This information is regulated by FERPA.

13

Planning for Instruction

PURPOSE FOR THE INSTRUCTIONAL PLANNING PROCESS

Planning for instruction is a complex process that most beginning teachers have not yet mastered. They usually understand the basics of lesson planning and design, yet when it comes to implementing a lesson and determining what students actually know and are able to do, beginning teachers find themselves overwhelmed when every student is not successful in their classroom. To accelerate a new teacher's instructional design skills, a mentor can guide him through the *Instructional Planning Process* by engaging him in conversations about well-written learning objectives, the depth of understanding and skill needed to meet the objectives, appropriate content to include in instruction for every student, and well-aligned instructional strategies and assessments. These conversations serve to deepen the beginning teacher's understanding of planning for instruction prior to developing lesson plans for a specific group of learners.

DESCRIPTION OF THE INSTRUCTIONAL PLANNING PROCESS

The eight-step *Instructional Planning Process* includes writing standards-based instructional objectives, conducting a task analysis, writing subobjectives, conducting a preassessment, identifying content, selecting instructional strategies and activities, identifying assessment strategies, and ensuring lesson element alignment, such as objectives, content, strategies, and assessments.

The details of what occurs during each of the eight steps in this Instructional Planning Process are described in the following pages. Completed examples of the tools used to facilitate each process are also provided.

Step 1: Writing Instructional Objectives

The *Learning Objective Worksheet* tool is used to provide a common language for the development of task objectives. This tool provides three examples of a learning objective broken down into three basic components: context of learning, student learning performance, and level of performance. The sample objectives are based on academic standards and performance objectives dictated by the state department of education and the district. At the bottom of the page are two blank rows in which the beginning teacher develops his own learning objectives (Figure 13.1).

Step 2: Conducting a Task Analysis

The *Task Analysis Part I* tool is used to record the learning objective as well as the prerequisite skills and knowledge identified by the beginning teacher during the conversation with the mentor. The mentor encourages the beginning teacher to brainstorm all of the prerequisite skills and knowledge that it takes for the students to be able to accomplish the objective. Once the prerequisite skills and knowledge are identified, the teacher reviews the list to identify the essential prerequisite skills and knowledge. The teacher places a star beside each identified essential prerequisite skills and knowledge. Mentors use this tool to help guide teachers through Steps 1–3 of the Task Analysis Part I process (Figure 13.2, page 174).

The beginning teacher sequences the starred essential prerequisite skills and knowledge using Step 4 of the *Task Analysis Part II* tool. For each entry, he describes the content it encompasses. This provides a more detailed list of the content that must be taught during the lesson. Mentors use this tool to help guide teachers through Steps 4 and 5 of the Task Analysis Part II process (Figure 13.3, page 175).

Figure 13.1 Learning Objectives Worksheet

Standard Upon which academic standard is this learning objective based?	Context of Learning What materials or resources are necessary for the learner to demonstrate knowledge? Where or how will the learning occur?	Student Learning Performance What will the learner know or do? Use specific verbs. Check the Bloom's level of thinking of the performance.	Level of Performance How well will the learner know or be able to do the performance at a minimal level? Make sure it is measurable.
R03-S2C1-02 Describe characters within a literary section.	When reading the story, *Stay Dog Stay*,	students will describe the physical attributes	by stating the hair color, height, age and weight of at least 2 characters.
M01-S1C2- 08 Count by multiples to show the process of multiplication.	Using manipulatives,	students will count by 2's	from 0 to 20 with 90% degree of accuracy.
2AM-E1-PO2 Compare/contrast the musical elements of various genres and cultures.	While listening to classical, rock, and rap music	students will compare tempo, pitch, and duration	to create a list of 5 differences and 5 similarities between the genres.
MA1-S2-PO5 Add two- and two-digit whole numbers with regrouping.	*Using regrouping strategies,*	*students will add two-digit plus two-digit numbers*	*with 90% accuracy.*
SCHS-S4LS-PO4 Diagram the energy flow in an ecosystem through a food chain.	*Using data for a known deer population,*	*students will diagram the energy flow in an ecosystem through a food chain*	*with 90% accuracy.*

Figure 13.2 Task Analysis: Part I

Step 1: Write your complete overall learning objective (i.e., learning task) below.

Step 2: Identify prerequisite skills and/or knowledge required to meet the objective. Review the list to identify essential skills and knowledge.

Step 3: Place a star by each essential prerequisite skills and knowledge that your students need to acquire in order to meet the objective.

Overall Learning Objective:

Using regrouping strategies, students will add two-digit plus two-digit numbers with 90% accuracy.

Prerequisite Skills and/or Prior Knowledge

Recognize numbers	*Number alignment for column addition*
Place value (ones and tens)	☆ *Two-digit plus two-digit column addition with regrouping using algorithms*
Single-digit addition	☆ *Proper number alignment for double-digit addition*
☆ *How to regroup using manipulatives*	☆ *Two-digit plus two-digit column addition with no regrouping using algorithms*

Figure 13.3 Task Analysis: Part II

Step 4: Sequence the essential prerequisite skills and knowledge in the appropriate boxes below.

Step 5: For each, describe the specific skill and knowledge content it encompasses.

Note: You may need to create your own version of this diagram to account for additional prerequisite skills and/or knowledge.

Prerequisite Skills and/or Prior Knowledge Sequence

1. Proper number alignment for double-digit addition *Ones and tens place value review* *How to align 2 two-digit numbers for addition* *Placement of addition sign*	*2. Two-digit plus two-digit column addition with no regrouping using algorithms* *Students add the numbers and record the number of ones and tens in the correct location under the horizontal equals sign*
3. How to regroup using manipulatives *Use tens and ones mat with unifix cubes to show how to regroup*	*4. Two-digit plus two-digit column addition with regrouping using algorithms* *Students add 2 two-digit numbers together and record the ones and the regrouped tends in the correct location*
5.	*6.*

Overall Learning Objective:
Using regrouping strategies, students will add two-digit plus two-digit numbers with 90% accuracy.

Step 3: Writing Subobjectives

Having identified, sequenced, and described the prerequisite skills and content needed on the Task Analysis Part II tool, the beginning teacher must now develop subobjectives to match these. These subobjectives are written in order on the *Lesson Element Alignment* tool (Figure 13.4).

Step 4: Writing a Preassessment

Determining how you will preassess students is a vital starting point in the development and design of an instructional plan. A preassessment is conducted once the subobjectives are identified. There are a wide variety of methods to preassess students ranging from informal KWL charts to formal pretests based on each subobjective. We do not provide a specific tool for preassessment; rather we encourage mentors to discuss preassessment ideas with beginning teachers after the subobjectives have been determined.

Step 5: Identifying Content

The beginning teacher identified much of the content to be taught when he identified the details of what prerequisite skills and knowledge must be taught during Step 2: Conducting a Task Analysis. This information, along with additional and relevant content, is written in the content box on the *Lesson Element Alignment* tool next to the corresponding subobjective.

Step 6: Selecting Instructional Strategies/Activities

Appropriate instructional strategies are described in the instructional strategies/activities box on the Lesson Element Alignment tool next to the corresponding subobjective and content.

Step 7: Identifying Assessment Strategies

Appropriate assessment strategies are described in the assessment strategies box on the Lesson Element Alignment tool following the corresponding subobjective, content, and instructional strategies/activities.

Step 8: Checking Lesson Element Alignment

This step of the Lesson Element Alignment tool completes the process. By looking across one row on the tool, a beginning teacher can check to make sure that each component (i.e., content, instructional strategies/activities, and assessment strategies) aligns with the others.

Figure 13.4 Lesson Element Alignment

> **Academic Standard:** *MA1-S2C4-PO 5. Add one- and two-digit whole numbers with regrouping.*
>
> **Overall Learning Objective:** *Using regrouping strategies, students will add two-digit plus two-digit numbers with 90% accuracy.*

Subobjectives	Preassessment Method	Content (See Task Analysis Part II)	Instructional Strategies/Activities	Assessment Strategies
1. Students will be able to write double-digit addition problems demonstrating the correct alignment of ones and tens as well as placement of the plus sign with 100% accuracy.	*Give the textbook chapter preassessment because it matches each sub-objective.*	*Place value (Ones and tens)* *Alignment of two double-digit numbers for column addition Placement of plus sign*	*Demonstrate how to align two double-digit numbers for column addition.* *Students write double-digit addition problem on individual whiteboards.*	*Observation of work done on whiteboards*
2. Given an individual whiteboard, students will demonstrate how to record the ones and ten(s) in the correct locations with no regrouping for a double-digit math problem.	*Give the textbook chapter preassessment because it matches each sub-objective.*	*Proper placement of ones below the horizontal equals sign* *Proper placement of tens below the horizontal equals sign*	*Model process of recording ones and tens.* *Demonstration using overhead projector, whiteboard, or interactive board* *Students practice on individual whiteboards and peer check*	*Observation of work done on whiteboard*
3. Given a ones and tens mat and unifix cubes, students will demonstrate how to regroup ones into tens and ones with 100% accuracy.	*Give the textbook chapter preassessment because it matches each sub-objective.*	*Manipulatives (Ones and tens mat plus unifix cubes)* *Exchanging ten ones for one ten*	*Sitting in a circle on the floor with individual mats and unifix cubes model regrouping for problem written on the board*	*Observation with unifix cubes*
4. Given an individual whiteboard, students will demonstrate how to record the ones and ten(s) with regrouping in the correct locations for a double-digit math problem.	*Give the textbook chapter preassessment because it matches each sub-objective.*	*Proper placement of ones below the horizontal equals sign* *Proper placement of tens above top number's tens digit*	*Model process of recording ones and placing tens above the top digit's tens digit.* *Demonstration using overhead projector, whiteboard or interactive board* *Students practice on individual whiteboards and peer check.*	*Observation of work done on whiteboard*
Overall objective: Using regrouping strategies, students will add two-digit plus two-digit numbers with 90% accuracy.				*Textbook end of chapter test*

HOW TO USE THE INSTRUCTIONAL PLANNING PROCESS

Based on feedback from a beginning teacher, a mentor may decide to go through the whole Instructional Planning Process or select relevant steps to discuss with the beginning teacher. The tools related to specific areas will be used to facilitate discussions.

If there is confusion regarding what the students are to learn, the mentor may opt to share the *Learning Objectives Worksheet* with the beginning teacher. Together they can review the examples provided and construct objectives for an upcoming lesson. The mentor can facilitate a discussion regarding each component of a complete objective through this process.

Step 3: Conducting a task analysis is a complex skill and therefore one which is perhaps skipped when planning a lesson. Looking at the process of completing a task analysis for the objective can lead to greater student and teacher success. A mentor can work with the beginning teacher to thoroughly determine what a learner must know and be able to do in order to meet the objective through using the Task Analysis: Parts I and II tools. These two tools allow the beginning teacher the opportunity to take an in-depth look at the stated learning objective.

This naturally leads to the writing of subobjectives. At this point, a beginning teacher might need a graphic organizer to assist in the alignment of the lesson elements, so the mentor may introduce the Lesson Element Alignment tool. The beginning teacher writes the initial learning objective at the top of the tool. Subobjectives, which result from the task analysis, are written in the appropriate column. Designing a preassessment for each of the subobjectives is another critical step that is often missed. The teacher needs to design a preassessment for each subobjective or use an assessment that measures each in order to identify what students know. From this point forward in the Instructional Planning Process, the mentor works with the beginning teacher to make sure each element of the design aligns with the other elements. Using the Lesson Element Alignment tool allows the beginning teacher to see all the related elements simultaneously to verify alignment.

INSTRUCTIONAL PLANNING PROCESS TOOLS IN ACTION

While reviewing "time-on-task" data collected in a previous lesson, Wanda, a first grade teacher, tells her mentor, "I see on the chart that my students were turning to one another and talking during the lesson. I do not understand why they were not paying attention." Wanda's mentor Barbara said "Let's look at your lesson plan to see what you expected them to do." "Well," said Barbara, "I didn't have time to write the lesson down. I knew in my head what I wanted them to learn."

This last comment by Wanda is a great entry point opening for instruction and discussion for Barbara regarding the value of developing a well-designed lesson plan. Barbara knows that begins with the Instructional Planning Process. She can introduce the process and guide Wanda through it to develop an upcoming lesson. When Wanda teaches this new lesson, Barbara can take the same "time-on-task" data. Here is what each step in the *Instructional Planning Process* might look like for Wanda.

Wanda determines that she wants to develop a lesson on equal fractions, which is identified in the academic standards. To begin the task analysis, Wanda writes the learning objective on the Task Analysis: Part I tool. By reading the objective, Barbara can see that Wanda has a sound understanding of constructing a measurable objective. She determines that they do not need to use the Learning Objective Worksheet. Barbara asks Wanda to brainstorm all the prerequisite knowledge her students must have in order to meet the overall learning objective. Wanda records each distinct piece of knowledge in a separate box on the Task Analysis: Part I. She is encouraged to write all her ideas and to think critically of the knowledge required. Wanda is asked to place a star by the essential prerequisite knowledge skills her students need to acquire in order to meet the objective (Figure 13.5).

To develop an instructional sequence, Wanda records the essential prerequisite knowledge skills she has starred, sequentially on *the Task Analysis: Part II* tool. She may choose to rewrite the overall learning objective on this tool as well to assist her in staying focused on the objective. In fact, the next step in the Instructional Planning Process is to write a subobjective for each piece of prerequisite knowledge skills. These subobjectives are recorded on the Lesson Element Alignment tool in the order in which they will be taught, for example, the sequence from the Task Analysis: Part II tool (Figure 13.6).

Barbara and Wanda begin discussing options for preassessing the students' knowledge of equal fractions for each subobjective written. The chosen method is a formal pretest that is provided by the school district and matches each subobjective Wanda has identified as important. Wanda writes the standard and the method of preassessment in the Lesson Element Alignment Worksheet. This will serve as a framework for organizing the elements of the lesson.

Using the data from her preassessment which measured each subobjective and her observations of the students in prior lessons and tasks, Wanda determines the prior knowledge her students' lack. She makes a student list and records the results of the preassessment for each subobjective next to the student's name. Wanda groups her students based on each subobjective. When developing her lesson, she needs to make sure she provides instructional time for each of these groups so that her students can meet the overall learning objective.

Wanda then transfers the content as she described on the Task Analysis: Part II tool to the corresponding column on the Lesson Element Alignment tool. Next, Wanda briefly describes what instructional activities will be implemented. These will be written in more detail on the lesson plan itself.

At this point in the process, Barbara encourages Wanda to make sure the students are learning and interacting with the content that reflects the learning objective. This is the first part of checking for alignment. She will determine if the content described aligns with the instructional strategies. Finally, Wanda identifies the assessment strategy for each subobjective as well as the overall learning objective. The task performed in the assessment matches the identified objective, instruction, and practice. Wanda is now ready to write a well-written and designed lesson plan (Figure 13.7).

Figure 13.5	Task Analysis: Part I

Step 1: Write your complete overall learning objective (i.e., learning task) below.

Step 2: Identify prerequisite skills and/or knowledge required to meet the objective. Review the list to identify essential skills and knowledge.

Step 3: Place a star by each essential prerequisite skill and knowledge that your students need to acquire in order to meet the objective.

Overall Learning Objective:

Given a series of diagrams, first grade students will be able to identify equal fractions with 90% accuracy (e.g., 2/4=1/2, 4/4=2/2, 2/8=1/4, 4/8=2/4=1/2, 6/8=3/4, 8/8=4/4=2/2).

Prerequisite Skills and/or Prior Knowledge (You may need more blocks)

☆ *Identify 1/2 and 2/2 with real objects*

☆ *Identify 1/4, 2/4, 3/4, and 4/4 real objects*

☆ *Identify 1/8, 2/8, 4/8, 6/8, and 8/8 real objects*

Identify shapes divided into equal parts

Can read fractions

☆ *Can identify diagrams that illustrate 1/8, 1/4, 1/2, 2/8, 2/4, 4/8, 6/8, 3/4, 8/8, 4/4, and 2/2*

☆ *Knows what equals means in terms of same parts of shapes shaded in*

Figure 13.6	Task Analysis: Part II

Task Analysis

Step 4: Sequence the selected essential prerequisite skills and/or knowledge in the appropriate boxes below.

Step 5: For each, describe the specific skill and/or content it encompasses.

Note: You may need to create your own version of this diagram to account for additional prerequisite skills and/or knowledge.

Prerequisite Skills and/or Prior Knowledge Sequence

1. *Identify 1/2 and 2/2 with real objects*

- Students need to be able to select 1/2 and 2/2 pieces of pie, pizza, a paper rectangle made from two squares of construction paper, etc.

2. *Identify 1/4, 2/4, 3/4, and 4/4 real objects*

-Students need to be able to select 1/4, 2/4, 3/4, and 4/4 pieces of pie, pizza, and a paper rectangle made from four equal pieces of construction paper, etc.

3. *Identify 1/8, 2/8, 4/8, 6/8, and 8/8 real objects*

-Students need to be able to select 1/8, 2/8, 4/8, 6/8, and 8/8 pieces of pie, pizza, and a paper rectangle made from eight equal pieces of construction paper, etc.

4. *Can identify diagrams that illustrate 1/8, 1/4, 1/2, 2/8, 2/4, 4/8, 6/8, 3/4, 8/8, 4/4, and 2/2*

- Looking at a diagram with shaded in sections students can circle the fraction that represents the quantity shaded

5. *Knows what equals means in terms of same parts of shapes shaded*

- Students shade areas of different shapes to represent 2/8, 1/4, 4/8, 2/4, 1/2, 6/8, 3/4, 8/8, 4/4, and 2/2.

6.

Overall Learning Objective:

Given a series of diagrams, first grade students will be able to identify equal fractions with 90% accuracy (e.g., 2/4=1/2, 4/4=2/2, 2/8=1/4, 4/8=2/4=1/2, 6/8=3/4, 8/8=4/4=2/2).

Figure 13.7 Lesson Element Alignment

Academic Standard: *MA1-SINS-PO15: Identify in symbols and in words a model that is divided into equal fractional parts.*

Overall Learning Objective: *Given a series of diagrams, first grade students will be able to identify equal fractions with 90% accuracy (e.g., 2/4=1/2, 4/4=2/2, 2/8=1/4, 4/8=2/4=1/2, 6/8=3/4, 8/8=4/4=2/2).*

Subobjectives	Preassessment Method	Content (See Task Analysis Part II)	Instructional Strategies/Activities	Assessment Strategies
1. Given real objects divided into two equal sections, students will select 1/2 and 2/2 pieces when instructed 5 out of 5 times.	Administered the district's preassessment for equal fractions which measured each sub-objective.	1/2 and 2/2 pieces of pie, pizza, a paper rectangle made from two squares of construction paper, etc.	Students manipulate objects to represent different fractions then to represent a given fraction.	Observation
2. Given real objects divided into four equal sections, students will select 1/4, 2/4, 3/4, and 4/4 pieces when instructed 5 out of 5 times.	Administered the district's preassessment for equal fractions which measured each sub-objective.	1/4, 2/4, 3/4, and 4/4 pieces of pie, pizza, a paper rectangle made from two squares of construction paper, etc.	Students manipulate objects to represent different fractions then to represent a given fraction.	Observation
3. Given real objects divided into eight equal sections, students will select 1/8, 2/8, 4/8, 6/8, and 8/8 pieces when instructed 5 out of 5 times.	Administered the district's preassessment for equal fractions which measured each sub-objective.	1/8, 2/8, 4/8, 6/8, and 8/8 pieces of pie, pizza, a paper rectangle made from two squares of construction paper, etc.	Students manipulate objects to represent different fractions then to represent a given fraction.	Observation
4. Looking at a diagram with shaded-in sections students will circle the fraction that identifies quantity shaded area represents (1/8, 1/4, 1/2, 2/8, 2/4, 4/8, 6/8, 3/4, 8/8, 4/4, and 2/2) with 100% accuracy.	Administered the district's preassessment for equal fractions which measured each sub-objective.	Variety of shapes divided into equal sections with shaded in representing 2/8, 1/4, 4/8, 2/4, 1/2, 6/8, 3/4, 8/8, 4/4, and 2/2 so students circle the fraction represented by the quantity shaded.	Using the overhead projector or interactive whiteboard, students circle the fraction represented by the diagram. In pairs students quiz each other using flash cards.	Observation
5. Given sets of diagrams of different shapes divided into two, four, and eight equal parts, students will shade in areas to represent 2/8, 1/4, 4/8, 2/4, 1/2, 6/8, 3/4, 8/8, 4/4, and 2/2 with 100% accuracy.	Administered the district's preassessment for equal fractions which measured each sub-objective.	Various shape diagrams with shaded sections representing the following quantities: 2/8, 1/4, 4/8, 2/4, 1/2, 6/8, 3/4, 8/8, 4/4, and 2/2	On the large white-board, students illustrate a given fraction. Students illustrate fractions using dry erase markers on individual whiteboards.	Observation
Overall Objective: Given a series of diagrams, first grade students will be able to identify equal fractions with 90% accuracy (e.g., 2/4=1/2, 4/4=2/2, 2/8=1/4, 4/8=2/4=1/2, 6/8=3/4, 8/8=4/4=2/2).		Various shape diagrams with shaded sections representing the following quantities: 2/8, 1/4, 4/8, 2/4, 1/2, 6/8, 3/4, 8/8, 4/4, and 2/2		District Posttest

NOTES FOR IMPLEMENTATION

This is an in-depth and time-consuming process. The mentor can spend more time on the areas that will have the most impact on instruction as she begins to know the needs of a specific beginning teacher. The mentor might emphasize that this detailed process may not be done on paper each and every time a lesson is planned, but all of these elements should, at least, be thought of during the instructional planning process to ensure engagement and learning.

Figure 13.8 Learning Objectives Worksheet

Standard	Context of Learning	Student Learning Performance	Level of Performance
Upon which academic standard is this learning objective based?	What materials or resources are necessary for the learner to demonstrate knowledge? Where or how will the learning occur?	What will the learner know or do? Use specific verbs. Check the Bloom's level of thinking of the performance.	How well will the learner know or be able to do the performance at a minimal level? Make sure it is measurable.
R03-S2C1-02 Describe characters within a literary section.	When reading the story, *Stay Dog Stay*,	students will describe the physical attributes	by stating the hair color, height, age, and weight of at least 2 characters.
M01-S1C2- 08 Count by multiples to show the process of multiplication.	Using manipulatives	students will count by 2's	from 0 to 20 with 90% degree of accuracy.
2AM-E1-PO2 Compare/contrast the musical elements of various genres and cultures.	While listening to classical, rock, and rap music	students will compare tempo, pitch, and duration	to create a list of 5 differences and 5 similarities between the genres.

Figure 13.9 Task Analysis: Part I

Step 1: Write your complete overall learning objective (i.e., learning task) below.

Step 2: Identify prerequisite skills and/or knowledge required to meet the objective. Review the list to identify essential skills and knowledge.

Step 3: Place a star by each essential prerequisite skill and/or knowledge that your students need to acquire in order to meet the objective.

Overall Learning Objective:

Prerequisite Skills and/or Prior Knowledge

Figure 13.10	Task Analysis: Part II

Task Analysis

Step 4: Sequence the selected essential prerequisite skills and/or knowledge in the appropriate boxes below.

Step 5: For each, describe the specific skill and/or content it encompasses.

Note: You may need to create your own version of this diagram to account for additional prerequisite skills and/or knowledge.

Prerequisite Skills and/or Prior Knowledge Sequence

1.	2.
3.	4.
5.	6.

Overall Learning Objective:

Figure 13.11 Lesson Element Alignment

Academic Standard:

Overall Learning Objective:

Subobjectives	Preassessment Method	Content (See Task Analysis Part II)	Instructional Strategies/ Activities	Assessment Strategies
1.				
2.				
3.				
4.				
5.				
Overall Objective:				

14

Lesson Design

PURPOSE FOR LESSON DESIGN

Lesson planning is taught in teacher education programs, yet it is not until beginning teachers are in charge of their own classrooms that many of them have a realistic opportunity to employ their skills as lesson designers. Experienced practitioners and researchers know that many classroom management and behavior issues can be averted by the successful implementation of a well-designed lesson. It is important that the mentor develop a common language for lesson development with beginning teachers since each teacher education program presents this task in its own way. It is equally important for a mentor to facilitate the connection to the lesson planning format and philosophy used in the beginning teacher's school system.

Different instructional situations lend themselves to different strategies. Providing beginning teachers with a variety of lesson plan designs to choose from allows a mentor to engage the beginning teacher in a conversation about the instructional approach that is the most appropriate for either the content or skills being taught.

DESCRIPTION OF LESSON DESIGN

Different instructional objectives require different approaches to presenting information and student activities. Using a lesson design format that matches the instructional approach provides a scaffold for designing a lesson. The lesson design templates that we have selected include the *Basic Lesson*, the *Inquiry Lesson*, and the *Essential Elements Lesson* that was first presented by Madeline Hunter (1989). The information presented here is not presented as thorough descriptions but rather as a narrative to the selection of lesson templates appropriate for classroom instruction.

The *Basic Lesson* plan includes generic lesson identification information: standard, rationale, objective, content, procedures that include teacher and student activities, assessment, and accommodations. This template is generic to basic teaching and can be adapted to accommodate various teaching styles. Most districts make internal decisions regarding the lesson template to be used by staff (Figure 14.1).

The *Inquiry Lesson* plan includes generic lesson identification information: standard, rationale, objective, and content; procedures that include inquiry question, exploration using hands-on materials to gather data, analyze data, and form preliminary conclusions, discussion, and explanation based on data; and expansion, assessment, and accommodations.

This lesson template is used to create an inquiry-based environment where students use various process skills. Students are naturally curious about their environment. Sustaining this curiosity and allowing students the opportunity to explore the content versus being informed about the content creates an inquiry-based environment. They have the opportunity to explore, build, and demonstrate their learning. Students are engaged in observation, collecting information, and organizing that information into data sets. They look for patterns, compare and analyze data sets, think critically, devise explanations, and create hypotheses for further investigation. From testing hypotheses or collecting data, they formulate explanations, and draw inferences. They are actively engaged in their own learning. Through students' discussions in presenting their data and teacher-guided explanation based on data, the students arrive at the desired outcome. The teacher provides an expansion of the concept for deeper learning as well as assessments and accommodations. This inquiry lesson has applications well beyond the science content and supports learning goals in all content areas (Figure 14.2).

The *Essential Elements Lesson* plan includes generic lesson identification information: standard, rationale, objective, task analysis, anticipatory set, input (content), model, understanding check, guided practice, independent practice, closure, assessment, and accommodations.

This lesson template is used when the teacher approaches academic content systematically and provides the content of the lesson directly to the students. This design generates and sustains motivation through pacing, reinforcement, success, and positive feedback. The teacher sets the stage for learning, provides the input, and checks for understanding. Students complete a task under the teacher's guidance prior to independent practice. Closure requires the students to tell the teacher what they have learned at the end of the lesson and allows for reflection. The teacher then has the opportunity to know what the students know and are able to do at the end of the lesson taught. This information can provide the teacher with next steps in her instruction. Assessment and accommodation follow (Figure 14.3).

The following examples use the same lesson content presented in three different lesson design formats: Basic Lesson, Inquiry Lesson, and Essential Elements Lesson. The mentor can use these tools to show the beginning teacher how instruction can be organized in different ways. The teacher may decide to utilize one of these suggested formats or identify various components to design a personalized lesson plan.

Figure 14.1 Basic Lesson Plan Format

Name/Grade Level/Content: Deborah, high school, American history

Title of Lesson: We Are at War: The Beginning of the Revolutionary War

Timeframe: Five class periods

Materials: Slideshow of the American Revolutionary War. Presentation on events leading to the Revolutionary War. Computer Lab, laptop, projector, printed copies of text and images, textbooks, reference books, and the National Park Service (NPS)

Websites of Lesson Resources:

http://www.nps.gov/history/nr/twhp/wwwlps/lessons/42bunker/42setting.htm, Setting the stage

http://www.nps.gov/history/nr/twhp/wwwlps/lessons/42bunker/42bunker.htm, Photo Analysis Worksheet

http://www.nps.gov/history/nr/twhp/PHOTOANA.HTM, Photo Analysis Graphic Organizer

Standard: H1.1 Research PO 3 Formulate questions that can be answered by historical study and research

Rationale:

This is required by the district curriculum and state academic standards. It lends itself well to the use of images as primary source documents.

Objective:

While viewing a slideshow, a historical photo, and reading text, students will be able to create questions that describe events that led to the American Revolutionary War at 90% accuracy.

Content:

Resources from websites mentioned above and adopted textbook on the Battle at Bunker Hill and the beginning of the revolutionary war, as well as resources located by students. Emphasis is on the use of images.

Procedures:

- Tell students the learning objective and academic standard.
- Show battlefield photo.
- Use Photo Analysis Worksheet from NPS to guide a discussion of the photo as a primary source of information. Students take notes.
- Individually students read the Setting Stage content and record their notes.
- As a class, view Locating the Site and discuss the provided questions, recording the answers in their notes.
- In pairs students read either Reading 1 or Reading 2 and discuss and answer questions. Each person presents the information to the other using the questions to guide the sharing of information.
- Teacher led discussion on the questions. Each person adds notes to their notes.
- Individually students read one of the three Visual Evidence pages and answer questions in their notes. This is followed by a class discussion of each piece of Visual Evidence led by a student volunteer.
- Students are randomly assigned to small groups. Each group chooses either Activity 1 or 2 from the NPS website.
- Groups present projects to the class.
- Clear up any misconceptions that might be presented.

Assessment:

Review student notes; Group project presentation; District common assessment

Accommodations:

Websites at different reading level or modify text to meet the reading levels of students in the class. Enable text-to-speech on computers so students can have the text read to them.

Allow students to use electronic Inquiry Journals and use speech-to-text software as needed.

Figure 14.2 Inquiry Lesson Plan Format

Name/Grade Level/Content: *Deborah, high school, American history*

Title of Lesson: *We Are at War: The Beginning of the Revolutionary War*

Timeframe: *Two 90-minute class periods*

Materials: *Slideshow of the American Revolutionary War, Presentation on events leading to the Revolutionary War. Computer Lab, laptop, projector, printed copies of text and images, textbooks, reference books, and the National Park Service (NPS).*

Websites of Lesson Resources:

http://www.nps.gov/history/nr/twhp/wwwlps/lessons/42bunker/ 42getting.htm, Inquiry Question

http://www.nps.gov/history/nr/twhp/wwwlps/lessons/42bunker/ 42setting.htm, Setting the stage

http://www.nps.gov/history/nr/twhp/wwwlps/lessons/42bunker/ 42bunker.htm, Photo Analysis Worksheet http://www.nps.gov/history/nr/twhp/PHOTOANA.HTM, Photo Analysis Graphic Organizer

Standard: *H1.1 Research PO 3 Formulate questions that can be answered by historical study and research*

Rationale:

This is required by the district curriculum and state academic standards. It lends itself well to the use of images as primary source documents.

Objective:

While viewing a slideshow, a historical photo, and reading text, students will be able to create questions that describe events that led to the American Revolutionary War at 90% accuracy. Emphasis is on the use of images.

Content:

Resources from websites mentioned above and adopted textbook on the Battle at Bunker Hill and the beginning of the revolutionary war, as well as resources located by students.

Procedures:

Inquiry Question(s): *"What events led to the American Revolutionary War?"*

Exploration and Gather Data:

- *View the photo. Use Photo Analysis Worksheet to analyze the photograph as a primary source of information. In small collaborative groups, students formulate a hypothesis based on the questions, "Which U.S. war is depicted in this battle scene? What famous battle might this be?" and record it in their Inquiry Journals.*
- *Individually students read the Setting Stage content and record their notes in the Inquiry Journals.*
- *Together they view Locating the Site and discuss the hypothesis recording their ideas based on data in their Inquiry Journals.*
  - ○ *Individually students read one of the three Visual Evidence pages and collect additional data to record in their Inquiry Journals. They then share this information with the rest of the group using the data to guide the sharing. Each person adds notes to their Inquiry Journals.*

Analyze Data and Form Preliminary Conclusions:

- *Groups choose either Activity 1 or 2 to guide the analysis of what information they have gathered.*

Discussion:

- *Groups share their projects with the class emphasizing discoveries, data collection, and preliminary conclusions.*

Explanation based on Data:

- *Based on the students' sharing their projects and their discussion, the teacher records and labels informational content.*

Expansion:

In pairs within the small groups, students read either Reading 1 or Reading 2, discuss and compare all events that led to the Revolutionary War. Each pair presents additional information not previously presented to the rest of the group using the readings to document data gathered. Each person adds notes to their Inquiry Journals. Students clear up any misconceptions that might be presented by asking for documentation of information presented.

Assessment:

The teacher asks the students to create questions that describe events that led to the American Revolutionary War. She also reviews their Inquiry Journal entries and their Group Project presentations.

Accommodations:

Websites at different reading levels, library books at different reading levels or modify text to meet the reading levels of students in the class. Enable text-to-speech on computers so students can have the text read to them. Allow students to use electronic Inquiry Journals and use speech-to-text software as needed.

Figure 14.3 Essential Elements Lesson Plan Format

Name/Grade Level/Content: *Deborah—high school—American History*

Title of Lesson: *We Are At War: The Beginning of the American Revolutionary War*

Timeframe: *Two 90-minute class periods*

Materials: *Slideshow of the American Revolutionary War, Presentation on events leading to the Revolutionary War. Computer Lab, laptop, projector, printed copies of text and images, textbooks, reference books, and the National Park Service (NPS).*

Websites of Lesson Resources:

http://www.nps.gov/history/nr/twhp/wwwlps/lessons/42bunker/ 42bunker.htm , Photo Analysis Worksheet

http://www.nps.gov/history/nr/twhp/PHOTOANA.HTM, Photo Analysis Graphic Organizer

Standard: *H1.1 Research PO 3 Formulate questions that can be answered by historical study and research*

Rationale:

This is required by the district curriculum and state academic standards. It lends itself well to the use of images as primary source documents.

Objective: *While viewing a slideshow, a historical photo, and reading text, students will be able to create questions that describe events that led to the American Revolutionary War at 90% accuracy.*

Task Analysis: *All steps of the task analysis have been completed and subobjectives written and preassessed.*

Anticipatory Set: *Show slideshow of images of events that led to the American Revolutionary War with powerful and relevant music.*

Input/Content:

- *Show single battlefield photo from NPS site.*
- *Use Photo Analysis Worksheet from NPS to guide a discussion of the photo as a primary source of information.*
- *Individually students read the Setting Stage content and record their notes.*
- *Review this content with the students eliciting from them key points from the text.*
- *As a class, view Locating the Site and discuss the provided questions, recording the answers in their notes.*
- *Presentation on events leading to the revolutionary war using same photos used in slideshow in participatory set.*
- *In pairs students read either Reading 1 or Reading 2 and discuss and answer questions. Each person presents the information to the other using the questions to guide the sharing of information.*
- *Teacher led discussion on the questions. Each person adds notes to their notes.*
- *Individually students read one of the three Visual Evidence pages and answer questions in their notes. This is followed by a class discussion of each piece of Visual Evidence led by a student volunteer.*

Model:

Select one event that led to the war. Model locating images in the public domain related to that event. Model the analysis process using the Photo Analysis Worksheet as a guide. Share a premade presentation that includes three images and bulleted information about the event and its connection to the revolutionary war.

Check for Understanding:

Critical questioning throughout discussions and observation of pair discussions

Guided Practice:

- *Select another event that led to the war. Show images from the slideshow related to this event. Show the Photo Analysis Worksheet on the screen for students to use as a guide. Provide students with a graphic organizer for recording the information they glean from the image.*
- *Students share their analysis with the class then turn them in for teacher feedback. Class discusses how this event contributed to the start of the war.*

Independent Practice:

Students are randomly assigned to small groups. Each chooses five events that led to the American Revolutionary War, locate at least three images for each event, complete an analysis of each image, and create a presentation (e.g., video, PowerPoint, poster, etc.). Groups present projects to the class.

Closure:

Summarize use of graphics as primary sources for providing evidence of events leading up to the Revolutionary War.

Assessment:

Review student notes: Group project presentation: District common assessment

Accommodations:

Websites at different reading level or modify text to meet the reading levels of students in the class. Enable text-to-speech on computers so students can have the text read to them. Allow students to use electronic Inquiry Journals and use speech-to-text software as needed.

HOW TO USE THE LESSON DESIGN TOOLS

Mentors can use any of the lesson design templates to engage beginning teachers in deeper discussions of developing lessons that will ensure student learning and engagement. Using the *Lesson Element Alignment* worksheet tool (see Chapter 13) provides the framework for the design of the lesson. The mentor assists the teacher in deciding which format to use for designing the lesson dependent on the style of the teacher and the intent of the lesson.

- The beginning teacher will use the Basic Lesson plan if he wants a generic lesson.
- The beginning teacher will use the Essential Elements Lesson plan if she wants to systematically present academic content by providing the content of the lesson directly to the students.
- The beginning teacher will use the Inquiry Lesson plan if he wants to create an inquiry-based environment where students use various process skills.

LESSON DESIGN TOOLS IN ACTION

Barbara, a mentor, continues the conversation she was having with her beginning teacher, Wanda, who teaches first grade from Chapter 13: Planning for Instruction. They had completed the *Instructional Planning* process. The next decision that needed to be made was what lesson design to use. Wanda has a framework for designing a set of lessons from the Lesson Element Alignment worksheet (see Chapter 13). When Wanda teaches this new lesson, Barbara can take the same "time-on-task" data to see if the *Instructional Planning* process and the *Lesson Design* process makes a difference.

Wanda's objective is that when given a series of diagrams, first grade students will be able to identify equal fractions with 90% accuracy; for example 2/4=1/2, 4/4=2/2, 2/8=1/4, 4/8=2/4=1/2, 6/8=3/4, and 8/8=4/4=2/2. Her second subobjective is that when given real objects divided into two equal sections, students will select 1/4, 2/4, 3/4, or 4/4 pieces when instructed five out of five times. All of her students know the first subobjective: 1/2 and 2/2. Eighty-five percent of her students did not know the second subobjective on the preassessment. Wanda makes the decision to use the Inquiry Lesson plan for the majority of the class since she wants to create an inquiry environment where students use various process skills. Wanda decides to make an accommodation activity for the 15% that already know the concept. Barbara guides Wanda through each step of the Inquiry Lesson plan, making sure that the materials and all procedures are listed (Figure 14.4). Wanda and Barbara set up a timeline for the lesson presentation.

Figure 14.4 Inquiry Lesson Plan Format

Name/Grade Level/Content: *Steve—1st Grade—Math: Fractions*

Title of Lesson: *Fraction Pizza Party*

Timeframe: *One lesson*

Materials and Resources: *1/4 and 2/4, 3/4, and 4/4 pieces of pie, pizza, candy bars, paper shapes made from two squares of construction paper. Each group of 4 students will need multiple copies of the pie, the pizza, and the candy bar. Set of magazines, scissors, pencils, and crayons.*

Standard: *MA1-SINS-P015: Identify in symbols and in words a model that is divided into equal fractional parts.*

Rationale: *Students need to understand the concept of fractions in the real world as they will be expected to use this skill when dividing groups of people into equal parts, cutting a pie for equal parts, etc.*

Objective: *Given real objects divided into two equal sections, students will select 1/4, 2/4, 3/4, and 4/4 pieces when instructed five out of five times.*

Content: *Students will identify 1/4, 2/4, 3/4, and 4/4 when given a set of materials (pie, pizza, candy bars)*

Procedures:

- *Inquiry Question(s): Ask students to set in groups of four. "I want to know how to divide this pizza into equal parts so each of you will have a piece."*
- *Exploration: Each group of students is given a paper pizza and have the opportunity to explore how to cut the pizza until they each have an equal piece.*
- *Gather Data: They make drawings of each attempt using a blank piece of paper. They already know the procedure for collecting data so that it is presentable to the group.*
- *Analyze Data and Form Preliminary Conclusions: As each group comes up with a solution, they paste their solution on a piece of paper and explain how they got their answers.*
- *Discussion: The class has a discussion and each group shows their solution. We discuss how many pieces it took to divide the pizza—4.*
- *Explanation based on Data: The teacher labels the pieces of her pizza based on what the students shared with her. She asks questions such as how many pieces would it take if we had divided the pizza into four parts but only 3 of you showed up, etc. until the concepts of 1/4, 2/4, 3/4, and 4/4 were discussed and labeled.*

Expansion: *Each student is given four pies and four candy bars. They are asked to divide their pie and their candy bars. After dividing the pie and candy bar into equal parts, they are to draw their solution and label each piece. The teacher observes and makes sure that every one is completing the assignment accurately. She then asks them to copy from the board questions in regard to 1/4, 2/4, 3/4, and 4/4. They use their pie and candy bar pieces to complete the assignment. If students need more materials, they get them from the bin in the back of the room.*

Assessment: *The teacher will use the data forms filled out by each child in the expansion activity as well as provide a written example of shaded shapes to label for each child to complete with 90% accuracy.*

Accommodations:

- *The students that already knew the subobjective are given a stack of magazines and asked to find pictures of equal parts for 1/4, 2/4, 3/4, and 4/4. They are to label the pictures and explain why they selected the picture. This assignment will be collected and assessed using 90% accuracy as the measure of success.*
- *For students who do not understand the concept, they will be provided with puzzle pieces and asked to record what they see. All puzzle pieces will be in fourths with some pieces missing.*

NOTES FOR IMPLEMENTATION

It is important for the mentor to assist the beginning teacher in transferring the lesson elements they created on the *Lesson Element Alignment* worksheet tool (see Chapter 13) to the appropriate lesson plan design. Mentors can offer beginning teachers different lesson plan designs to support a beginning teacher's desire to try different approaches to instruction. Mentors can support teachers in matching the elements of these lesson plan formats to the teachers' instructional style as well as looking at the developmental needs of the students in the classroom. Lesson design requirements that might be set forth by the school district or site administrator can be used to incorporate these different instructional styles.

Figure 14.5	Basic Lesson Plan Format

Name/Grade Level/Content:

Title of Lesson:

Timeframe:

Materials and Resources:

Standard:

Rationale:

Objective:

Content:

Procedures:

Assessment:

Accommodations:

Figure 14.6 Inquiry Lesson Plan Format

Name/Grade Level/Content:

Title of Lesson:

Timeframe:

Materials and Resources:

Standard:

Rationale:

Objective:

Content:

Procedures:

- Inquiry Question(s):
- Exploration:
- Gather Data:
- Analyze Data and Form Preliminary Conclusions:
- Discussion:
- Explanation based on Data:

Expansion:

Assessment:

Accommodations:

Figure 14.7 Essential Elements Lesson Plan Format

Name/Grade Level/Content:

Title of Lesson:

Timeframe:

Materials and Resources:

Standard:

Rationale:

Objective:

Task Analysis:

Anticipatory Set:

Input/Content:

Model:

Check for Understanding:

Guided Practice:

Independent Practice:

Closure:

Assessment:

Accommodation:

15

Videotaping as a Process for Reflection

PURPOSE FOR VIDEOTAPING AS A PROCESS

The most powerful form of reflection is to watch a videotape of one's practice. According to Stigler and Hiebert (1999, p. 9), "Video provides us with a unique way of gathering the information we need to examine our current practices and then improve them." Documenting evidence through videotape allows observers to see practices and behaviors with an objective lens. Seeing *is* believing! All beginning teachers are videotaped by their mentors as a part of the data collection process. There are several tools that serve to guide this process. These tools are *Video Preparation Checklist, Videotaping Guidelines,* and *Videotape Reflection.* The videotaped lesson is linked to the beginning teacher's *Professional Growth plan.*

DESCRIPTION OF VIDEOTAPING AS A PROCESS

During a planning conference (see Chapter 2) a mentor and beginning teacher determine when the videotaping session will take place. This is the first step of the *Video Preparation Checklist,* a tool that guides rather than serves to collect data (Figure 15.1). The beginning teacher uses this tool to ensure all steps are taken when preparing for videotaping session.

Figure 15.1	Video Preparation Checklist

☑ During a *Planning Conference,* set date and time for videotaping. Make sure you give yourself enough time to collect Student Release forms and secure equipment.

Date: *October 15ᵗʰ* Time: *10:00am*

☑ During a *Planning Conference*, determine the focus of lesson. Next, determine which data collection tool will best capture the desired behaviors. The tool will be used while viewing the videotape.

Focus: *Teacher student interactions regarding questioning strategies during a Social Studies lesson.*

☑ Locate the required student release form. Check with your site administrator or district legal office.

Location: *Signed Parent Handbook forms*

☑ Send home the student release forms.   Date: *October 8ᵗʰ*

☑ Locate needed equipment (e.g., video camera, tri-pod, high quality video tape, power cord, lapel microphone – optional, etc).

Location: *Mentor has camera, tripod, power cord, and videotape. I need to find a microphone. I will ask the media specialist and site administrator.*

☑ Collect the student release forms and file them in your room. Make sure you identify whom you CANNOT film.   Due Date: *October 7ᵗʰ*

☑ Confirm your mentor will be coming to your room on the set date and time to videotape your lesson.

Date: *October 7ᵗʰ*

☑ Plan the lesson that will be presented during the videotaping session.

Date Complete: *October 13ᵗʰ*

☑ On the day of the videotaping, arrange students so that those who cannot be videotaped will be out of the camera shot. You MUST not exclude them from the lesson nor make them feel identified in any way.

☑ Make sure the person videotaping the lesson knows who cannot be videotaped.

☑ Test the equipment to make sure it is working!

☑ Take a deep breath; this is not going to be seen by anyone expect you and your mentor.

The *Videotaping Guidelines* tool is designed to support mentors and beginning teachers in capturing the best quality video possible. This includes capturing audio of both the teacher and the students. This tool explains the process of how to take a video in the classroom. Since some students' parents have not signed the release form, place those students out of view of the camera but do not leave them out of the lesson. Let your mentor know which students are without parent permission so they will not be in the video. As you prepare to video the lesson, let the tape run for a few minutes before actually starting the lesson. This short timeframe will allow the teacher's opening remarks to be taped. It is important to let the students know why you as the beginning teacher are being videotaped. If you feel that the majority of the students have never been videotaped, a preliminary tape can be made as a practice session. This practice session will allow the mentor, the teacher, and the students to become familiar with this experience in the classroom (Figure 15.2).

The mentor and the teacher review the process using the Videotaping Guidelines tool and discuss any of the components. Remember to:

- Place the video recorder away from the light since light can interfere with the recording device
- Conduct a sound check for quality sound
- Know how to start and end the videotaping
- Practice videotaping before using in the classroom
- Make adjustments as needed prior to taping the lesson in the classroom
- Hear and see as much as possible in the classroom to provide the mentor and the beginning teacher a tool for a reflective discussion

Thoughtful and purposeful reflection on the contents of the videotape is vital to achieve the maximum impact on instructional practice. During the reflective conference, the mentor and the beginning teacher view the tape. Both use the data collection tool identified during the planning conference to capture the specific data related to the professional growth goal. After the viewing and a discussion between the two, the teacher completes the *Videotape Reflection* (Figure 15.3).

Figure 15.2	Videotaping Guidelines

Preparing to Videotape

- Set up camera on a tripod.
- Let the tape run for the first two minutes of the session.
- Share with your students why you are being videotaped.

Establishing the Camera

- Set up the camcorder in a place in the room that allows the greatest range of visibility as the teacher works with students.
- For PE teachers, shoot from an angle, rather than head-on, for the most attractive video.
- Try to have the camera no more than 20 feet away.
- Focus on the students as well as the teacher.
- Make sure shoots are well framed before you begin. Be aware of headroom. You want to be able to see the teacher in the scene.
- Extreme high angles or low angles in shooting will not produce the best quality.

Lighting

- Main source of light should be behind the camera operator, illuminating the instructor.
- Poor lighting causes poorer quality in videotape pictures than anything else.
- Pointing the video recorder toward the windows will cause a lighting problem. Either cover the windows or put the camera in front of them and shoot away from them.
- Shooting into the sun or into bright lights when videotaping PE candidates and others outdoors will cause a lighting problem.

Conducting a Sound Check

- Use a lavaliere microphone plugged into the camcorder if the built-in microphone in the camcorder is not providing enough volume.

Recording

- Starting: Push the record button at least five seconds before you want your actual "scene" to begin. It gives camera time to get up to the proper speed and it assures that you won't lose the speakers' first few words.
- During: You may want to repeat student questions or statements if they are inaudible.
- Ending: Allow an additional minute or two of taping at the end of the lesson. The tape is not finished at the exact same time you think the lesson is over.

Figure 15.3 Videotaping Reflection

This completed reflection page should accompany a copy of your videotape.

Description: The description explains the *"what."* Be concise and clear about your instruction and student learning so that an outsider could "see as you see" what you are describing.	**Describe what you saw or heard in your video that demonstrates effective instruction?** • *Most of my students were looking in the appropriate direction when I or another student was talking. A couple of students in the back were chatting on and off.* • *Students were writing on their whiteboards when directed to do so. One student was drawing pictures.* • *During independent work most students were really working on the assignment. A few were playing around with pencils and scraps of paper.* • *The scripting data collection tool confirmed my description.*
Analysis: Analysis deals with reasons, motives, and interpretation. Any analysis you provide should be supported by concrete examples.	**What evidence shows that decisions or instructional methods had a positive or negative impact on the students in your classroom? What did you see or hear in your video that demonstrates evidence of students' learning? What were the results of what you described?** • *Using the individual whiteboards and allowing them to choose the color marker they wanted to use seemed to work well in holding their attention.* • *Students were solving the problems correctly on their whiteboards.* • *When the students returned to their tasks several were distracted by papers that were already on their desks. These papers kept them from starting to do their work right away.*
Reflection: Your reflection provides the basis for starting the learning cycle over. Give specific details and concrete examples.	**Based on your analysis, what did you learn about your students? What did you learn about your instruction? Explain what changes you will make to your instructional practice based on what you observed in your videotape. Will you do something different? Why or why not?** • *I will use the individual whiteboards again. This helped keep them engaged and gave me a quick way to "see" if they were solving the problems correctly.* • *In the future, I will have students clear off their desks before they come to the group area for the math lesson. This way they will not be distracted by papers or other items on their desk when they return for independent practice.*

HOW TO USE THE VIDEOTAPING TOOLS

During a planning conference, the mentor gives the beginning teacher copies of the video preparation checklist, videotaping guidelines, and the videotape reflection. They set a date for the videotaping and the reflective conference. They talk through the elements of each tool. Together they complete the first two items on the checklist. The mentor may be able to assist in locating the student release form. It is the beginning teacher's responsibility to complete the remaining items on the video preparation checklist. The mentor will check out and bring the video camera.

As they plan for the videotaping event, certain decisions need to be made. The teacher shares what the lesson objectives are for the lesson that day. Together they determine which data collection tool they will use during the viewing of the video to capture the desired student and teacher behaviors.

On the day of the videotaping, the beginning teacher and mentor reference the videotaping guidelines tool as they prepare to record the lesson. This ensures they will acquire the most useful video possible.

If possible, the mentor and the beginning teacher view the videotape the same day that it is made. Often the beginning teacher likes to view the video alone first, and then review it with the mentor. Prior to watching the video with the mentor, the beginning teacher should review the lesson plan, the selected data collection tool, and the videotape reflection tool. The beginning teacher and the mentor use the data collection tool while viewing the video to help guide the discussion during the reflective conference. The teacher may also reference the data collection tool when writing the reflection.

VIDEOTAPING TOOLS IN ACTION

In a planning conference, first year teacher Sam indicated to his mentor Joseph that he was getting frustrated with many of his students not paying attention during his tenth-grade social studies lecture. He said he had been using multimedia slideshows so they should be paying attention. Joseph had already collected time-on-task data for Sam on several occasions. Each time Sam identified a different reason for the data Joseph collected. This time Joseph suggested videotaping Sam's lesson so he could see and hear what was happening during a lesson. Although hesitant, Sam agreed seeing the video for himself might be helpful. Joseph pulled out a copy of the videotaping preparation checklist for him and Sam to review (Figure 15.4).

Sam decided to focus on student engagement as measured by their time-on-task. He wanted to lecture using a multimedia slideshow so he could see why the slideshow itself was not engaging the students. Together they completed the first three items of the videotaping checklist. Sam would work through the rest of the items on the checklist as he prepared for the videotaping session. After reviewing the checklist, Joseph gave Sam a copy of the videotaping guidelines. They reviewed each item and

Figure 15.4 Video Preparation Checklist

☑ During a *Planning Conference* set date and time for videotaping. Make sure you give yourself enough time to collect Student Release forms and secure equipment.

Date: *November 20ᵗʰ* Time: *1:00pm*

☑ During a *Planning Conference*, determine the focus of lesson. Next, determine which data collection tool will best capture the desired behaviors. The tool will be used while viewing the videotape.

Focus: *Student engagement measured by student behaviors during a lecture along with a multimedia slideshow*

☑ Locate the required student release form. Check with you site administrator or district legal office.

Location: *School website in the Forms section*

☑ Send home the student release forms. Date: *November 12ᵗʰ*

☑ Locate needed equipment (e.g., video camera, tripod, high quality video tape, power cord, lapel microphone – optional, etc).

Location: *I need to check out the equipment from the media.*

☑ Collect the student release forms and file them in your room. Make sure you identify whom you CANNOT film. Due Date: *November 10ᵗʰ*

☑ Confirm your mentor will be coming to your room on the set date and time to videotape your lesson.

Date: *November 10ᵗʰ*

☑ Plan the lesson that will be presented during the videotaping session.

Date Complete: *November 11ᵗʰ*

☑ On the day of the videotaping, arrange students so that those who cannot be videotaped will be out of the camera shot. You MUST not exclude them from the lesson nor make them feel identified in any way.

☑ Make sure the person videotaping the lesson knows who cannot be videotaped.

☑ Test the equipment to make sure it is working!

☑ Take a deep breath; this is not going to be seen by anyone expect you and your mentor.

Figure 15.5 Videotaping Reflection

This completed reflection page should accompany a copy of your videotape.

Description: The description explains the *"what."* Be concise and clear about your instruction and student learning so that an outsider could "see as you see" what you are describing.	**Describe what you saw or heard in your video that demonstrates effective instruction?** • *Me talking and talking and talking and talking…* • *By the end of the class they were talking a lot. I do not think it was about my lecture.* • *Each time I changed slides they looked up and were quiet for a few minutes.* • *They were quiet during the shorter video segments.* • *I asked a lot of yes/no questions or other one-word answer questions.*
Analysis: Analysis deals with reasons, motives, and interpretation. Any analysis you provide should be supported by concrete examples.	**What evidence shows that decisions or instructional methods had a positive or negative impact on the students in your classroom? What did you see or hear in your video that demonstrates evidence of students' learning? What were the results of what you described?** • *The more I talked the less they paid attention and the more they talked.* • *They seemed to attend to the slideshow each time a new visual was presented: however, the longer I just spoke with that one image displayed the less they paid attention.* • *Some of the students answered the basic questions correctly, but they could have been guessing.* • *A review of the seating chart time-on-task data collection tool confirmed my analysis.*
Reflection: Your reflection provides the basis for starting the learning cycle over. Give specific details and concrete examples.	**Based on your analysis, what did you learn about your students? What did you learn about your instruction? Explain what changes you will make to your instructional practice based on what you observed in your videotape. Will you do something different? Why or why not?** • *Need to be more precise in my speaking.* • *If I am going to use a slideshow I need to offer more images.* • *I need to ask questions that require higher-level thinking.* • *I need to think more about the differences between paying attention and student engagement.* • *Providing a graphic organizer for note taking would allow me to see if they are at least organizing the information correctly.* • *The multimedia is not enough. I need to use engagement strategies and lecture for shorter periods of time. Perhaps some pair-share or jigsaw type activities.*

discussed how to best set up for the videotaping and decided to use the *Logging Student Engagement* tool (see Chapter 16).

On the day of the taping, Sam and Joseph set up the camera and lapel microphone together referencing the videotaping guidelines. When the lesson was complete, Joseph took the tape with him as the two of them would review it together the next day.

Joseph and Sam watched the video together the next day, both taking data using a *Logging Student Engagement* tool (see Chapter 16) during the reflective conference. They discussed the data each one collected. Joseph guided the conversation for Sam to "see" clearly who was engaging in the learning and who was not. Sam made decisions for his seating arrangement based on the data collected. Sam also saw the need to implement additional engagement strategies as he recorded the percentage of students engaged during various segments of the lesson. Sam will complete his videotape reflection to share with his mentor at their next meeting (Figure 15.5).

NOTES FOR IMPLEMENTATION

Sometimes beginning teachers cannot see in themselves what an objective observer can see. This is a good time to use videotaping as a tool for collecting data about the beginning teacher's practice. In order for beginning teachers to feel comfortable being videotaped, they must trust the mentor that the video will not be shared with anyone else. The tools are introduced prior to videotaping. The process keeps the teacher and the mentor focused on the task of observing the teacher's practice in the classroom. The mentor and the beginning teacher use a data collection tool while viewing the videotape together. This process allows the mentor and the beginning teacher to be objective in their observations. This data tool is the foundation for the conversation during the reflective conference. An action plan is produced during the reflective conference and the Conference Data Conference (CDC) Cycle begins again (see Chapter 3).

Figure 15.6 Video Preparation Checklist

☐ During a *Planning Conference,* set date and time for videotaping. Make sure you give yourself enough time to collect Student Release forms and secure equipment.

Date: _____ Time:_____

☐ During a *Planning Conference*, determine the focus of lesson. Next, determine which data collection tool will best capture the desired behaviors. The tool will be used while viewing the videotape.

Focus: _____

_____

☐ Locate the required student release form. Check with your site administrator or district legal office.

Location: _____

☐ Send home the student release forms.   Date: _____

☐ Locate needed equipment (e.g., video camera, tripod, high quality video tape, power cord, lapel microphone – optional, etc).

Location: _____

☐ Collect the student release forms and file them in your room. Make sure you identify whom you CANNOT film.   Due Date: _____

☐ Confirm your mentor will be coming to your room on the set date and time to videotape your lesson.

Date: _____

☐ Plan the lesson that will be presented during the videotaping session.

Date Complete: _____

☐ On the day of the videotaping, arrange students so that those who cannot be videotaped will be out of the camera shot. You MUST not exclude them from the lesson nor make them feel identified in any way.

☐ Make sure the person videotaping the lesson knows who cannot be videotaped.

☐ Test the equipment to make sure it is working!

☐ Take a deep breath; this is not going to be seen by anyone expect you and your mentor.

Figure 15.7 Videotaping Guidelines

Preparing to Videotape

- Set up camera on a tripod.
- Let the tape run for the first two minutes of the session.
- Share with your students why you are being videotaped.

Establishing the Camera

- Set up the camcorder in a place in the room that allows the greatest range of visibility as the teacher works with students.
- For PE teachers, shoot from an angle, rather than head-on, for the most attractive video.
- Try to have the camera no more than 20 feet away.
- Focus on the students as well as the teacher.
- Make sure shoots are well framed before you begin. Be aware of headroom. You want to be able to see the teacher in the scene.
- Extreme high angles or low angles in shooting will not produce the best quality.

Lighting

- Main source of light should be behind the camera operator, illuminating the instructor.
- Poor lighting causes poorer quality in videotape pictures than anything else.
- Pointing the video recorder towards the windows will cause a lighting problem. Either cover the windows or put the camera in front of them and shoot away from them.
- Shooting into the sun or into bright lights when videotaping PE candidates and others outdoors will cause a lighting problem.

Conducting a Sound Check

- Use a lavaliere microphone plugged into the camcorder if the built-in microphone in the camcorder is not providing enough volume.

Recording

- Starting: Push the record button at least five seconds before you want your actual "scene" to begin. It gives camera time to get up to the proper speed, and it assures that you won't lose the speakers' first few words.
- During: You may want to repeat student questions or statements if they are inaudible.
- Ending: Allow an additional minute or two of taping at the end of the lesson. The tape is not finished at the exact same time you think the lesson is over.

Figure 15.8	Videotaping Reflection

This completed reflection page should accompany a copy of your videotape.

Description: The description explains the *"what."* Be concise and clear about your instruction and student learning so that an outsider could "see as you see" what you are describing.	**Describe what you saw or heard in your video that demonstrates effective instruction?**
Analysis: Analysis deals with reasons, motives, and interpretation. Any analysis you provide should be supported by concrete examples.	**What evidence shows that decisions or instructional methods had a positive or negative impact on the students in your classroom? What did you see or hear in your video that demonstrates evidence of students' learning? What were the results of what you described?**
Reflection: Your reflection provides the basis for starting the learning cycle over. Give specific details and concrete examples.	**Based on your analysis, what did you learn about your students? What did you learn about your instruction? Explain what changes you will make to your instructional practice based on what you observed in your videotape. Will you do something different? Why or why not?**

16

Collecting Evidence

Student Engagement

PURPOSE FOR COLLECTING EVIDENCE: STUDENT ENGAGEMENT

Engaging students in learning activities is a challenging task for even the most experienced teachers. Beyond classroom management, being able to engage students is the most identified need for beginning teachers (Horn & Metler-Armijo, 2009). Beginning teachers want to know how to effectively connect students to content and motivate them to learn. This desire is one indication that teachers are transforming from *role focused* to *practice focused.* Teachers want to engage students in the learning and want to see evidence that learning is occurring.

One of the early steps for teachers in moving in this direction is to distinguish between students paying attention and students engaging in the learning. Danielson (2009) states, "Engagement is not the same as busy nor is physical activity sufficient. An activity might involve students working with physical materials, as in a science lesson. But the key to student engagement is not physical but mental activity; an activity may be hands-on but it must be minds-on" (p. 55). Teachers need to recognize overt behaviors that indicate students are exercising their minds and not just playing the role of student.

The purpose for developing our *Student Engagement* tools is for mentors to help teachers see evidence of student engagement in the classroom.

With these tools, data can be collected that demonstrates how well students are engaged in the learning activities provided during a specific time span. Data can also be collected to show specific overt student and teacher behaviors occurring during instructional time. Presenting this evidence can help teachers visualize how to better meet the needs of their students.

DESCRIPTION OF COLLECTING EVIDENCE: STUDENT ENGAGEMENT

There are two tool formats mentors use to collect data on student engagement in the classroom: *Logging Student Engagement* and *Logging Engaging Behavior.*

The *Logging Student Engagement* tool is used to identify the amount of time students are actively engaged within the learning activities. Many tools focus on identifying those behaviors that demonstrate unengaged behaviors. This tool is a quick and easy way for both beginning teachers and mentors to visually recognize areas in which the students are engaged in the activities during a specific time span.

The Logging Student Engagement tool is divided into four different informational sections:

1. Student Behavior

2. Time and Lesson Components

3. Number of Students

4. Reflection

The left-hand column, student behavior, is divided into six sections that describe demonstrated engaged behavior. These sections focus on those overt behaviors that indicate students are engaging their brains rather than just paying attention. While it is often difficult to know what goes on in students' brains, there are some behaviors that students demonstrate that show they are actively engaging in the learning.

- Active listening: How well the students are listening to the instruction, such as leaning forward, tracking teacher movement, head nodding, and paraphrasing
- Signaling: How the students are communicating understanding to the teacher and each other, such as thumbs up/thumbs down and whiteboards

- Verbalizing: How the students are communicating verbally about the learning, such as student questioning, student response, and group discussion
- Writing: How the students are communicating in written format about the learning, such as journaling and recording observations
- Manipulating: How the students are communicating using manipulatives during learning, such as making suggestions for use, hands-on, and creativity in use
- Other engagement data: This section is open to defining any other areas of engagement the mentor or beginning teacher feels are necessary to add to the data

The center column consists of two sections:

- Time and lesson components are broken up to identify the time segment that allows multiple lesson components to be described during that same time segment
- Number of students performing student behaviors described in the left column during allotted time segments

The far right-hand column, reflection, is for the mentor to record any teacher reflection that is pertinent to moving the teacher's practice forward. This portion of the tool is completed during the reflective conference. Mentors capture the reflective comments with quotation marks to indicate it is a direct quote from the teacher (Figure 16.1).

The *Logging Engaging Behavior* tool is used to identify student and teacher behaviors occurring during a lesson. This tool can help the teacher see connections between her actions and students' behavioral responses. She can begin to identify if her behaviors elicited engaged or disengaged student behavior. Three types of behaviors are observed throughout the lesson, which is divided into five segments of time:

1. Teacher Behavior: What the teacher is doing to facilitate learning, such as direct instruction, modeling, student conferencing, and using proximity

2. Engaged Student Behavior: What students are doing that demonstrates a connection to the learning and instruction, such as active listening, signaling, verbalizing, writing, and manipulating

3. Disengaged Student Behavior: What students are doing that demonstrates a detachment from the learning and instruction, such as talking out of turn, getting out of seats, or sleeping (Figure 16.2)

Figure 16.1 Logging Student Engagement

Teacher: *Bernice*   **Mentor:** *Steve*   **Date:** *10/2*

Lesson Focus: *Going beyond the Great Barrier Reef whole class lecture.*   **Number of Students:** *32*

Student Behavior	Time and Lesson Component						Reflection
	9:10-9:15	9:15-9:20	9:20-9:25	9:25-9:30	9:30-9:35	9:35-9:40	
	Intro & Set	Lecture Check for understanding	Lecture	Lecture	Independent work directions	Independent work time	
	Number of Students						Reflection
A. Active Listening —leaning forward, tracking teacher movement, head nodding, paraphrasing	✓✓✓✓✓ ✓✓✓✓✓ ✓✓✓✓✓ ✓✓✓✓✓ ✓✓✓✓✓ ✓✓✓✓✓ ✓✓	✓✓✓✓✓ ✓✓✓✓✓ ✓✓✓✓✓ ✓✓✓✓✓ ✓✓✓	✓✓✓✓✓ ✓✓✓✓✓ ✓✓✓✓✓ ✓✓✓✓✓ ✓✓	✓✓✓✓✓ ✓✓✓✓✓ ✓✓✓✓✓ ✓✓	✓✓✓✓✓ ✓✓✓✓		"I notice that all my students were engaged at the beginning. Then I seemed to lose them a few at a time."
B. Signaling —thumbs up and whiteboards		✓✓✓✓✓ ✓✓✓✓✓ ✓✓✓✓✓ ✓✓✓✓✓ ✓✓✓✓✓ ✓✓✓✓✓ ✓✓					"I really like using whiteboards to check for understanding. All of my students did what they were supposed to."
C. Verbalizing —student questioning, student response, group discussion	✓✓✓	✓✓✓✓✓ ✓✓✓✓✓			✓✓✓✓✓ ✓✓✓✓✓ ✓✓✓✓✓ ✓✓✓✓✓ ✓✓		"It seems like when I was giving directions and had them partner share, most students did what I asked."
D. Writing —journaling, recording observations						✓✓✓✓✓ ✓✓✓✓✓ ✓✓✓✓✓ ✓✓✓✓✓ ✓✓✓✓	"Wow! Only 24 of my students were doing work. I wonder why."
E. Manipulating —suggestions for use, hands-on, creativity in use							
F. Other Engagement Data							

Figure 16.2 Logging Engaging Behavior

Teacher: _Rod_   **Mentor:** _Ronnie_   **Date:** _11/4_

Lesson Focus: _Chapter 20 in Social Studies_   **Number of Students:** _32_

Time	# of Engaged Students	Teacher Behaviors	Engaged Student Behaviors	Disengaged Student Behaviors
2:00-2:05	✓✓✓✓✓✓✓ ✓✓✓✓✓✓✓ ✓✓✓✓✓✓✓ ✓✓✓	*T began lesson with questions to get the students involved in the chapter *T moved around the room *T wrote questions on board	*S raised their hands to answer the questions	*1 S texting on cell phone *1 S sleeping
2:05-2:10	✓✓✓✓✓✓✓ ✓✓✓✓✓✓✓ ✓✓✓✓✓	*T asked students which question they would like to investigate *T assigned each student to one of the six questions *T assigned chapter pages for each group to read and discuss	*S got into groups	*3 S texting on cell phone *1 S sleeping *2 S talking *4 S were not engaged in group discussion
2:10-2:15	✓✓✓✓✓✓✓ ✓✓✓✓✓✓✓ ✓✓	*T at desk looking at computer	*S reading aloud to partner *S answering assigned question	*1 S wandering room *6 S talking *2 S sleeping *1 S texting on cell phone
2:15-2:20	✓✓✓✓✓✓✓ ✓✓✓✓✓✓✓ ✓✓✓✓✓✓✓ ✓✓✓✓✓✓	*T roaming around room *T redirects 1 sleeping student and wanderer *T stops at 4 students' desks to check for understanding	*S reading aloud to partner *16 students working on questions at end of chapter.	*1 S sleeping
2:20-2:25	✓✓✓✓✓✓✓ ✓✓✓✓✓✓✓ ✓✓✓✓✓✓✓ ✓✓✓✓✓✓✓ ✓✓	*T roaming around room *T stopping at 12 students' desks to check for understanding	*S reading silently *S working on questions at end of chapter	

HOW TO USE THE STUDENT ENGAGEMENT TOOLS

During the collaborative planning conference (see Chapter 2), the beginning teacher and mentor determine a focus for the observation. They decide which tool will best fit their needs and will best capture the student engagement data they desire. If the teacher wishes to see how students are responding behaviorally to her actions, the Logging Engaging Behavior tool is used. If the teacher wishes to see an overall picture of what engagement behaviors are occurring, the mentor will use the Logging Student Engagement tool.

During the planning conference, the teacher identifies whether she wishes the mentor to capture evidence on all students or just a few select individuals. They also decide which specific behaviors the mentor should capture. If the teacher or mentor wishes for a behavior to be addressed that is not identified on the Logging Student Engagement tool, the mentor should identify that specific behavior in the Other box.

Together, the pair agrees on how often the mentor will collect data. This generally goes hand in hand with the length of time intervals necessary for collecting the desired observation data. The longer the interval time, the fewer sets of data there will be. Typically, five-minute intervals provide an adequate amount of data for reflection.

During the scheduled observation, the mentor watches the predetermined students for behaviors that exhibit engagement. She logs the number of students demonstrating engagement for each predetermined time interval by placing a tally mark in the appropriate box. When using the Logging Engaging Behavior tool, the mentor will also describe any evident behaviors for the teacher, engaged students, and disengaged students.

During the reflective conference, the teacher and mentor discuss the number of students who were engaged versus those who were not and behaviors that were exhibited. If the Logging Engaging Behavior tool was used, they also compare and contrast the behaviors the teacher exhibited during times when students were engaged with times when the students were disengaged. It is the mentor's responsibility to help the teacher make the distinction between students just paying attention and students who are actively engaging in the learning.

STUDENT ENGAGEMENT TOOLS IN ACTION

Marvin, a first year ninth-grade Spanish teacher, was distraught because his students kept falling asleep during class. He tried several different instructional strategies that other teachers had suggested but did not see success with any of them. He and his mentor, Gayle, met and discussed his concerns. They created a plan of action that included Marvin trying one of the strategies he thought had worked better than the others. It was determined that Gayle would collect data on how his behaviors during instruction impacted his students.

During their reflective conference, Gayle presented the data she had collected to Marvin (Figure 16.3). "What do you notice about your students in this data?"

"The partner reading strategy worked better this time than last time. My students were more engaged in the reading and question answering," answered Marvin.

"What were you doing during the lesson when your students were the most engaged?" questioned Gayle.

"I was roaming the room and checking for understanding," responded Marvin.

"What do you notice about your actions during the second and third data collection interval in comparison to your students' behaviors?" Gayle questioned.

"It seems that when I was putting grades into the computer, there were more students off task, but I had to get those done! They were due that morning, and I was already late. I figured this was my good class so it would be okay. Only a few of my students were off task. That is better than before!" Marvin stated.

Gayle knew that Marvin struggled with time management issues and that this was a major concern for his principal. Several times already that year, he had been reprimanded for paperwork tardiness. She thought that perhaps this was an entry point to address both the time management and instructional issues that Marvin was having. Gayle responded, "I know that student engagement is a top priority for your school, and they have a goal of all students engaged 85% of the time. What could you have done differently to ensure that your students met this goal?"

Marvin was quiet for a few moments and then stated hesitantly, "Well I guess I could have been roaming the room more and not sitting at my desk."

Gayle knew that she had reached a milestone with Marvin and that it was time to stretch his growth. "What would it take for you to ensure that all of your students are engaged more than 85% of the time? Could you have your paperwork deadlines completed before they are due, so then you would have all of your instructional time dedicated to your students?"

"I could definitely try," Marvin acknowledged.

"How about if we get your calendar out and create a timeline of deadlines so that way you know how much time you will need to be ready for them?" Gayle asked. Even though this was something they had done in a small group at the beginning of the year, she felt this would benefit Marvin greatly.

"Sure, that would be great. I also would like for us to look at my lesson plans and see what other strategies I could try. I like this data collection. I think it will really help me be a better teacher," Marvin stated.

| Figure 16.3 | Logging Engaging Behavior |

Teacher: _Marvin_   **Mentor:** _Gayle_   **Date:** _10/17_

Lesson Focus: _Chapter 7_   **Number of Students:** _28_

Time	# of Engaged Students	Teacher Behaviors	Engaged Student Behaviors	Disengaged Student Behaviors
2:00–2:05	✓✓✓✓✓✓✓✓ ✓✓✓✓✓✓✓✓ ✓✓✓✓✓✓✓✓ ✓✓	*T began lesson with direct instructions as to how the chapter discussion would go. *T stood in front of room. *T modeling finding correct chapter	*S retrieved textbooks from under seats *S open books to correct page	*1 S texting on cell phone *1 S sleeping
2:05–2:10	✓✓✓✓✓✓✓✓ ✓✓✓✓✓✓✓✓ ✓✓✓✓✓✓	*T at desk looking at computer *T redirected S talking	*S reading aloud to partner *7 S using finger to follow text	*3 S texting on cell phone *1 S sleeping *2 S talking
2:10–2:15	✓✓✓✓✓✓✓✓ ✓✓✓✓✓✓✓✓ ✓✓✓	*T at desk looking at computer	*S reading aloud to partner *4 students answering questions at end of chapter	*1 S wandering room *6 S talking *2 S sleeping *1 S texting on cell phone
2:15–2:20	✓✓✓✓✓✓✓✓ ✓✓✓✓✓✓✓✓ ✓✓✓✓✓✓✓✓ ✓✓✓	*T roaming around room *T redirects 1 sleeping student and wanderer *T stops at 4 students desks to check for understanding	*S reading aloud to partner *16 students working on questions at end of chapter.	*1 S sleeping
2:20–2:25	✓✓✓✓✓✓✓✓ ✓✓✓✓✓✓✓✓ ✓✓✓✓✓✓✓✓ ✓✓✓✓	*T roaming around room *T stopping at 12 students desks to check for understanding	*S reading silently *S working on questions at end of chapter	

NOTES FOR IMPLEMENTATION

The teacher is recognizing certain student behaviors that are of concern to her during the time she is teaching. As the teacher brings her concern to the attention of the mentor, this gives the mentor the opportunity to introduce the variety of student engagement tools. Usually this occurs around the fifth month of the school year. The teacher feels confident that her lessons are well planned, her classroom management plan is working well, but she feels that her students should be more engaged during the teaching of the lesson itself. Once the teacher and the mentor begin to look at the student engagement data, action plans can be implemented. The teacher uses new engagement strategies and begins to transform her teaching with the support of the mentor.

Figure 16.4 Logging Student Engagement

Teacher: _____ Mentor: _____ Date: _____

Lesson Focus: _____ Number of Students: ___

Student Behavior	Time and Lesson Component						Reflection
	Number of Students						
A. Active Listening —leaning forward, tracking teacher movement, head nodding, paraphrasing							
B. Signaling —thumbs up and whiteboards							
C. Verbalizing —student questioning, student response, group discussion							
D. Writing —journaling, recording observations							
G. Manipulating —suggestions for use, hands-on, creativity in use							
H. Other Engagement Data							

Figure 16.5	Logging Engaging Behavior

Teacher: _____ **Mentor:** _____ **Date:** _____

Lesson Focus: _____ **Number of Students:** ___

Time	# of Engaged Students	Teacher Behaviors	Engaged Student Behaviors	Disengaged Student Behaviors

17

Probing Higher Level Thinking

Once teachers are familiar with general instructional practices and classroom management is no longer the focus of all conversations, novice teachers begin to shift their thinking toward how they can engage students more effectively. This is a time for mentors to help those teachers think about how they can challenge their students' thinking and learning through questioning strategies. It is also a time for mentors to help expand their teachers' thinking and move them toward independent practice.

To help mentors accomplish this high level of facilitation, we created several tools that capture specific questioning data, student responses, and levels of Bloom's Taxonomy. We also developed a series of question word banks to help mentors and teachers create question stems to facilitate learning at a deeper level. These tools are broken into two categories, *Questioning Skills* and *Questioning Word Banks*.

PURPOSE FOR QUESTIONING SKILLS

Mentors often script questions beginning teachers ask students. This allows for the beginning teacher to see the types of questions being asked, and how they are related to higher level thinking. The purpose of these tools is to label which level of Bloom's Taxonomy teachers are asking questions and ensure that the teacher is giving students opportunities to think at all levels. The questions can be recorded with their direct relationship to Bloom's Taxonomy to show the level of thinking asked of students.

During the reflective conference, the beginning teacher can see the level of questioning and determine if he was asking for higher level thinking skills. The mentor can offer support during the reflection by asking how lower level questions could be restated to reach a higher level. The mentor may collaborate with the teacher to brainstorm ways of changing the question or adding to the question. The result is the beginning teacher analyzing his questioning skills and gaining insight on how to maximize his questioning skills to obtain higher level thinking.

The Questioning Skills—Student Response tool provides mentors with a format to collect data regarding the questions teachers ask students and the responses students give. This allows for teachers to see connections between the types of questions they are asking and the level thinking students are obtaining. This tool is also used as a reflection instrument to help teachers analyze how their instruction is impacting student learning.

DESCRIPTION OF QUESTIONING SKILLS

There are three data collection tools that incorporate Bloom's Taxonomy for mentors to label the type of questions asked by the teacher, tally the total number of questions asked at each level, or capture student responses:

- Questioning Skills—Levels of Knowledge
- Questioning Skills—Levels of Knowledge Totals
- Questioning Skills—Student Response

At the bottom of each of the tools, the Bloom's Taxonomy levels identified in 1956 and revised in 2001 (Anderson & Krathwohl) are listed. During the planning conference, the teacher and mentor determine which Bloom's Taxonomy they will use.

The *Questioning Skills—Levels of Knowledge* tool is divided into two sections. The first section is for data collection. The mentor records questions that are asked during an observation. The second section is for data reflection. The mentor and teacher reflect on the level of Bloom's Taxonomy and the types of questions asked (Figure 17.1).

The *Questioning Skills—Levels of Knowledge Totals* tool is an extension of the *Questioning Skills—Levels of Knowledge* tool. This tool is divided into two sections as well. The first section is intended for mentors and teachers to record the number of questions asked in each Bloom's Taxonomy level. The second section is to be utilized for recording questions that are asked or for developing new questions that reflect higher level thinking. This tool is intended to be used in conjunction with the Questioning Skills—Levels of Knowledge tool during a reflective conference and is not intended for mentors to collect observation data. It is more meaningful for the teacher to determine the level of questioning (Figure 17.2).

The *Questioning Skills—Student Response* tool is designed to capture three types of information: purpose and Bloom's Taxonomy level, teacher question and student response, and teacher reflection. The tool is divided into columns to provide space to capture all pertinent information. At the bottom of the tool is a code key that can act as a guide for determining the purpose of questions and responses as well as the Bloom's Taxonomy level of both (Figure 17.3).

Figure 17.1 Questioning Skills—Levels of Knowledge

Teacher: _Bryce_   **Mentor:** _Josie_   **Date:** _1/12_

Grade/Subject: _6th American History_   **Lesson Topic:** _Causes of the Civil War_

Data Collected: Question Asked by Teacher = T	*Code: Level of Question*	Teacher Reflection: Comments and Questions
• Why was the Civil War fought?	C	"It seems like I was asking a lot of comprehension level questions. I was really hoping to go for higher level questions, since that is what I was working on."
• What did your textbook say were the major causes of the Civil War?	K	
• Did the socioeconomic differences between North and South have any impact on the division of states?	C	"I really like the last three questions. I got those from that Understanding by Design questioning stuff you gave me last week. Those questions really got my student going!"
• What was President Lincoln's major concern about slavery?	K	
• Was the war over just slavery?	A	
• What is secession?	C	"But, I don't think they really demonstrated what the kids knew about the causes of the Civil War."
• What was the South so mad at?	C	
• How could the South and North have settled their issues without going to war?	S	"How can I get better at asking questions?"
• Could we ever have another Civil War?	S	
• How do we prevent a Civil War from happening again?	E	

*Levels Code Key Bloom's 1956		*Levels Code Key Bloom's 2001	
K = Knowledge	**AN** = Analysis	**R** = Remember	**AN** = Analyze
C = Comprehension	**S** = Synthesis	**U** = Understand	**E** = Evaluate
A = Application	**E** = Evaluation	**AP** = Apply	**C** = Create

Figure 17.2 Questioning Skills—Levels of Knowledge Totals Bloom's 1956

Teacher: _Brandi_ **Mentor:** _Carrie_ **Date:** _1/12_

Grade/Subject: _8th Grade Language Arts_ **Lesson Topic:** _Persuasive Essay Components_

KNOWLEDGE Total: 4 **COMPREHENSION** Total: 3	**Knowledge** Questions that **check** the basic facts. _Who can tell me what the components of a persuasive essay are?_	**Comprehension** Questions that check your **understanding** of the facts. _How and why might we use persuasion as writers?_
APPLICATION Total:1 **ANALYSIS** Total:1	**Application** Questions that test your ability to **use** your knowledge to solve problems. _Can you tell me some ways you have used persuasion in your life recently?_	**Analysis** Questions, in which you **select** information, **examine** it and break it apart into **separate** parts. _Based on the essay we just read, what are elements of persuasion the author used that you could use to convince someone to change the school calendar?_
SYNTHESIS Total:0 **EVALUATION** Total:0	**Synthesis** Questions in which you put the basic information back together **but** in a new or different way. _What persuasive techniques will you use in your essay that will be effective in changing a person's mind?_	**Evaluation** Questions that stimulate, **evaluative** thinking and help you decide whether to accept or reject your facts. _Based on the persuasive techniques you have identified, how will you know whether they are effective or not?_

Next Steps:

"Plan to include these questions when I have students read the 'Changing School Calendar' essay. I want to make up note cards to help me remember these questions."

| Figure 17.3 | Questioning Skills—Student Response Bloom's 1956 |

Teacher: _Rod_ **Mentor:** _Ronnie_ **Date:** _11/2_

Grade/Subject: _7th/American History_ **Lesson Topic:** _Civil War_

Code: Purpose & Level of Question*	Data Collected:		Code: Purpose & Level of Response*	Teacher Reflection: Comments and Questions
	Question Asked by Teacher	Response to the Teacher's Question		
2/C	What can you tell me about the Civil War?	It was between the North and South	2/K	_I wanted to find out what the students knew about the Civil War before we started the unit. Before the student answered the questions, the other students were answering the questions on the whiteboard so I could see what the majority of the students knew._
2,3/C,R	Why was there a war between the North and the South?	The South wanted slavery and the North did not	2,3/C	
2/K	Who can name two of the famous generals?	General Lee and Andrew Jackson	2/K	_I wanted the students to be reflective about their responses as well as tell me what they already knew._
2,4/K	What was the Underground Railroad?	A railroad under the ground	2,4/K	_I did not want to give clues to right answers or not so I redirected the question._
				After these questions, I gave the students a preassessment so I could tell what they already knew and what they needed to know. This information also allowed me to begin to think about grouping my students.

* Purpose Code Key		*Levels Code Key Bloom's 1956	
1 = Check for understanding **2** = Prior learning/ knowledge **3** = Reflective Thinking	**4** = Re-direction **5** = Extension question **6** = Reminding students of expectations question **7** = Self-Assessment	**K** = Knowledge **C** = Comprehension **A** = Application	**AN** = Analysis **S** = Synthesis **E** = Evaluation

HOW TO USE QUESTIONING SKILLS

The Questioning Skills—Levels of Knowledge tool is used both for observation data collection and as a means to capture reflective conversation. During an observation, the mentor uses this tool to record the questions asked by the teacher. During a reflective conference, the teacher and the mentor determine what knowledge level each question is according to Bloom's Taxonomy. As the beginning teacher reflects on the questions and the impact those questions might have had on their students, the mentor captures the teacher's ideas in the far right column. The beginning teacher then plans their next steps while reflecting on the data.

The Questioning Skills—Levels of Knowledge Totals tool is used during a reflective conference. Together, the mentor and beginning teacher sort the questions recorded on the Questioning Skills—Levels of Knowledge tool according to Bloom's Taxonomy. The total number of questions is recorded on the left side of the paper. Seeing the total number of questions asked can help the teacher assess whether he is asking his students to think critically or just recall information.

The mentor and teacher next determine if the recorded questions could be rewritten to address the different levels of Bloom's Taxonomy, or the pair decides that new questions need to be written. All questions are placed in a corresponding box according to Bloom's Taxonomy. Based on this conversation, the teacher determines what next steps are necessary in order to deepen their students thinking and learning.

The Questioning Skills—Student Response tool is used during both observational data collection and reflective conference conversations. During data collection, the mentor records questions asked by the teacher and student responses to those questions. It is important that the mentor captures the exact wording of the questions asked and the responses to help clarify intent.

During the reflective conference following the data collection, the mentor and teacher discuss the purpose for each question asked and student responses. The teacher should determine whether the question was intended to engage students in higher level thinking or had some other purpose. If the question was intended to induce student learning, then the mentor and teacher should determine what level of Bloom's Taxonomy the question addresses.

How the student responds to the question is compared to the purpose of the question and the level of Bloom's Taxonomy. The overall goal is congruency between purpose and response. If there is a higher level question asked, it should be followed by a higher level thinking response. Examining student responses helps teachers see how they are impacting student learning.

Finally, the mentor can offer support during the reflection by asking how lower level questions can be restated to reach a higher level response from the student. The mentor can brainstorm with the teacher ways of changing the question or adding to the question. This collaboration results in the beginning teacher gaining insight on strategies to maximize his questioning skills and obtain higher level thinking among the students.

PURPOSE FOR QUESTIONING WORD BANKS

The *Questioning Word Banks* are useful tools that are intended for two purposes:

1. Mentor prompts

2. Teacher prompts

One purpose is to provide mentors with prompts to guide their questioning during information gathering, data analysis, and promoting action. Phases of conferencing prompts can help beginning mentors go beyond initial clarifying questions. Initial responses are just that, initial. People's first thoughts are not necessarily their final thoughts or their best thoughts. Inviting elaboration causes beginning teachers to reconceptualize and assess their own language, concepts, and strategies.

Another purpose is to provide teachers with prompts that help build their questioning skills for student learning. Asking higher level questions can be a challenging skill for many teachers to develop. This set of Questioning Word Banks can help teachers design questions that will engage students in higher level thinking.

DESCRIPTION OF QUESTIONING WORD BANKS

The Questioning Word Banks were derived from the work of Garmston (2000) and Barkley (2004). As Garmston states, "Of all the tools in a staff developer's repertoire, a good question is probably one of the most important" (p. 73). Our thinking is that knowing how to ask good questions is the most essential tool for mentors, teachers, and students. If we know how to ask good questions, then we are constantly seeking ways to improve our understanding of the world around us.

There are three different Questioning Word Banks we have developed as tools for mentors and teachers:

1. Word Bank for Questions Used to Gather Information

2. Word Bank for Questions Used to Analyze Data

3. Word Bank for Questions Used to Promote Action

Each word bank is comprised of verbs to address different cognition levels of learners, synonyms for the different cognition level, and a space for questions to be generated. Having and using a consistent vocabulary that promotes critical thinking is one element that constitutes good questioning skills.

The Word Bank for Questions Used to Gather Information addresses thinking skills for the purpose of data collection. This tool can be used by mentors to help teachers identify what data might be collected that would promote their professional practice. Teachers can use this word bank to help students identify what skills and knowledge are essential for their academic growth. Four different cognition levels are addressed in this tool: *awareness*, *generalization*, *comprehension*, and *comparison* (Figure 17.4).

The Word Bank for Questions Used to Analyze Data addresses cognitive levels for the purpose of data analysis. This tool can be used by mentors to help teachers assess and evaluate their professional practice based on the evidence presented in data collection tools. Teachers can use this tool to help students distinguish between what is clear and compelling information and information that is vague and irrelevant to their understanding of essential skills and knowledge. Four different cognition levels are addressed in this tool: *inference*, *summarization*, *appraisal*, and *evaluation* (Figure 17.5).

The Word Bank for Questions Used to Promote Action addresses thinking skills for the purpose of taking action. This tool can be used by mentors to help teachers identify what their next steps might be based on the evidence presented. Teachers can use this word bank to help students identify how they will demonstrate the essential skills and knowledge learned. Three different cognition levels are addressed in this tool: *ideas*, *predictions*, and *actions* (Figure 17.6).

HOW TO USE QUESTIONING WORD BANKS

Before meeting with teachers, mentors should brainstorm potential question stems to use during the conference. Having those stems predetermined and ready will enable mentors to push their teacher's thinking deeper and facilitate growth. Mentors should deliberately choose words to activate and engage mental processes. Finding relationships, predicting outcomes, and analyzing and synthesizing data are mental processes that require others to draw forth their knowledge, make connections, and create new understandings.

Mentors should encourage beginning teachers to utilize the Question Word Banks when planning and designing questions for their instruction. Teachers should use mediational questioning and problem solving to stimulate the brain and to engage students in higher order, creative cognitive functions.

Figure 17.4 Word Bank for Questions Used to Gather Information

Awareness		Generalization	
Verbs for Cognition	**Synonyms**	**Verbs for Cognition**	**Synonyms**
detect feel hear notice observe picture see smell taste touch	acuity discernment insight observation opinion perception sensitivity view	describe enumerate identify label list match name read record reproduce select state	common frequent generality on the whole overview pattern simplification sweeping statement universal
• *What do you picture/envision as the end result of changing your math instruction?* • *What do you notice when you are observing students in groups?* • *In your opinion, what would your class look like and sound like if you had changed this strategy?* • *What do you notice about the student's behavior after he is aware of the consequences?*		• *How would you describe your students' understanding of the objective on the whole?* • *Can you describe any patterns that you see in your questioning of students?* • *Could you list for me some general ways students could demonstrate their understanding of the objective?* • *Can you identify for me the number of students who worked on Bell Work?*	
Comprehension		Comparison	
Verbs for Cognition	**Synonyms**	**Verbs for Cognition**	**Synonyms**
classify cite describe discuss estimate explain generalize give example make sense out of understand	be aware of command conception grasp identify with intellectual capacity knowledge realize recognize understanding value	articulate assess chart collect construct determine differentiate extend informs relate show	alike different diverse equal like parallel related same similar unlike varied
• *Could you describe some ways teachers can check all students' comprehension?* • *Describe for me the level of understanding you were wanting your students to achieve.* • *Can you discuss with me what patterns you recognize in how you develop performance objectives?*		• *How could you differentiate the lesson to meet the varying needs of your students?* • *Can you articulate parallels between your class and the veteran teacher's class we observed last week?* • *What are various ways you could determine the learning styles your students possess?* • *How can you determine the diverse needs of your students?*	

Figure 17.5 Word Bank for Questions Used to Analyze Data

Inference		Summarization	
Verbs for Cognition	**Synonyms**	**Verbs for Cognition**	**Synonyms**
assume connect deduce expect figure out infer presume realize reason suppose work out	assumption conclusion conjecture connection deduction implication insight presumption suggestion supposition	break down compose establish extend focus illustrate include inform instructs reframe	condense focus in a nutshell main idea main point paraphrase reiterate restate in own words sum up summary
• *What might you infer about the reasons your students did (poorly/well) on the last test?* • *Suppose you decided to implement one new idea/strategy we saw from our veteran teacher observation. What kind of implication/impact would that have on your classroom?*		• *How can you break down the results of this quiz? What does it sum up about what the students know?* • *Can you reframe the lesson so that you can focus on what worked and what didn't work?*	
Appraisal		**Evaluation**	
Verbs for Cognition	**Synonyms**	**Verbs for Cognition**	**Synonyms**
appraise assess consider grade judge prioritize rank by value rate value weigh	assessment belief estimation finding judgment measurement opinion priority review	appraise compare & contrast conclude criticize decide defend interpret judge justify support	belief conclusion critique decision opinion viewpoint
• *How would you rate the lesson yesterday based on how it affected the behavior within your classroom?* • *In what ways could you judge a student's review of peer work?* • *In your belief, are the students' grades on this assessment an accurate reflection of their understanding?*		• *When you compare the behavior of the students in this group to the students in the other class, what conclusions can you make?* • *What can you interpret from the students' critiques of the project?*	

Figure 17.6 Word Bank for Questions Used to Promote Action

Ideas		Predictions	
Verbs for Cognition	**Synonyms**	**Verbs for Cognition**	**Synonyms**
adapt adjust alter amend change fine tune modify promote revise transform vary	aim ambition aspiration end goal objective opportunities options possibilities purpose target ways	affect anticipate calculate effect estimate expect foresee predict project	anticipation be hopeful for calculation estimation expectation forecast foretell guess hypothesize projection

- *If you want to promote change in engagement, what goal could you create that would cause that change?*
- *Based on what we've seen, what options do we have to meet the target set by your administrator?*
- *In what ways will you adjust your lesson to address different learning styles in your classroom?*
- *How are you going to fine tune your objectives so students can apply their learning?*

- *Can you predict your students' reaction to this lesson?*
- *Can you anticipate how meeting your PTG goal will improve your overall effectiveness as a teacher?*
- *In anticipation of your questioning strategies on the reading selection, what student behaviors do you expect to see?*

Action		
Verbs for Cognition		**Synonyms**
apply build combine compose compute construct create design do draft draw	graph make plan produce report role play interview simulate use write	accomplishment achievement attainment do something feat realization success take steps triumph

- *How could you construct a lesson plan that will enable you to effectively implement your classroom management plan?*
- *Would you like to role-play the possible outcomes and steps in dealing with difficult parents?*
- *Which of the identified steps on our action plan will we take first to produce a lesson your students will benefit from?*
- *How can you use the results from this test to determine how you will ensure student success?*

PROBING HIGHER LEVEL THINKING TOOLS IN ACTION

Third grade teacher Danielle was concerned that her students were not engaged during whole class discussion time. She voiced her concerns to her mentor, Breanna, in an e-mail. Her mentor replied that they could definitely discuss that concern during their next collaborative conference. In preparation for the meeting, Breanna spent some time thinking about the questions she would ask and used the Word Bank for Questions Used to Gathering Information to help her generate questions she could use.

Their collaborative conference began with Danielle sharing her successes and then moved toward her concern. "My students are just not going where I want them to during whole class discussion," Danielle stated.

"What is it that you envision your students doing during whole class discussions?" Breanna asks.

"I want my students to be thinking. You know when they look up at the ceiling, and you can see the wheels turning in their heads! I want them to give answers that show they understand what I have been teaching them. I want them to all nod in agreement that yes that is a great answer!" Danielle responds.

"It sounds like you really want your students to have a deep understanding of the content. How would you describe the types of questions you are asking?"

"Well I have worked really hard to create questions that will make them think harder and hopefully engage their brains. I used my Bloom's Taxonomy wheel to help me think of higher level questions, but they are just not answering the questions. Most of the time they just sit there," Danielle shares.

Breanna thinks for a moment about the direction she should move toward with Danielle and then proceeds with the conversation. "When you think about your students and the level of understanding you are striving for, how are you building the questioning from a basic understanding to more abstract thinking?"

Danielle is quiet for a minute. She then states, "I am not sure I am! I have been so focused on higher level questions that I probably have not even been asking comprehension and application questions first. Maybe that is why my students look so confused. How do I know for sure what questions I am asking?"

This is the entry point that Breanna has been waiting for. She suggests that she come in to observe Danielle during a whole group questioning session and capture what questions she is asking of her students. "The Questioning Skills—Levels of Blooms tools can help us see what types of questions you are asking. From there, we can use the Questioning Word Banks to help us develop some questions in order to scaffold the learning."

Both Breanna and Danielle left the collaborative conference feeling satisfied and accomplished that they were on the right track.

NOTES FOR IMPLEMENTATION

Probing for higher level thinking is typically introduced during the fifth month of teaching. Mentors and teachers need to be aware of the levels of cognition their learners have attained before moving into the more abstract concepts of questioning.

Figure 17.7 Questioning Skills—Levels of Knowledge

Teacher: _____ **Mentor:** _____ **Date:** _____

Grade/Subject: _____ **Lesson Topic:** _____

Data Collected: Question Asked by Teacher = T	*Code: Level of Question*	Teacher Reflection: Comments and Questions

*Levels Code Key Bloom's 1956		*Levels Code Key Bloom's 2001	
K = Knowledge	**AN** = Analysis	**R** = Remember	**AN** = Analyze
C = Comprehension	**S** = Synthesis	**U** = Understand	**E** = Evaluate
A = Application	**E** = Evaluation	**AP** = Apply	**C** = Create

Figure 17.8 Questioning Skills—Levels of Knowledge Totals Bloom's 1956

Teacher: _____ Mentor: _____ Date: _____

Grade/Subject: _____ Lesson Topic: _____

KNOWLEDGE Total:_____ COMPREHENSION Total:_____	**Knowledge** Questions that **check** the basic facts.	**Comprehension** Questions that check your **understanding** of the facts.
APPLICATION Total:_____ ANALYSIS Total:_____	**Application** Questions that test your ability to **use** your knowledge to solve problems.	**Analysis** Questions, in which you **select** information, **examine** it, and break it apart into **separate** parts.
SYNTHESIS Total: _____ EVALUATION Total:_____	**Synthesis** Questions in which you put the basic information back together **but** in a new or different way.	**Evaluation** Questions that stimulate **evaluative** thinking and help you decide whether to accept or reject your facts.
Next Steps:		

Figure 17.9	Questioning Skills—Levels of Knowledge Totals Bloom's 2001

Teacher: _____ **Mentor:** _____ **Date:** _____

Grade/Subject: _____ **Lesson Topic:** _____

REMEMBER Total:_____ **UNDERSTAND** Total:_____	**Remember** Retrieve relevant knowledge from long term memory.	**Understand** Construct meaning from instruction.
APPLY Total:_____ **ANALYZE** Total:_____	**Apply** Carry out or use a procedure in a given situation.	**Analyze** Break material into its constituent parts, determine their relationships, and relate back to whole.
EVALUATE Total: _____ **CREATE** Total:_____	**Evaluate** Make judgments based on criteria.	**Create** Reorganize elements into a new pattern or structure.
Next Steps:		

Figure 17.10 Questioning Skills—Student Response Bloom's 1956

Teacher: _____ **Mentor:** _____ **Date:** _____

Grade/Subject: _____ **Lesson Topic:** _____

Code: Purpose & Level of Question*	Data Collected:		Code: Purpose & Level of Response*	Teacher Reflection: Comments and Questions
	Question Asked by Teacher	Response to the Teacher's Question		

* Purpose Code Key		*Levels Code Key Bloom's 1956	
1 = Check for understanding **2** = Prior learning/ knowledge **3** = Reflective Thinking	**4** = Redirection **5** = Extension question **6** = Reminding students of expectations question **7** = Self-Assessment	**K** = Knowledge **C** = Comprehension **A** = Application	**AN** = Analysis **S** = Synthesis **E** = Evaluation

Figure 17.11	Questioning Skills—Student Response Bloom's 2001

Teacher: _____ **Mentor:** _____ **Date:** _____

Grade/Subject: _____ **Lesson Topic:** _____

Code: Purpose & Level of Question*	Data Collected:		Code: Purpose & Level of Response*	Teacher Reflection: Comments and Questions
	Question Asked by Teacher	Response to the Teacher's Question		

* Purpose Code Key		*Levels Code Key Bloom's 2001	
1 = Check for understanding	**4** = Redirection	**R** = Remember	**AN** = Analyze
2 = Prior learning/ knowledge	**5** = Extension question	**U** = Understand	**E** = Evaluate
3 = Reflective Thinking	**6** = Reminding students of expectations question	**AP** = Apply	**C** = Create
	7 = Self-Assessment		

Figure 17.12 Word Bank for Questions Used to Gather Information

Awareness		Generalization	
Verbs for Cognition	**Synonyms**	**Verbs for Cognition**	**Synonyms**
detect feel hear notice observe picture see smell taste touch	acuity awareness discernment insight observation opinion sensitivity view	describe enumerate identify label list match name read record reproduce select state	common frequent generality on the whole overview pattern simplification sweeping statement universal
Comprehension		**Comparison**	
Verbs for Cognition	**Synonyms**	**Verbs for Cognition**	**Synonyms**
classify cite describe discuss estimate explain generalize give example make sense out of understand	be aware of command conception grasp identify with intellectual capacity knowledge realize recognize understanding value	articulate assess chart collect construct determine differentiate extend informs relate show	alike different diverse equal like parallel related same similar unlike varied

Figure 17.13	Word Bank for Questions Used to Analyze Data

Inference		**Summarization**	
Verbs for Cognition	**Synonyms**	**Verbs for Cognition**	**Synonyms**
assume	assumption	break down	condense
connect	conclusion	compose	focus
deduce	conjecture	establish	in a nutshell
expect	connection	extend	main idea
figure out	deduction	focus	main point
infer	implication	illustrate	paraphrase
presume	insight	include	reiterate
realize	presumption	inform	restate in own words
reason	suggestion	instructs	sum up
suppose	supposition	reframe	summary
work out			

Appraisal		**Evaluation**	
Verbs for Cognition	**Synonyms**	**Verbs for Cognition**	**Synonyms**
appraise	assessment	appraise	belief
assess	belief	compare & contrast	conclusion
consider	estimation	conclude	critique
grade	finding	criticize	decision
judge	judgment	decide	opinion
prioritize	measurement	defend	viewpoint
rank by value	opinion	interpret	
rate	priority	judge	
value	review	justify	
weigh		support	

Figure 17.14 Word Bank for Questions Used to Promote Action

Ideas		Predictions	
Verbs for Cognition	**Synonyms**	**Verbs for Cognition**	**Synonyms**
adapt adjust alter amend change fine tune modify promote revise transform vary	aim ambition aspiration end goal objective opportunities options possibilities purpose target ways	affect anticipate calculate effect estimate expect foresee predict project	anticipation be hopeful for calculation estimation expectation forecast foretell guess hypothesize projection

Actions		
Verbs for Cognition		**Synonyms**
apply build combine compose compute construct create design do draft draw	graph make plan produce report role play interview simulate use write	accomplishment achievement attainment do something feat realization success take steps triumph

Section III

Learner Focused Transformational Learning Stage

The third stage is *learner focused*. During this stage, the transformation occurs when the novice teacher and mentor begin to realize the impact they have had on the individuals with whom they have been directly working. Both individuals are able to move toward more abstract concepts, such as differentiation. Novice mentors examine how to meet the needs of individual teachers through self-assessment of practices and reflection. Mentors utilize tools to plan how to differentiate for their teachers based on evident growth. Novice teachers recognize the importance of focusing on the academic and social needs of a class as a whole and students as individuals. Teachers begin to see their practices of analyzing student work, differentiating instruction, and using formative assessment as effective practices to meet student needs.

Each chapter in this stage becomes the final transition for the mentor role or the teacher role as each focuses on the learner. Chapters 18–22 analyze student work, plan for differentiating instruction, analyze student assessments, plan for differentiating mentoring, and reflect on one's own practice. These chapters answer the questions: What does analyzing student work reveal about teaching and the students' learning? How does the teacher plan for differentiating instruction based on the diversity of the students? Do analyzing student assessments provide the opportunity for the teacher to analyze instruction? Was the student assessment in alignment with the teacher's objective and instruction? How does the mentor plan for differentiating mentoring based on the diversity of the teachers? Does the reflection on one's own practice document the transformation on entering the learner focused stage? What are the plans for the future?

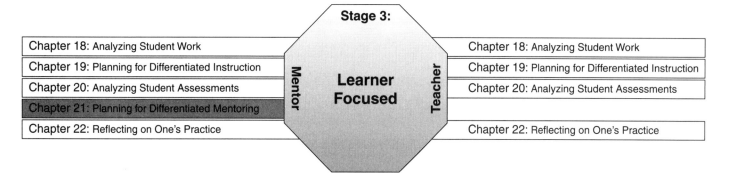

Chapter Introduced	Practices and Tools
Chapter 18	1. Analysis of Student Work Steps 1–5—NCR
Chapter 19	2. Instructional Groups for Differentiated Instruction
	3. Differentiated Lesson Plan Organizer
	4. Lesson Plan Differentiation Template—NCR
Chapter 20	5. Formative Assessment of Student Practice—NCR
	6. Formative Assessment Protocol
	7. Assessing Student Learning
Chapter 21	8. Differentiated Mentoring Analysis of Beginning Teacher Development Steps 1–5
Chapter 22	9. A Look Back: Then and Now
	10. Transformational Learning Stages: Reflection for Beginning Teachers
	11. Transformational Learning Stages: Reflection for Beginning Mentors
	12. Beginning Teacher New Year Action Plan: Continuing the Transformation
	13. Mentor New Year Action Plan: Continuing the Transformation
NCR = No Carbon Required paper. NCR copies are made for the mentor and the beginning teacher to provide each with a copy of the tool.	

18

Analyzing Student Work

PURPOSE FOR ANALYZING STUDENT WORK

Teaching is a dynamic decision-making process in which teachers are constantly making both macrodecisions and microdecisions. What teachers have planned for a lesson may not be the reality of what occurs during the lesson. Think for a moment about a teacher presenting a lesson, responding to students' questions, and students' statements. What is a teacher thinking while she is teaching? Perhaps a few questions that might be going through her mind include:

- Why isn't Jan paying attention?
- Is Juan tired or hungry, as his head is on his desk?
- How can I make sure that everyone understands what I am presenting?
- Can I help all of these students in such a short time?
- How can I challenge Steve? He is already finished with the assignment.

Teachers weigh all of these questions with lots of evidence about what students know and are able to do. Teachers use questions about their students to make difficult instructional decisions. The process of analyzing student work is a meaningful and challenging way to be data driven and to reflect critically on instructional practices.

Analyzing student work helps teachers understand what students are thinking and what connections they are making. Analyzing student work helps teachers provide an enriched environment for students as their individual needs become more apparent. The proof of teaching and student learning is in the work the students produce. Students' work lets teachers know if they are teaching to standards at a high level and if students are learning. Looking at student work is a window into the strengths and weaknesses of the lessons and assignments teachers design (Nolan, n.d.).

Teachers see student work every day, but *Looking at Student Work (LASW)* refers to a process that helps educators improve teaching and learning by reflecting deeply on teacher lessons and student work. The results from analyzing student work give teachers a picture of how well students perform against the intended learning objectives. Beginning teachers need tools and support to help build the practice of analyzing student work. The *Analysis of Student Work* tool was created to provide a structured process for the mentor to assist the beginning teacher in having a clearer understanding of teaching targets and more consistency in evaluating student learning against academic standards.

DESCRIPTION OF ANALYZING STUDENT WORK

Various organizations have developed protocols to examine student work. A protocol is a structure and a guide for building the skills and culture necessary for collaborative work. Some analyzing student work protocols were developed by the Education Trust, Coalition of Essential Schools, Annenberg Institute for School Reform, and the National School Reform Faculty for the purpose of providing protocols for groups of teachers who decided to share their student work collectively and have collaborative conversations. There are numerous protocols for this purpose available on the web.

The *Analysis of Student Work* tool in this chapter was developed for the individual teacher. Various agencies have developed this type of protocol, such as the *Beginning Teacher Support and Assessment (BTSA)*, which is a state-funded induction program cosponsored by the California Department of Education and the Commission on Teacher Credentialing, the New Teacher Center at the University of California, Santa Cruz, and the National Board for Professional Teaching Standards. Our work is a compilation from the collaboration with various organizations and our mentors. The following is a five-step process to complete the Analysis of Student Work tool:

1. Performance Expectations and Assessment Criteria (Figure 18.1)

2. Student Work Samples (Figure 18.2)

3. Description of Student Performance (Figure 18.2)

4. Diagnosis and Interpretation (Figure 18.3)

5. Action Plan for Meeting Student Needs (Figure 18.4)

Figure 18.1	Analysis of Student Work

Name: *Emily*	**Date:** *2/18*	**Mentor:** *Jessica*

Grade Level/Subject Area: *High School Chemistry* **Content Standard(s)**: *SCHS-CI-PO3*

Lesson/Unit Objective(s): *Given a set of household substances, students will use*

supporting evidence to determine the pH of the substance and to identify if those

substances are acids or bases.

Step 1: Performance Expectations and Assessment Criteria
A. Clarify Expectations for Students' Performance:
- – What is the purpose of the lesson?
- – Is the assignment aligned with the standard and the objective?
- – What evidence of learning do you expect the students to produce? Be specific and give examples.

Use 5 common household materials to:
- *Predict whether 5 common household materials are acids or bases*
- *Demonstrate how to measure the pH of substances*
- *Determine the pH of substances*
- *Use supporting evidence to identify acid or bases*
- *Yes, assignment is aligned*
- *To perform experiments, collect data, identify substances as acid or base, and use evidence in support of their conclusion*
- *Example:*

Material	pH litmus paper	pH meter	Observations
Liquid soap			
lemon juice			

B. Identify Assessment Criteria:
- – What grading criteria did you use for assessing the assignment?
- – How did you inform the students of the grading criteria you would use?
- – If you only used a numerical grading scale, how do you know the student has mastered the standard and the objective?
- – Did you use a rubric to analyze this work?
- – Does the rubric or grading criteria align with the standard and the objective?
- – Is the assessment appropriate for the objective, the developmental level of students, the teaching strategies, and the learning activities?

- A 3 point rubric is used for assessment aligned with standards, objective, and expectations
- Points were allocated based on the rubric: 3 points = 93% to 100%; 2 points = 92% to 80%; 1 points = 79% or below performance
- Each student was given the rubric before they began experiments
- The assessment is appropriate

Figure 18.2   Analysis of Student Work

Step 2: Student Work Samples

A. Sorting Student Work:

– Did the students master the standard that was being taught? Divide the student work samples into four columns: Exemplary, Meets Objective, Almost Meets Objective, and Does Not Meet Objective.

– Do the various groups match the assessment criteria established?

B. Write students' names in the columns below.

Exemplary	Meets Objective	Almost Meets Objective	Does Not Meet Objective
Terry	Samatha	Kara	Tony
Bryce	Butch	Christy	Joyce
Kaden	Sara	Grace	Kim
Brooke	Angela	Terrell	Jami
Brooklyn	Cindy	Tim	
Harleigh	Steve		
Rod	Deb		
Lori	George		
Manny	Jason		
Ron	Maria		

Step 3: Description of Student Performance

– Describe the student performance for each level. Specifically, which expectations criteria for the standard, objective, and assessment does the work match?

– Describe the student performance for each level that does not match the expectations criteria set for the standard, objective, and assessment

Exemplary	Meets Objective	Almost Meets Objective	Does Not Meet Objective
Students could use 5 common household materials to: – Predict whether 5 common household materials are acids or bases – Demonstrate how to measure the pH of substances – Determine the pH of substances – Use supporting evidence to identify acid or bases – Perform experiments, collect data, identify substances as acid or base, and use evidence in support of their conclusion.	Students met everything in exemplary column but they had a few errors for measuring pH; therefore they could not achieve 100% but they achieved 80%.	Students did not achieve 80% on the expectations. Many did not know how to measure the pH, but they could record the experiment information.	Students could not perform at a satisfactory level on any of the expectations except prediction. They did not know how to measure the pH, nor could they accurately record what they did in the experiment.

| Figure 18.3 | Analysis of Student Work |

Step 4: Diagnosis and Interpretation

A. Diagnosing Student Work:

- Which knowledge and skills did the students know and were able to do well?
- Which knowledge and skills did the students not know or do well?
- What did you see in the students' work that was surprising?
- What did you learn about how your students think and learn?

Exemplary	Meets Objective	Almost Meets Objective	Does Not Meet Objective
Met all expectations. Their thinking was explicit and their records were exemplary and descriptive.	*Met most expectations. Their thinking was analytical and they could explain what happened during the experiment. Few errors in measuring pH.*	*Their records were descriptive, but they do not know how to measure pH.*	*Their records were not descriptive. They could not describe what they did. They did not know how to measure pH.*

B. Interpreting Student Work:

- Based on the above student performance descriptions, what are the learning needs for each group of students?
- Why do you think the standard and objective of the lesson were not met?
- What patterns of understandings or misunderstandings do you see?
- Are there prerequisite skills and/or knowledge students have not mastered?
- Are any specific groups of students (e.g., boys or girls, special education, English language learners, etc.) not meeting the standard?
- What percentage of students is in each column?

Exemplary	Meets Objective	Almost Meets Objective	Does Not Meet Objective
Need extension activity to determine the composition of other household items.	*Need 5 additional household items to practice measuring pH.*	*Need to learn how to measure pH.*	*They need to learn how to:* *- Demonstrate how to measure the pH of substances* *- Determine the pH of substances* *- Use supporting evidence to identify acid or bases* *- Perform experiments, collect data, identify substances as acid or base, and use evidence in support of their conclusion.*
34.5 %	*34.5 %*	*17 %*	*14 %*

I don't see any special groups of students in any one column. My ESL students are in each column. The two prerequisite skills they have not mastered are measuring pH and writing accurate records.

| Figure 18.4 | Analysis of Student Work |

Step 5: Action Plan for Meeting Student Needs

A. Questions related to teaching and learning:
- As a result of analyzing students' work, are there any questions about teaching and assessment that come to mind? What are those questions?
- How will you build bridges between what the students know and are able to do with what they will know and be able to do?

B. Next Steps for your teaching and your students' learning:
- What extension or reteaching do you need to do?
- What type of lesson will you design to meet the needs of your students?
- Were there gaps in the students' learning? Were the prerequisite skills and/or knowledge mastered? How do you know? Do you need to complete a task analysis?
- What resources or personnel do you need to find in order to meet your students' needs?
- How can your mentor assist you?

Identified Students	Next Steps	Resources Needed (R)/ Mentor Assistance (M)
Exemplary Terry Harleigh Rod Bryce Lori Kaden Manny Brandi Ron Brooklyn	*Plan extension activity to discover some household items and their chemical composition.*	**R** *Check web site connection for American Chemistry Society.* **M**
Meets Objective: Samatha Steve Butch Deb Sara George Angela Jason Cindy Marie	*Recreate the experiment discussing how to measure pH prior to using 5 different household items.*	**R** **M**
Almost Meets Objective: Kara Christy Grace Terrell Tim	*Present how to measure pH and have 10 items for them to determine pH.*	**R** **M**
Does Not Meet Objective: Tony Joyce Kim Jami	*3 Step process:* - *Present how to measure pH and have 10 items for them to determine pH.* - *Use supporting evidence to identify acid or bases* - *Perform experiments, collect data, identify substances as acid or base, and use evidence in support of their conclusion.*	**R** *Materials for learning stations* **M** *Brainstorm ideas with me on learning stations*

HOW TO USE THE ANALYZING STUDENT WORK TOOLS

The mentor asks the beginning teacher to identify a lesson that required students to submit a piece of their work that demonstrated how well the students learned the skills or knowledge that was presented. This request happens during a planning conference, which usually occurs in the spring. During the conference, the teacher shared that she wants to know more about her students' learning. Once the beginning teacher has identified the students' work, the mentor invites the teacher to a conference to analyze the selected student work samples. The mentor asks the teacher to bring a copy of the corresponding lesson plan and any assessment materials used to grade the students' performance to the conference.

The mentor conducts a reflective conference using the student work samples as the data. When the conference begins, the mentor introduces the Analysis of Student Work tool and gives an overview of the five-step process. Guiding questions prompt the beginning teacher's thinking as the mentor moves through each step of the process.

Step 1: Performance Expectations and Assessment Criteria

This step is used to clarify the expectations the teacher has for the students' performance and to identify the assessment criteria. Some guiding questions to clarify expectations for students' performance include:

- What is the purpose of the lesson?
- Is the assignment aligned with the standard and the objective?
- What evidence of learning do you expect the students to produce? Be specific and give examples.
- Some guiding questions to identify assessment criteria include:
  - What grading criteria did you use for assessing the assignment?
  - How did you inform the students of the grading criteria you would use?
  - If you only used a numerical grading scale, how do you know the student has mastered the standard and the objective?
  - Did you use a rubric to analyze this work?
  - Does the rubric or grading criteria align with the standard and the objective?
  - Is the assessment appropriate for the objective, the developmental level of students, the teaching strategies, and the learning activities?

Step 2: Student Work Samples

The mentor asks the teacher to sort the students' work into four groups: *exemplary, meets objective, almost meets objective,* and *does not meet objective.* Once the expectations and assessment criteria have been described, Sorting Student Work samples will be based on that criteria. Guiding questions the mentor will ask include:

- Did the students master the standard that was being taught?
- Do the various groups match the assessment criteria established?

The teacher will write each student's name in the designated columns. This allows the teacher to see which students were proficient, met, almost met, or did not meet the objective.

Step 3: Description of Student Performance

The third step is a description of the students' performance. As the teacher examines each set of student work, the mentor asks the teacher to describe the student performance for each level. The mentor specifically asks the teacher to look at the expectations and criteria set for the standard, the objective, and the assessment. The guiding question is, "Does the work match the criteria?" The mentor asks the teacher to describe each level of the student performance that does not match the criteria. The teacher can see what each student knows and does not know as the criteria and the work is compared.

Step 4: Diagnosis and Interpretation

After the teacher has described the students' performance in each category, it is time for the teacher to begin to diagnose what happened between the time the teacher taught the lesson and the students completed the work assigned. The mentor asks the teacher the following guided questions:

- Which knowledge and skills did the students know and do well?
- Which knowledge and skills did the students not know and do well?
- What did you see in the students' work that was surprising?
- What did you learn about how your students think and learn?

By reflecting on the previous questions, the teacher will begin to see her students in a different way based on what they know or don't know, how the students think, how the students express themselves as individuals, and how the student's work mirrors her practice.

The next activity in Step 4 is to interpret the student work. Some guiding questions the mentor will ask include:

- Based on the above student performance descriptions, what are the learning needs for each group of students?
- Why do you think the standard and objective of the lesson were not met?
- What patterns of understandings or misunderstandings do you see?
- Are there prerequisite skills and knowledge students have not mastered?
- Are any specific groups of students, such as boys or girls, special education, and English language learners, not meeting the standard?
- What percentage of students is in each column?

Step 5: Action Plan for Meeting Student Needs

The teachers have determined the performance expectations and reviewed the assessment criteria, sorted the student work into categories of how well they achieved the objective, described their students' performance, and diagnosed and interpreted their students' work samples. Step 5 involves writing an action plan for meeting the students' needs. There are some guiding questions the mentor asks the teachers related to teaching and learning:

- As a result of analyzing students' work, are there any questions about teaching and assessment that have come to mind? What are those questions?
- How will you build bridges between what the students know and are able to do with what they will know and be able to do?

The mentor assists the teacher in building the next steps for her teaching and her students' learning by asking additional questions to guide the teachers thinking and planning.

- What extension or reteaching do you need to do?
- What type of lesson will you design to meet the needs of your students?
- Were there gaps in the students' learning?
- Were the prerequisite skills and/or knowledge mastered? How do you know?
- Do you need to complete a task analysis?
- What resources or personnel do you need to find in order to meet your students' needs?
- How can your mentor assist you?

Depending on the answers the teacher gives, she may need to complete a task analysis or review the process of Planning for Instruction as described in Chapter 13.

As the mentor moves through each step with her beginning teacher, the teacher will begin to recognize the different learning needs of her students. Specific strategies can be identified that will meet the needs of her diverse student populations. After completing the process, the mentor will be able to support the beginning teacher as she begins to plan for supporting her students.

The mentor will gain new insights into the teacher's thinking as they complete this process together and collaborate on the next steps.

ANALYZING STUDENT WORK TOOLS IN ACTION

When Jamie met with Jim, the beginning art teacher at the high school, Jim was concerned that his students did not complete the assignment successfully. Jamie suggested, "Would you like for us to look at those student work samples?" Jim responds that would be a great idea, and he pulls out the papers from his desk. Jamie states that they need more time than they have right now, so she makes an appointment with Jim for the end of the week. Jamie asks Jim to bring the student work samples he has from today, his lesson plan, and the criteria he used to grade the work.

Jamie enters Jim's room at the end of the week and shares with Jim the Analysis of Student Work tool. Jamie generally reviews the five steps, and they get to work. Jamie asks Jim the guiding questions through each of the steps (Figures 18.5, 18.6, 18.7, and 18.8). As Jim responds verbally, Jamie suggests that Jim write his response as they go through each step. Jim is more than happy to do so and is beginning to see what the actual problem is in the classroom. He sees that 60.8% of his students did meet the standard and approximately 39% did not. He has great ideas for those students who did meet the objective but needs assistance from Jamie in creating an action plan for the others. Jim identifies the main problem—his students do not know how to write descriptive words for the art they are viewing. They also do not know how to distinguish similarities and differences between the Impressionist and the Post-Impressionist artists. Jim feels confident that he can teach his students to look at the artists, but he has concerns in regard to teaching descriptive words. Jamie knows a master writing teacher and offers to set up an appointment between the three of them so Jim can get some ideas.

Jim feels like he has a plan to assure that his students can be successful when he and Jamie complete all five steps of the process. He also thinks he knows his students better by actually looking at what they were able to do and creating a plan for them to acquire the skills they were not able to do. Jim will continue to look at his students' work every four weeks to see if his teaching practices have improved over time. Jamie assures Jim she will be there to assist him, encourage him, and collaborate with him whenever he needs to complete the Analysis of Student Work process.

Figure 18.5 Analysis of Student Work

Name: *Jim*	**Date:** *3/10*	**Mentor:** *Jamie*

Grade Level/Subject Area: *High School Art* **Content Standard(s):** *VAHS3-2-PO401*

Lesson/Unit Objective(s): *After viewing a video on Impressionism, the students will compare the style and technique of Impressionist and Post-Impressionist paintings with 90% accuracy.*

Step 1: Performance Expectations and Assessment Criteria

A. Clarify Expectations for Students' Performance:
- What is the purpose of the lesson?
- Is the assignment aligned with the standard and the objective?
- What evidence of learning do you expect the students to produce? Be specific and give examples.

- *Impressionists redefined art with their images of light and color and therefore thought beyond the limits of realism.*
- *Yes, the assignment is aligned with the standard and the objective*
- *Expectations:*
  - *Search the web for the assigned artist or explore the Impressionist and Post-Impressionist paintings to identify at least two artists or each era*
  - *Label, compare, and contrast the paintings of the artists from Impressionist and Post-Impressionist*
  - *Develop a clear, thoughtful, description of the artistic styles and techniques*
  - *Describe at least one similarity and one difference between the two*

B. Identify Assessment Criteria:
- What grading criteria did you use for assessing the assignment?
- How did you inform the students of the grading criteria you would use?
- If you only used a numerical grading scale, how do you know the student has mastered the standard and the objective?
- Did you use a rubric to analyze this work?
- Does the rubric or grading criteria align with the standard and the objective?
- Is the assessment appropriate for the objective, the developmental level of students, the teaching strategies, and the learning activities?

- *Rubric was given to each student before the assignment*
- *The rubric aligns with the standard and the objective*
- *The assessment is appropriate*
- *The rubric was a 4 point rubric: 4 points=Clear, concise, thoughtful description of the artistic styles and techniques of Impressionist and Post-Impressionist paintings with examples by at least 2 artists; 3 points=Basic description; 2 point=Poor description; 1 points=Little description or no description*

| Figure 18.6 | Analysis of Student Work |

Step 2: Student Work Samples

A. Sorting Student Work:

– Did the students master the standard that was being taught? Divide the student work samples into four columns: Exemplary, Meets, Almost Meets, and Does Not Meets.

– Do the various groups match the assessment criteria established?

B. Write students' names in the columns below.

Exemplary	Meets Objective	Almost Meets Objective	Does Not Meet Objective
David Wendy Katilyn Rebecca Mitch Joshua Manuel Julie	Cynthia Sara Angela Kelsy Michael Tom Kelly	Geneva Jose Grace Cindy Sam	Matt Robert Sally Sue

Step 3: Description of Student Performance

– Describe the student performance for each level. Specifically, which expectations criteria for the standard, objective, and assessment does the work match?

– Describe the student performance for each level that does not match the expectations criteria set for the standard, objective, and assessment.

Exemplary	Meets Objective	Almost Meets Objective	Does Not Meet Objective
• Search the web for the assigned artist or explore the Impressionist and Post-Impressionist paintings to identify at least two artists or each era • Label, compare, and contrast the paintings of the artists from Impressionist and Post-Impressionist • Develop a clear, thoughtful, description of the artistic styles and techniques • Describe at least one similarity and one difference between the two	• Search the web for the assigned artist or explore the Impressionist and Post-Impressionist paintings to identify at least two artists or each era • Label, compare, and contrast the paintings of the artists from Impressionist and Post-Impressionist • Describe at least one similarity and one difference between the two	• Search the web for the assigned artist or explore the Impressionist and Post-Impressionist paintings to identify at least two artists or each era • Label, compare, and contrast the paintings of the artists from Impressionist and Post-Impressionist	• Search the web for the assigned artist or explore the Impressionist and Post-Impressionist paintings to identify at least two artists or each era

| Figure 18.7 | Analysis of Student Work |

Step 4: Diagnosis and Interpretation

A. Diagnosing Student Work:

- Which knowledge and skills did the students know and do well?
- Which knowledge and skills did the students not know and not do well?
- What did you see in the students' work that was surprising?
- What did you learn about how your students think and learn?

Exemplary	Meets Objective	Almost Meets Objective	Does Not Meet Objective
Met all of the expectations. The depth of their thinking was surprising. They are a group of students who want to succeed and can find the information they need on the web site easily.	Met the objective but their writing was not as concise and clear as I would have liked. They just wrote basic facts and did not elaborate.	There were no similarities or differences identified. Their writing was not complete in descriptions. They do know how to search the web.	Can search the web for the two eras. Did not write about what they learned. There were no similarities or differences identified.

B. Interpreting Student Work:

- Based on the above student performance descriptions, what are the learning needs for each group of students?
- Why do you think the standard and objective of the lesson was not met?
- What patterns of understandings or misunderstandings do you see?
- Are there pre-requisite skills and/or knowledge students have not mastered?
- Are any specific groups of students (e.g., boys or girls, special education, English language learners, etc.) not meeting the standard?
- What percentage of students is in each column?

Exemplary	Meets Objective	Almost Meets Objective	Does Not Meet Objective
Extensions of learnings	Writing descriptive words	Writing descriptive words Distinguish between similarities and differences between the two eras	Label, compare, and contrast Writing descriptive words Distinguish between similarities and differences between the two eras
Prerequisites not met are writing skills rather than artistic knowledge. No specific groups of students are evident in groupings.			
___30.4___ %	___30.4___ %	___22___ %	___17.2___ %

Figure 18.8 Analysis of Student Work

Step 5: Action Plan for Meeting Student Needs

A. Questions related to teaching and learning:

- As a result of analyzing students' work, are there any questions about teaching and assessment that have come to mind? What are those questions?
- How will you build bridges between what the students know and are able to do with what they will know and be able to do?

B. Next Steps for your teaching and your students' learning:

- What extension or reteaching do you need to do?
- What type of lesson will you design to meet the needs of your students?
- Were there gaps in the students' learning? Were the prerequisite skills and/or knowledge mastered? How do you know? Do you need to complete a task analysis?
- What resources or personnel do you need to find in order to meet your students' needs?
- How can your mentor assist you?

Identified Students	Next Steps	Resources Needed (R)/ Mentor Assistance (M)
Exemplary David Manuel Wendy Julie Katilyn Rebecca Mitch Joshua	*Extension – Create an art gallery of the artists for display in the classroom different from those previously found. Searching the web for the culture of the times.*	R M
Meets Objective: Cynthia Tom Sara Angela Kelsy Michael Kelly	*Work on writing descriptive words for the style and techniques of the two eras using the art gallery as it is posted by the exemplary group.*	R M – *Can help me find an outstanding writing teacher for tips*
Almost Meets Objective: Geneva Jose Grace Cindy Sam	*Work with meets objective group on writing descriptive words. Make a list of those words that compare and contrast the two eras. Make a list of similarities and differences. Put those words into paragraph form.*	R M
Does Not Meet Objective: Matt Robert Sally Sue	*Print out artist and at least one of their paintings from each era. Write words that describe the artist and the painting. Make a list of those words that compare and contrast the two eras. Make a list of similarities and differences. Put those words into paragraph form.*	R M

NOTES FOR IMPLEMENTATION

A mentor will implement the Analysis of Student Work tool when the teacher she is working with has solid instructional planning skills, can implement the plan but has questions, and concerns about the work that the students produce. This is a time when the teacher has successfully completed Stage 1: Role Focused and Stage 2: Practice Focused of the Transformational Learning Stages and is ready to enter the first part of Stage 3: Learner Focused.

Figure 18.9 Analysis of Student Work

Name:	**Date:**	**Mentor:**
Grade Level/Subject Area:	**Content Standard(s):**	
Lesson/Unit Objective(s):		

Step 1: Performance Expectations and Assessment Criteria

A. Clarify Expectations for Students' Performance:

- What is the purpose of the lesson?
- Is the assignment aligned with the standard and the objective?
- What evidence of learning do you expect the students to produce? Be specific and give examples.

B. Identify Assessment Criteria:

- What grading criteria did you use for assessing the assignment?
- How did you inform the students of the grading criteria you would use?
- If you only used a numerical grading scale, how do you know the student has mastered the standard and the objective?
- Did you use a rubric to analyze this work?
- Does the rubric or grading criteria align with the standard and the objective?
- Is the assessment appropriate for the objective, the developmental level of students, the teaching strategies, and the learning activities?

Step 2: Student Work Samples

A. Sorting Student Work:

– Did the students master the standard that was being taught? Divide the student work samples into four columns: Exemplary, Meets, Almost Meets, and Does Not Meets.

– Do the various groups match the assessment criteria established?

B. Write students' names in the columns below.

Exemplary	Meets Objective	Almost Meets Objective	Does Not Meet Objective

Step 3: Description of Student Performance

– Describe the student performance for each level. Specifically, which expectations criteria for the standard, objective, and assessment does the work match?

– Describe the student performance for each level that does not match the expectations criteria set for the standard, objective, and assessment.

Exemplary	Meets Objective	Almost Meets Objective	Does Not Meet Objective

Step 4: Diagnosis and Interpretation

A. Diagnosing Student Work:

- Which knowledge and skills did the students know and do well?
- Which knowledge and skills did the students not know and not do well?
- What did you see in the students' work that was surprising?
- What did you learn about how your students think and learn?

Exemplary	Meets Objective	Almost Meets Objective	Does Not Meet Objective

B. Interpreting Student Work:

- Based on the above student performance descriptions, what are the learning needs for each group of students?
- Why do you think the standard and objective of the lesson were not met?
- What patterns of understandings or misunderstandings do you see?
- Are there prerequisite skills and/or knowledge students have not mastered?
- Are any specific groups of students (e.g., boys or girls, special education, English language learners, etc.) not meeting the standard?
- What percentage of students is in each column?

Exemplary	Meets Objective	Almost Meets Objective	Does Not Meet Objective
_____%	_____%	_____%	_____%

Step 5: Action Plan for Meeting Student Needs

A. Questions related to teaching and learning:

- As a result of analyzing students' work, are there any questions about teaching and assessment that have come to mind? What are those questions?
- How will you build bridges between what the students know and are able to do with what they will know and be able to do?

B. Next Steps for your teaching and your students' learning;

- What extension or reteaching do you need to do?
- What type of lesson will you design to meet the needs of your students?
- Were there gaps in the students' learning? Were the prerequisite skills and/or knowledge mastered? How do you know? Do you need to complete a task analysis?
- What resources or personnel do you need to find in order to meet your students' needs?
- How can your mentor assist you?

Identified Students	Next Steps	Resources Needed (R)/ Mentor Assistance (M)
Exemplary		R
		M
Meets Objective:		R
		M
Almost Meets Objective:		R
		M
Does Not Meet Objective:		R
		M

19

Planning for Differentiated Instruction

PURPOSE FOR PLANNING FOR DIFFERENTIATED INSTRUCTION

Meeting the needs of a variety of different learners is essential skill for all teachers. For beginning teachers, this is a constant challenge during the Transformational Learning stages. Differentiated instruction requires effective classroom management, effective assessment strategies, and effective data analysis knowledge. It also requires that teachers constantly be thinking about who their students are and how they learn best. Tomlinson (2000) states, "What we call differentiation is not a recipe for teaching. It is not what a teacher does when he or she has time. It is a way of thinking about teaching and learning. It is a philosophy" (p. 6).

In order to establish a common language within our program, we have adopted Tomlinson's work as the basis for differentiated instruction. Her body of work describes the basic principles of differentiated instruction as flexible grouping, respectful tasks, and ongoing assessment and adjustments of instruction. Teachers can differentiate what content students will be learning, how students will acquire the new learning, or how students will demonstrate understanding of the new learning. Once teachers identify what they will differentiate, they need to determine whether they will differentiate by readiness, interest, or learning profile. Communicating this set of beliefs and principles to teachers; and creating a common language as to what differentiation is and is not, becomes a focus for mentors when differentiated instruction is the topic for conversation.

Differentiated instruction is introduced to beginning teachers when they have moved into the learning focused stage. It is in this stage that teachers are more aware of who their students are and how they learn best. The complexity of differentiation is fueled by the desire to meet the needs of the students in their classrooms. Teachers are also more prepared to shift their instruction from whole group lessons to flexible group instruction.

In order to help teachers overcome the daunting but necessary task of differentiated instruction, we have created several tools that mentors use to assist teacher through the process. These tools provide a visual and structural support to help teachers differentiate content, process or product according to their students' readiness, interests or learning profiles. They help build the process of recognizing and planning to meet the needs of diverse learners.

DESCRIPTION OF PLANNING FOR DIFFERENTIATED INSTRUCTION

The first tool mentors introduce to teachers who are preparing to differentiate instruction is the *Instructional Groups for Differentiated Instruction* tool. This tool is intended to be used to visually determine which students belong to like groups based on readiness, interest, or learning profile.

This tool has two major components designed to help teachers. The first is a space where the lesson objectives are written to help teachers maintain a focus when designing instructional groups. In this section, teachers also indicate how they are planning to differentiate. Whether teachers are going to differentiate based on readiness, learning profile, or interest, it is important to maintain high academic expectations for all learners.

The second component is for teachers to record student names and visually arrange like groups of students. Teachers describe common readiness levels, preferred learning styles, modes of learning, or interests. Underneath, there are boxes for teachers to list students who fit the descriptions (Figure 19.1).

The second tool mentors introduce to teachers is the *Differentiated Lesson Plan Organizer*. This tool was developed to help teachers create instructional activities focused on academic standards. It helps teachers to address the complexities of planning for differentiation by providing space for the activity, assessment criteria, and materials necessary to be described (Figure 19.2).

The third tool to assist teachers in differentiating instruction is the *Lesson Plan Differentiation* template. The template is similar to other lesson planning formats, with the additional component of differentiation details. On this tool, teachers can describe how they will provide different avenues for students to learn content, process information, or demonstrate understanding (Figure 19.3).

Figure 19.1	Instructional Groups for Differentiated Instruction

Date: _2/17_   **Teacher:** _Laura_   **Mentor:** _Tyler_

Grade Level/Subject: _7th Language Arts_   **Date for Lesson Implementation:** _2/23_

Lesson Objective(s): SW demonstrate understanding of a nonfiction text selection.	What I will differentiate: ☐ Content ☑ Process ☐ Product	How I will differentiate: ☐ Readiness ☐ Interest ☑ Learning Profile
Group Identifier: _Musical/Rhythmic_	**Group Identifier:** _Verbal Linguistic_	**Group Identifier:** _Visual Spatial_
Dusty _Macy_ _Anthony_ _Jessica_ _James_ _Vance_ _David_ _Juan_	_Emily_ _Andrea_ _Breeana_ _Danielle_ _Laura_ _Mike_ _Greg_	_Jason_ _Matthew_ _Ron_ _Patty_ _Sandy_ _Audrey_ _Lisa O._
Group Identifier: _Bodily Kinesthetic_	**Group Identifier:**	**Group Identifier:**
Julia _Lisa B._ _Jane_ _Rick_ _Austin_ _Troy_ _Sabrina_ _Lorin Mae_		
Group Identifier:	**Group Identifier:**	**Group Identifier:**

| Figure 19.2 | Differentiated Lesson Plan Organizer |

Date: _2/16_   Teacher: _Emily_   Mentor: _Colton_

Grade Level/Subject: _3rd Grade Math_   Date for Lesson Implementation: _2/23_

1. Performance Objective(s):
The students will create a model of a given fraction.

2. State Standards Addressed:
Third Grade Math: Strand 1 Number Sense- PO 10 (create a model that represents a proper fraction)

3. Differentiation:
Differentiated by (What): ☐ Content – ☑ Process – ☐ Product
Based on Student (How): ☑ Readiness – ☐ Interest – ☐ Learning Profile

4. Instructional Activities for Differentiation:

Group Identifier: Does Not Meet Objective	Group Identifier: Almost Meets Objective	Group Identifier: Meets Objective	Group Identifier: Exemplary
Assessment: Matching game worksheet	**Assessment:** Colored shapes worksheet	**Assessment:** Fractions worksheet	**Assessment:** Fractions worksheet
Assessment Criteria: Accurately match fraction to pictorial w/ 90% accuracy	**Assessment Criteria:** Accurately shade shape to match numerical fraction with 90% accuracy	**Assessment Criteria:** Accurately divide fraction and shade to match numerical fraction with 90% accuracy	**Assessment Criteria:** Create numerical fractions with matching model with 90% accuracy
Activity: Students will be given a fraction in numerical form. TSW choose the correct pictorial representation of the fraction.	**Activity:** Students will be given a fraction in numerical form. TSW use shapes that are already divided into equal parts. TSW shade the appropriate part(s) to represent the fraction.	**Activity:** Students will be given a fraction in numerical form. TSW use blank shapes to divide and shade to represent the fraction.	**Activity:** Students will create their own numerical fraction. TSW create a shape; divide it into equal parts and shade to represent the fraction.
Materials: Various fractions represented in pictorial form using various shapes. i.e. circle, rectangle	**Materials:** Various shapes divided into equal parts	**Materials:** Various blank shapes	**Materials:** Blank paper

Figure 19.3	Lesson Plan – Differentiation Template

Learning Objective(s): *TSW locate facts in expository text. TSW distinguish between fact and opinions in persuasive text.*

	Differentiation Details
Anticipatory Set: *"Brussel Sprouts are the best food ever!" Whole class discussion of fact and opinion.* **Building Background/Prior Knowledge** (check all that apply) ☑ Student experience ☐ KWL charts ☑ Brainstorm ☐ Visuals/illustrations ☐ Webbing ☐ Story ☑ Small group talk ☐ Vocabulary ☐ Metaphor ☐ Partner talk development ☐ Realia ☑ Other *Brainstorming/Discussion* **Teacher Instruction:** *Advertisement –Talk about Lunchables Ad – "Kids love them" – Think Aloud about a friend who doesn't like them – opinion. Model listing facts and opinions.*	**Content:** ☑ Readiness ☐ Interest ☐ Learning Profile *During independent practice, students must read expository text and record facts and opinions. I am providing different leveled reading material to meet the varying reading levels of my students as determined by the district reading assessment.*
Guided Practice: *Explain components of advertisements* *Model listing facts & opinions with kids* *Mixed ability groups list facts and opinions about their ad – then present to class. Class signals whether each list has facts or opinions.* **Independent Practice:** *Students use leveled reading books to locate facts and opinions in expository text. Record findings on sheet provided.*	**Process:** ☐ Readiness ☐ Interest ☐ Learning Profile

Closure of Lesson:
 	
 Review facts and opinions and expository text.
 	
 Assessment:
 Completed facts and opinion record sheets from leveled readers.
 	
 Assessment Criteria: *(Grades for all students)*
    A – Lists 6 facts, 6 opinions
    B – List 4 facts, 4 opinions
    C – List 5 facts, 5 opinions
    D – List 3 facts, 3 opinions
    F – fewer than 3 facts, and 3 opinions
	Product:
	 ☐ Readiness
	 ☐ Interest
	 ☐ Learning Profile

HOW TO USE THE PLANNING FOR DIFFERENTIATED INSTRUCTION TOOLS

When working with teachers to differentiate instruction, mentors utilize a backwards planning process to help facilitate the conversation. During a planning conference, the mentor first helps the teacher clarify learning outcomes. It is essential that teachers know what students will know and be able to do as a result of the lesson before they begin planning the learning activities. Some questions that mentors ask during this portion of planning for differentiated instruction are as follows:

- Tell me about this lesson and how it relates to your students' needs?
- Where does it fit relative to student content or grade level standards?
- What essential understanding do you want your students to gain?
- What do you want students to be able to do?
- How might these be modified to address your students' various needs?
- I'm interested in any preassessments that might have contributed to your understanding of your students' learning needs.
- What are the most important concepts your students need to understand?
- What are the essential skills they need to achieve your outcomes?
- To what extent do you want to differentiate the content according to your students' needs?
- What essential questions will guide your teaching and your students' learning?

Once teachers have an idea of what students will know and be able to do as a result of the lesson, teachers can begin to formulate a plan and begin to design for differentiated instruction. Teachers choose *what* they will differentiate (content, process, or product). Do they want to differentiate what students will be learning, how students will acquire the learning, or how students will demonstrate the learning?

The first tool mentors might introduce to teachers when planning for differentiation is Instructional Groups for Differentiated Instruction. When using this tool, teachers decide *how* they wish to meet the needs of the students in their classroom. Will they differentiate by readiness, learning profile, or interest? Once this has been determined, teachers need to examine student data information. Teachers might utilize the student data maps (see Chapter 12), student work analysis (see Chapter 18), compiled student interest surveys, or identified learning styles for students. This information is then used to determine specific Group Identifiers. These should pertain to readiness levels, student interests, or learning styles.

Teachers list students by name under the Group Identifier that best meets individual student's needs. Not all students will fit exactly into one of the groups. Teachers need to recognize that they are trying to best meet students' needs. If a student does not match the group identifier exactly, they should use a second or even third description for students. New teachers should try to form no more than 3 or 4 groups the first time they differentiate with small groups.

Once groups are organized, teachers can then begin to plan and design the assessment expectations and learning activities for students. The Differentiated Lesson Plan Organizer tool helps teachers with this step. On the top of the tool, teachers write the Performance Objectives identified for the lesson, the academic State Standard Addressed, Differentiation components, and the Group Identifiers. The sample Differentiated Lesson Plan Organizer tool that follows shows the teacher will differentiate the lesson process by readiness.

Teachers are ready to determine how each group will be assessed. This follows the backwards planning philosophy that learning events should only be designed once the end result has been determined. Some questions mentors may ask during this part of the planning conferences include:

- What will success look like?
- How can students demonstrate their understanding or their learning?
- What might be different ways in which they could do this?
- How will you know your students are reaching the desired outcomes?
- What evidence will show that students understand?
- Tell me about the criteria you might use to assess student responses and products.

Once teachers determine how they will assess students and by what criteria they will be assessed by, they describe this information in the assessment and assessment criteria sections of the tool.

Teachers can then begin to plan the activities and identify any materials that are necessary for students to accomplish the activities. When conferencing with teachers, we utilize strategies from the Tomlinson and Edison (2003) book, *Differentiation in Practice: A Resource Guide for Differentiating Curriculum Grades 5–9*. Mentors may ask the following questions during this portion of the planning conference to help guide the teacher's thinking:

- How might you draw students into the lesson? What are some ways to pique student interest or curiosity? How do you plan to communicate learning outcomes to your students?
- Describe for me how you might link this lesson to your students' prior knowledge or experiences?

- Tell me what you already know about your students' current knowledge, skills, and interest in this topic?
- Let's think about different ways to engage students in this learning! To what extent will these strategies support different types of learners?
- What instructional strategies might help students understand the key concepts? How might you model what you want students to do?
- What visual prompts might support students in answering the question, "How do I do this?"
- How will your instruction support different groups of students as identified in our analysis of student work? What sort of materials will you need?
- What might be the ways to support English language learners and special education students?
- Tell me about how you might check for understanding during the lesson?
- What challenges or possible confusion might you anticipate? How might you prepare for them?
- How might you transition from one activity to the next?
- Describe how the learning activities build upon one another.
- What visual supports might help students answer the question, "What do I do next?"
- Let's think about how students might progress from one activity to the next. How do you propose to link these concepts and activities? What is important to review or summarize?
- How might you assess students understanding or applications of learning? How might you help students process their learning? Or their group behavior?
- What can students do independently that will reinforce what they've learned? How can students apply and extend their learning?

The third tool we have developed to assist teachers in differentiating instruction is the Lesson Plan Differentiation template. This template can be used when designing a differentiated lesson. The beginning teacher decides if he will be differentiating by content, process, or product. Then they can describe how they will differentiate by the students' readiness, interests, or learning profiles. Based upon this information, the mentor and the beginning teacher can collaboratively design a differentiated lesson to meet the needs of the students.

PLANNING FOR DIFFERENTIATED INSTRUCTION TOOLS IN ACTION

Alison, a first year teacher, was concerned that some of her students did not seem to be achieving the way that she felt they could. She met with her mentor, Dana, to discuss her concerns.

"Some of my students are just not performing the way that I know they can perform. I am worried because the state test is coming up in a couple of months and not all of my students are going to be performing well."

Dana knows how passionate Allison is about her students. She has expressed a desire to meet the needs of her students during the second month of school but was not ready to try small group differentiation. Because Allison now has classroom management under way and has begun to do some student work analysis, Dana feels that she is ready to try small groups and thinks this might be an opportunity for her to explore differentiation with Allison.

"I know that you have worked really hard this fall to become the best teacher you can be. We have spent a lot of time looking at how you can improve your practice with whole group instruction, and now your students are doing what you expect. We have seen significant growth in most of your students. How do you think looking at creating some small groups would impact student learning?"

Allison responded with a smile on her face, "Yes! I think that is just where we need to go. I saw Mr. Jones work with small groups last week and was really excited to see how well his students did on their writing assignment. I want to try that with my students. Where do we begin?"

"Well, from what we have talked about today and the past few weeks, it sounds like you are most interested in meeting students' readiness levels. In other words, providing them a learning experience right at the level they are ready to learn. Is this where you would like to begin?" Dana asked.

"I am pretty sure that is where I would like to start. What do we need to have in order to get going?"

"We have talked about the unit you would like to start next week, and you did a preassessment for that unit a few days ago. Have you analyzed those student results yet?" Dana questioned.

Shaking her head excitedly, Allison said, "Yes! I finished that yesterday. You know, it is almost like you have been leading me to this point!"

Together, the pair examines the student work analysis data.

"If you look closely, you can see that based on your data, you have already identified several groups. There are several students who have very little understanding of the concepts necessary for your next unit. There are a few students who have an average understanding, and the majority of your students have some knowledge and skill necessary. You have identified the strengths and challenges for each of those groups and based on what you have written here, you have identified some patterns of your learners. What do you see from these patterns as possible groups based on skill and knowledge readiness?," Dana inquires.

"Well I see that there are a lot of students who really do not know what ending punctuation is. In their writing, they have used periods where question marks need to go and question marks where periods should go. Some students even used commas as ending punctuation," Allison responds. "I do see that some students are not using correct paragraph structure. They did not indent, and they just have one large body of writing, although they did know how to use ending punctuation. Then, I see I have a few students who have both of those concepts down. Those are actually my advanced students. I would like to try to challenge them more this time. They get so bored when we practice what they already know. Maybe I can have them really work on building their ideas."

Dana agrees, "It does look like you have three very distinct groups of readiness levels for your next writing unit. Let's capture that information onto an Instructional Groups for Differentiated Instruction tool so that we can visually begin to see the make-up of your groups" (Figure 19.4).

NOTES FOR IMPLEMENTATION

We often suggest that when teachers are first trying to differentiate, they look first at learning styles and examine their own preferred mode of teaching. Typically, we teach in the same way we learn, so we ask teachers to try a new strategy that incorporates a different learning style during their whole group instruction. In this way, they are becoming familiar with the differentiated instructional strategies and building their repertoire of instructional tools in preparation for small group work.

| Figure 19.4 | Instructional Groups for Differentiated Instruction |

Date: _3/11_   **Teacher:** _Allison_   **Mentor:** _Dana_

Grade Level/Subject: _5th Language Arts_   **Date for Lesson Implementation:** _3/18_

Lesson Objective(s): _SW write a personal experience narrative that utilizes correct conventions._	**What I will Differentiate:** ☑ Content ☐ Process ☐ Product	**How I will differentiate:** ☐ Readiness ☐ Interest ☑ Learning Profile
Group Identifier: _Paragraph Structure_	**Group Identifier:** _Ending Punctuation_	**Group Identifier:** _Building Ideas_
Dusty _Macy_ _Anthony_ _Jessica_ _James_ _Vance_ _David_ _Juan_	_Emily_ _Julia_ _Andrea_ _Lisa B._ _Breeana_ _Jane_ _Danielle_ _Rick_ _Laura_ _Austin_ _Mike_ _Troy_ _Patty_ _Sabrina_ _Sandy_ _Lorin Mae_	_Jason_ _Matthew_ _Ron_ _Audrey_ _Lisa O._
Group Identifier:	**Group Identifier:**	**Group Identifier:**
Group Identifier:	**Group Identifier:**	**Group Identifier:**

| Figure 19.5 | Instructional Groups for Differentiated Instruction |

Date: _____ **Teacher:** _____ **Mentor:** _____

Grade Level/Subject: _____ **Date for Lesson Implementation:** _____

Lesson Objective(s):	What I will Differentiate:	How I will differentiate:
	☐ Content ☐ Process ☐ Product	☐ Readiness ☐ Interest ☐ Learning Profile

Group Identifier:	Group Identifier:	Group Identifier:

Group Identifier:	Group Identifier:	Group Identifier:

Group Identifier:	Group Identifier:	Group Identifier:

| **Figure 19.6** | Differentiated Lesson Plan Organizer |

Date: _____ Teacher: _____ Mentor: _____

Grade Level/Subject: _____ Date for Lesson Implementation: _____

1. Performance Based Objective(s):

2. State Standards Addressed:

3. Differentiation:
    Differentiated by (What): ☐ Content – ☐ Process – ☐ Product
    Based on Student (How): ☐ Readiness – ☐ Interest – ☐ Learning Profile

4. Instructional Activities for Differentiation:

Group Identifier:	**Group Identifier:**	**Group Identifier:**	**Group Identifier:**
Assessment:	**Assessment:**	**Assessment:**	**Assessment:**
Assessment Criteria:	**Assessment Criteria:**	**Assessment Criteria:**	**Assessment Criteria:**
Activity:	**Activity:**	**Activity:**	**Activity:**
Materials:	**Materials:**	**Materials:**	**Materials:**

| Figure 19.7 | Lesson Plan Differentiation Template |

Learning Objective(s):

Anticipatory Set:	**Differentiation Details**
Building Background/Prior Knowledge (check all that apply) ☐ Student experience ☐ KWL charts ☐ Brainstorm ☐ Visuals/illustrations ☐ Webbing ☐ Story ☐ Small group talk ☐ Vocabulary ☐ Metaphor ☐ Partner talk development ☐ Realia ☐ Other_____ **Teacher Instruction:**	**Content:** ☐ Readiness ☐ Interest ☐ Learning Profile
Guided Practice: **Independent Practice:**	**Process:** ☐ Readiness ☐ Interest ☐ Learning Profile
Closure of Lesson: **Assessment:** **Assessment Criteria:**	**Product:** ☐ Readiness ☐ Interest ☐ Learning Profile

20

Analyzing Student Assessments

PURPOSE FOR ANALYZING STUDENT ASSESSMENTS

When analyzing student assessments, teachers need to identify whether the assessment is formative or summative. Both assessments are an integral part of gathering information about students. Summative assessments are used to find out what a student knows and does not know at a specific point in time. Some examples include end of unit tests, state assessments, district benchmarks, and scores that are used to create a student report card. These assessments are given after instruction and only assess certain aspects of the learning process.

Formative assessment is part of the instructional process. This assessment informs the teacher of his students' learning for the purpose of adjusting his teaching while the process is occurring. Adjustments can be made in a timely manner to ensure that students achieve the objective within a set frame of time. Formative assessments allow the students the opportunity to practice what they are learning.

A mentor can work with beginning teachers to determine the most appropriate type of assessment to use or to encourage the teacher to develop assessment tasks that provide evidence of student learning in order to inform their instruction. It is vital that beginning teachers develop the practice of identifying the evidence of students' performance to adjust their ongoing instructional procedures or to assist students so they will adjust their current learning tactics (Popham, 2008). For our purposes, we emphasize formative student assessments.

DESCRIPTION OF ANALYZING STUDENT ASSESSMENTS

The three tools in this chapter are designed for mentors to help teachers uncover how they assess their students and how the results of those assessments impact their instruction. The *Formative Assessment of Student Practice* and *Formative Assessment Protocol* tools can be used independent of one another. The *Assessing Student Learning Continuum* is a reference tool that serves as an informative resource during the use of the two aforementioned tools.

Many types of student-generated information can be used as assessment data. The use of the *Formative Assessment of Student Practice* tool can assist the beginning teacher in identifying various forms of assessment data she can collect throughout a lesson or a unit.

The *Formative Assessment of Student Practice* tool helps clarify specific data and evidence a teacher has collected for her students. It helps to focus attention on the analysis of that data and the importance of using a process to determine growth. The tool focuses attention on what growth has been made and what next steps need to occur by the teacher and students. The formative assessments inform the teacher how to adjust her instruction and inform students how to adjust their learning (Figure 20.1).

Alignment between content, strategies, assessment, and evaluation is crucial to effective instruction as discussed in Chapter 13. The Formative Assessment Protocol tool provides a format for analyzing assessment alignment among the content taught, the instructional strategies used, the type of assessment created, the evaluation tool used, and the feedback provided to students (Figure 20.2).

The Assessing Student Learning is a tool adapted from McTighe & Wiggins (2004) that the mentor can use with the beginning teacher to determine if the teacher wants to create an assessment that is simple or complex. Three basic decisions are made prior to the teacher creating an assessment for his students:

1. Do I want my assessment to be simple or complex?

2. What product or performance do I want my students to complete that demonstrates understanding of the learned skills and knowledge?

3. Which evaluation tool will you use to judge student how well students did on the given assessment?

Once the teacher makes those three decisions, he is ready to create an assessment for his students that will reflect what they learned from his teaching and how he can adjust his instruction (Figure 20.3).

Figure 20.1 Formative Assessment of Student Practice

Beginning Teacher: _Joshua_   Mentor: _Lauren Rose_
Academic Standard: _HS Science: S1C4 PO1-4 and S5C4 PO 11_   Date: _4/5_

Growth

- 90% of students use lab journal successfully
- 95% of students acquired the ability to acquire vocabulary using nonlinguistic representation and in-context usage
- 90% use of note cards successfully

Next Steps

- Reteach objectives 2, 3, & 5 to those that were not successful
- Reteach objective 4 to those that were not successful
- Challenge the 90% that were using the lab journal successfully to extend their scientific writing by submitting article to the school newspaper
- Work with specific students on the use of the lab journal that represented those 10%
- Use similar vocabulary activity in future units
- Involve the students in their own assessments and record keeping

Analysis

- Need extra time on Objective 4 for those 40% that misunderstood
- 90% of students understand how to use note cards and illustrations in lab journals
- 10% need additional instructions regarding lab journals
- Just-in-time discussion revealed additional teaching needs for objectives 1 & 3
- Vocabulary activity was helpful and engaging to students
- Need to reteach objectives 2, 3, & 5 to specific students

Collection of Data

Pretest from textbook
- Poor overall performance on the pretest
- Misunderstandings of objectives 1-5

Hands-on Lab & Report
- 80% scored met all objectives
- 10% met 4 out of 5; 5% met 3 out of 5; 5% met 2 out of 5
- Objective 1 was met by 100%; Objective 2 was missed by 5%; Objective 3 was missed by 5%; Objective 4 was missed by 40%; Objective 5 was missed by 10%

Lab Journal
- 85% of students turned in accurate information through written responses or diagrams
- 10% misunderstood objectives 1 & 2
- 5% misunderstood objectives 1, 2, 4, & 5

Just-in-Time Discussion to Teacher Questions
- Responses varied in depth and accuracy
- Objectives 1 & 3 need reteaching activities
- Objectives 2, 4, & 5 need further analysis

Vocabulary Activity – Nonlinguistic Representation and In-context usage
- Most students increased their skills
- Comments made by students regarding the use of note cards and diagrams were positive
- Successful use of objectives 1, 2, 3, & 5
- Only 5% were successful on objective 4

Figure 20.2 Formative Assessment Protocol

1. How did this assessment link to your lesson's objectives and activities?

The multimedia projects required students to communicate the objectives effectively via a multimedia presentation, thus demonstrating their level of mastery of both the academic and technology objectives.

2. What type of assessment did you use? Did it measure the lesson objective?

I used the multimedia projects as a part of the formative assessments. The requirements of the multimedia project were aligned to three of the five technology objectives and three of the six academic objectives. A rubric was developed based on a 3 point scale for the presentation and the content.

3. What evaluation tool did you use to evaluate student performance on the assessment?

The students and I developed a rubric adapted from one provided by our school district based on three of the five technology objectives and three of the six academic objectives.

4. What feedback did you provide to your students?

I provided the students with a copy of the rubric, which included their score for each evaluation criterion and comments.

5. How did your students' learning benefit from this assessment?

They had to look at the score on the rubric, the content of their project, and determine their level of mastery on each objective. This was a way for them to know which objectives they knew and which objectives they did not know.

6. Can this assessment be considered a performance assessment? Use specific criteria to explain why or why not.

Yes, this is a performance assessment because the students had to create a project and communicate their understanding of the content through their presentation. The students also assisted in the development of the rubric.

7. Select one area where you could improve your assessment and write ideas for improvement:
    ☐ Alignment to Objectives
    ☐ Type of Assessment
    ☐ Evaluation Tool
    ☑ Feedback – *Be more descriptive in providing feedback. Ask students to also become involved in determining their level of mastery.*
    ☐ Benefit to Students

Figure 20.3 Assessing Student Learning

1. Do I want my assessment to be simple or complex? *More complex*

Simple	⬅━━━━━━━━━━➡			Complex
Informal check for understanding	Observation or dialogues	Formative check for mastery	Essay or other writing prompt	Performance Task
☐	☐	☒	☐	☐

2. What product or performance do I want my students to complete that demonstrates understanding of the learned skills and knowledge?

☐ Selected-response format (e.g., multiple choice, true-false statements)

☐ Extended written products (e.g., essays, lab reports)

☐ Visual products (e.g., PowerPoint show, mural)

☐ Oral performances (e.g., oral report, foreign language dialogues, debate)

☐ Student demonstrations (e.g., skill performance in P.E.)

☐ Student self-assessments

☐ Just-in-time assessments (e.g.,

☒ Written responses to academic prompts (i.e., short answer format)

☐ Reflective journals or learning logs

☐ Informal or formal, on-going observations of students

☐ Peer reviews and peer response groups

☐ Long-term, 'authentic' assessment projects (i.e., senior exhibit)

☐ Portfolios (collections of student work over time)

☐ Other_____

3. What evaluation tool will you use to judge how well students did on the given assessment?

☐ Criterion-based performance list

☐ Teacher checklist

☐ Answer Key

☐ Holistic rubric

☒ Analytic rubric

☐ Longitudinal rubric

☐ Student generated rubric

☐ Other _____

My Assessment:

My prompt: What was the sequence of events that led to the discovery of the lightbulb? Be specific in your response and provide examples.

I will develop an analytical rubric that depicts the sequence of events (that led to the discovery of the light-bulb) chronologically. The rubric will reflect factual information and accurate examples. The rubric will be a five point rubric

HOW TO USE THE ANALYZING STUDENT ASSESSMENT TOOLS

A mentor and a beginning teacher collaborate in the use of the Formative Assessment of Student Practice tool. This tool is mainly used during either a planning conference or a reflection conference. The beginning teacher identifies the different assessments used during a lesson or a unit by writing the name of each in a separate box on the left of the tool. At this point the mentor might provide a copy of the Assessing Student Learning Continuum to support the identification of assessment data. Next, the beginning teacher enters the student performance data that each assessment activity generated.

Once all the data is recorded, the two discuss what the data means. This analysis is recorded in the *analysis* box. The mentor may need to ask probing questions to encourage a thorough exploration of what the data means in terms of practice for mastery of the instructional objectives. Any student growth is recorded in the *growth* box. A discussion of the impact of this assessment analysis leads to identifying the next steps.

The beginning teacher records the data-driven instructional decisions in the *next steps* box of the Formative Assessment of Student Practice tool. Future instruction is then planned with the next steps serving as the road map.

The Formative Assessment Protocol tool is used to facilitate the analysis of the effectiveness of a formative assessment a teacher has created or used. When first introduced, the tool can be used to guide the discussion between the mentor and beginning teacher regarding a particular assessment created by the teacher. Later, a beginning teacher can use the tool alone to assist herself in analyzing the appropriateness of the assessments she makes. In either scenario, the beginning teacher answers the questions based on the assessment itself and the students' performance on the assessment.

The Assessing Student Learning is a tool that the mentor can use with the beginning teacher to determine the type of assessment the teacher wants to create. The first decision the teacher makes is to determine the simplicity or the complexity of the assessment. The second decision the teacher makes is to decide what product or performance he wants his students to complete that demonstrates understanding of the learned skills and knowledge. The third decision to be made is to decide what evaluation tool will be used to judge how well students did on the given assessment. Once the teacher makes those three decisions, he is ready to create an assessment for his students that will reflect what they learned from his teaching.

ANALYZING STUDENT ASSESSMENT TOOLS IN ACTION

Jerry, a first-year fifth grade teacher, really enjoyed teaching science. He especially enjoyed teaching science through inquiry. He was frustrated because the only materials provided to him for science was a textbook.

Through much effort he acquired the materials he needed in order to provide his students with some hands-on experiences. During a planning conference with his mentor, he expressed a concern that the only assessment he had for his students was the end of chapter test from the textbook. Jerry said he did not want to wait until the end of a unit to determine if the students understood the content because by then it was too late to help those who did not get it.

Jerry's mentor, Tom, took out a copy of the Assessing Student Learning Continuum reference tool and shared it with him. They discussed the different types of assessments that can serve to inform instruction. Reflecting on the last science unit Jerry taught, the two of them identified examples of assignments or tasks Jerry could have used as formative assessments.

Next Tom brought out a copy of the Formative Assessment of Student Practice tool (Figure 20.4). Jerry identified five types of assessment he could conduct during the next unit. He described the type of data that he would collect from each. After each assessment he replaced the description with the actual data. At the end of the unit, Tom and Jerry planned to meet to analyze the data, look for growth, set next steps, and discuss the effectiveness of the assessments.

NOTES FOR IMPLEMENTATION

Each of these tools can be used in a variety of ways to meet the needs of the individual beginning teacher. In the Tools in Action scenario, the mentor chose to use the Formative Assessment of Student Practice tool as scaffolding for the beginning teacher to reference throughout the planning and teaching of one unit. Using this tool provides the students with the practice that they need prior to the end of the unit test or the summative assessment. It allows the teacher to know what additional instruction his students need for mastery.

Figure 20.4 Formative Assessment of Student Practice

Beginning Teacher: _Jerry_   Mentor: _Tom_   Date: _1/21_
Standard: _Science Grade 5: S1C1 PO1&2; S1C2 PO1-5; S1C4 PO1; and S5C1 PO2_

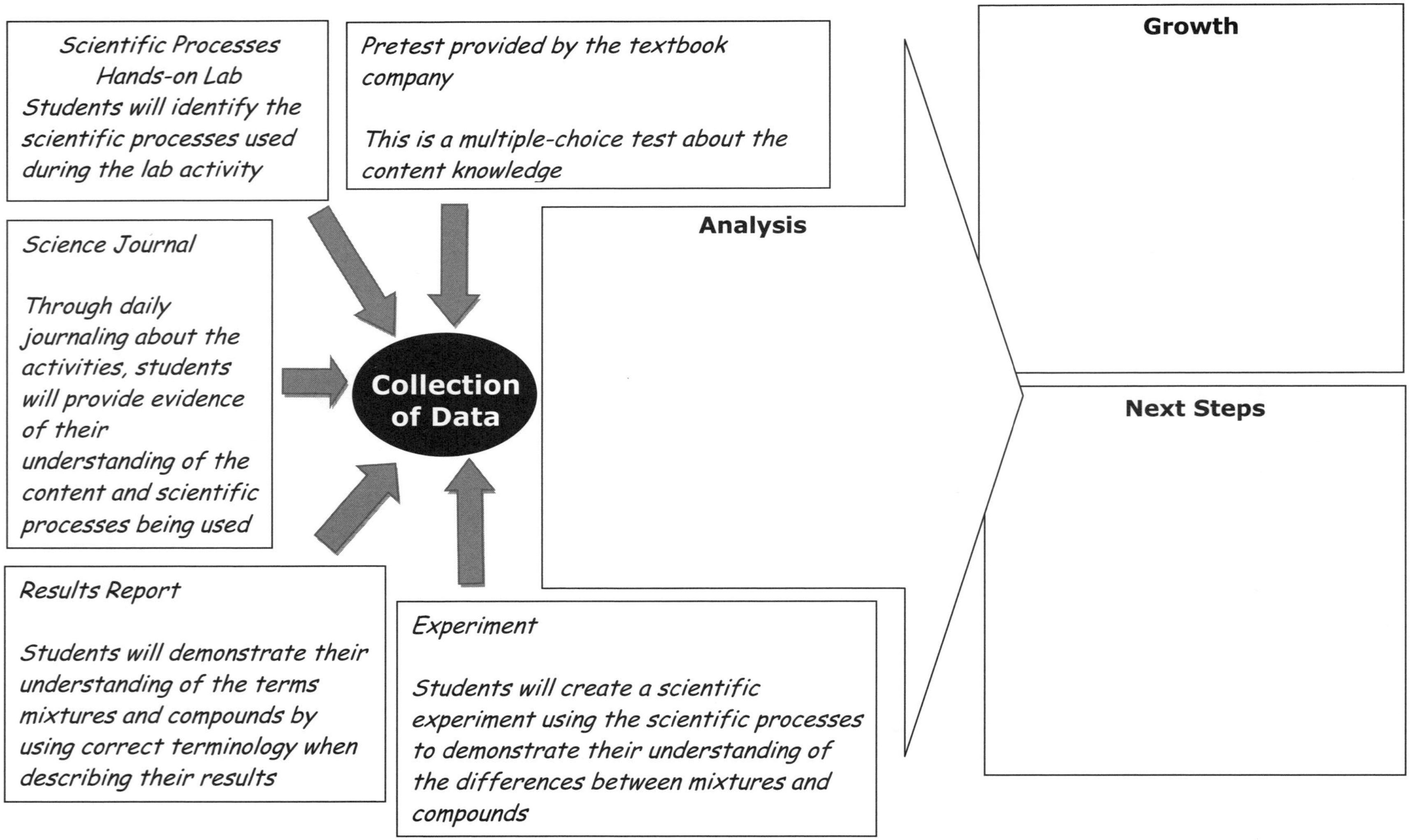

Growth

Next Steps

Analysis

Collection of Data

Scientific Processes
Hands-on Lab
Students will identify the scientific processes used during the lab activity

Pretest provided by the textbook company

This is a multiple-choice test about the content knowledge

Science Journal

Through daily journaling about the activities, students will provide evidence of their understanding of the content and scientific processes being used

Results Report

Students will demonstrate their understanding of the terms mixtures and compounds by using correct terminology when describing their results

Experiment

Students will create a scientific experiment using the scientific processes to demonstrate their understanding of the differences between mixtures and compounds

Figure 20.5 Formative Assessment of Student Practice

Beginning Teacher: _____ Mentor: _____ Date: _____
Standard: _____

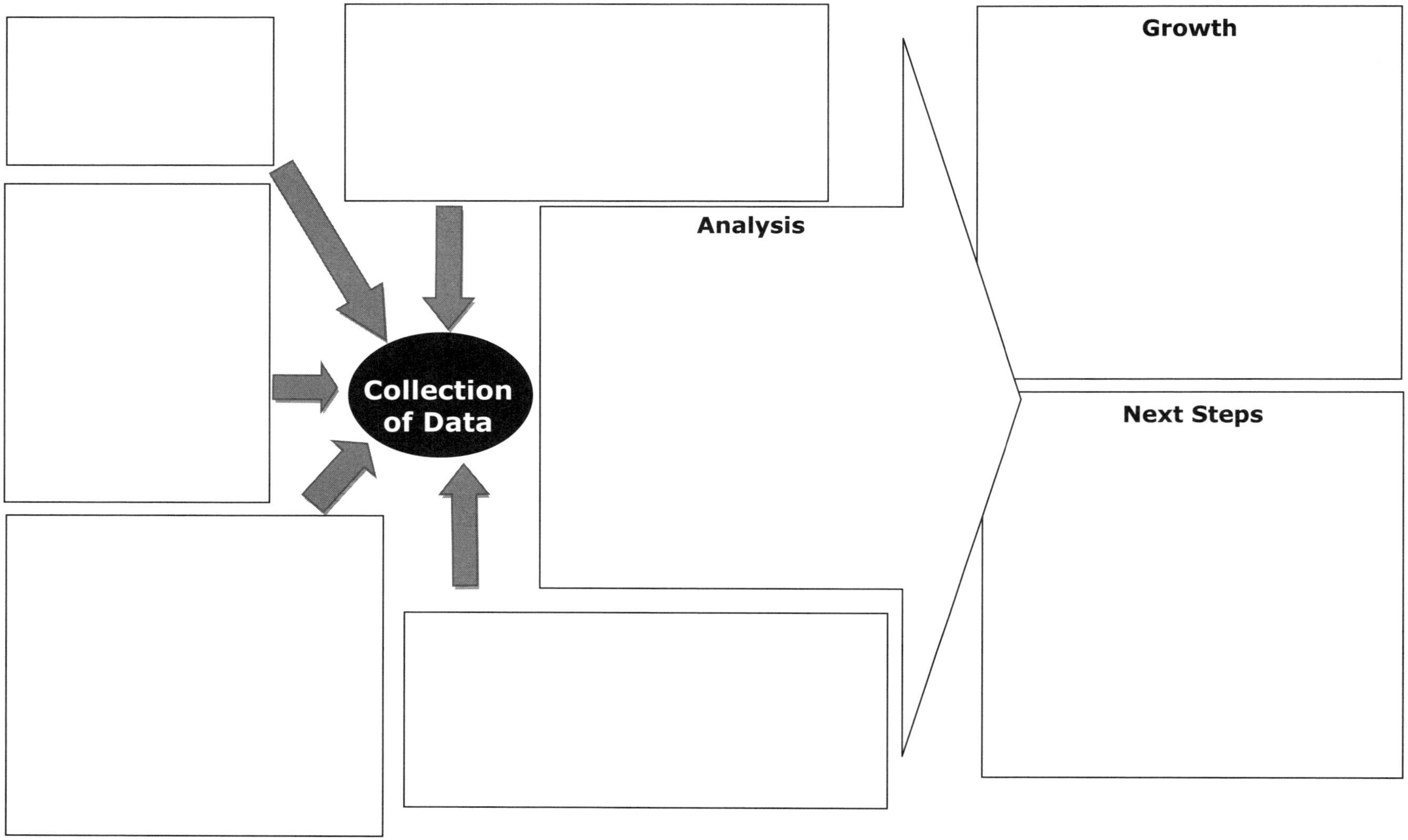

Growth

Next Steps

Analysis

Collection of Data

Figure 20.6	Formative Assessment Protocol

1. **How did this assessment link to your lesson's objectives and activities?**

2. **What type of assessment did you use? Did it measure the lesson objective?**

3. **What evaluation tool did you use to evaluate student performance on the assessment?**

4. **What feedback did you provide to your students?**

5. **How did your students' learning benefit from this assessment?**

6. **Can this assessment be considered a performance assessment? Use specific criteria to explain why or why not.**

7. **Select one area where you could improve your assessment and write ideas for improvement:**
   - ☐ Alignment to Objectives
   - ☐ Type of Assessment
   - ☐ Evaluation Tool
   - ☐ Feedback
   - ☐ Benefit to Students

Figure 20.7 Assessing Student Learning

1. Do I want my assessment to be simple or complex?

Simple ←————————————————→ Complex

Informal check for understanding	Observation or dialogues	Formative check for mastery	Essay or other writing prompt	Performance task
☐	☐	☐	☐	☐

2. What product or performance do I want my students to complete that demonstrates understanding of the learned skills and knowledge?

☐ Selected-response format (e.g., multiple choice, true-false statements)

☐ Extended written products (e.g., essays, lab reports)

☐ Visual products (e.g., PowerPoint show, mural)

☐ Oral performances (e.g., oral report, foreign language dialogues, debate)

☐ Student demonstrations (e.g., skill performance in P.E.)

☐ Student self-assessments

☐ Just-in-time assessments (e.g.,

☐ Written responses to academic prompts (i.e., short answer format)

☐ Reflective journals or learning logs

☐ Informal or formal, on-going observations of students

☐ Peer reviews and peer response groups

☐ Long-term, 'authentic' assessment projects (i.e., senior exhibit)

☐ Portfolios (collections of student work over time)

☐ Other_____

3. What evaluation tool will you use to judge student how well students did on the given assessment?

☐ Criterion-based performance list

☐ Teacher checklist

☐ Answer key

☐ Holistic rubric

☐ Analytic rubric

☐ Longitudinal rubric

☐ Student-generated rubric

☐ Other _____

My Assessment:

21

Planning For Differentiated Mentoring

PURPOSE FOR DIFFERENTIATED MENTORING

The mentor has been meeting with his beginning teachers for six months. At this time, he is wondering why some of his beginning teachers are not transforming their practice. Just as teaching is a dynamic decision-making process so is mentoring. Mentors are constantly making both macrodecisions and microdecisions. The mentor is constantly thinking about conversations with his beginning teachers. Perhaps a few questions that might be going through his mind include:

- Which data collection tool should I suggest in this situation?
- What should I say to the teacher so that my words lead to actions that are meaningful to the teacher?
- Why does Samuel always cancel our appointments?
- Do I spend two hours per week with each of my beginning teachers?
- How can I challenge each of my teachers to transform their practice?

Mentors weigh all of these questions. Mentors are data driven and reflective yet still have questions about their teachers on how to support their transformation. The process of differentiated mentoring is a meaningful and challenging way to be data driven and to reflect critically on mentoring practices.

The success of the mentor depends on the success of the teacher who in turn impacts student learning. The process of differentiated mentoring helps mentors assess whether transformation of teacher's practice is occurring.

DESCRIPTION OF DIFFERENTIATED MENTORING

The mentor uses a collection of two tools to provide data for each beginning teacher. The first collection of tools is the Conference Data Conference (CDC) journals. These journals contain information regarding professional teacher standards and the focus of the conversation. The second collection of tools is the monthly schedule, which documents the amount of time spent with each beginning teacher. Using these tools in much the same way as a teacher analyzes student work will provide the mentor with the foundational data needed to look at his beginning teachers in order to differentiate the mentoring process. It will take several sessions before the process is completed. The process for the collections of those two data tools includes the following steps:

1. Organization of CDC Journal Records and time spent (Figure 21.1)

2. Description of the data (Figure 21.2)

3. Analysis of data (Figure 21.3)

4. Diagnosis of data (Figure 21.4)

5. Action plan for meeting beginning teachers' needs (Figure 21.5)

| Figure 21.1 | Differentiated Mentoring Analysis of Beginning Teacher Development |

Mentor: _____ *Bryce*_____ Date: *2/28*_____

Step 1: Organization of *CDC Journal Records* and Time Spent

A. Professional Teaching Standards

- Separate your *CDC Journal Records* according to the *Professional Teaching Standards* recorded.
- Review each *Professional Teaching Standard*.
- List the first name of each beginning teacher under each of the standards that has been discussed during the *CDC Cycle*. If you have spent more than one session discussing one standard, put a ✓ by the name of the teacher.
- Write the total number of *CDC Journal Records* for each teacher. If you meet with your beginning teacher every week for six months, you will have a total of 24 journal records. Not every calendar week is viable for conferencing so look at the total weeks possible and use that number as your possible number of journal records. Write that number at the top of the column.

Designs and Plans Instruction	Creates and Maintains Learning Environment	Implements and Manages Instruction	Assesses Learning	Possible # of *CDC Journal Records* = 20
Aiden ✓✓✓	Aiden ✓✓✓	Aiden ✓✓✓✓✓✓	Aiden ✓✓✓✓✓	19
Anna✓✓✓✓✓✓	Anna ✓✓	Anna ✓✓✓	Anna ✓✓✓✓ ✓✓ ✓✓	20
Butch ✓✓✓	Butch ✓✓✓✓✓✓	Butch ✓✓✓✓	Butch ✓✓✓✓	18
Charisa ✓✓✓	Charisa	Charisa ✓✓✓✓✓✓	Charisa	10
Dakota ✓✓✓	Dakota ✓✓✓✓✓✓	Dakota✓✓✓✓✓✓✓	Dakota✓✓✓✓✓✓✓	26
Gary ✓✓✓✓	Gary✓✓✓✓	Gary ✓✓✓✓	Gary✓✓✓✓✓	18
Greg ✓✓✓✓✓✓	Greg ✓✓✓✓✓✓✓	Greg✓✓✓✓✓✓✓✓	Greg✓✓✓✓✓✓✓	29
Jack ✓✓	Jack✓✓✓	Jack ✓✓✓✓✓✓✓	Jack✓✓✓✓✓✓	19
Karen ✓ ✓✓	Karen ✓✓✓✓✓	Karen ✓✓✓✓✓	Karen ✓✓✓✓✓✓✓	20
Mika ✓✓✓✓✓	Mika ✓✓✓	Mika ✓✓✓✓✓	Mika ✓✓✓✓✓✓✓	20
Malin ✓✓✓	Malin ✓✓	Malin ✓✓✓	Malin ✓✓	10
Sandy ✓	Sandy ✓✓	Sandy ✓✓✓✓✓✓✓	Sandy ✓✓	12
Scott ✓	Scott ✓✓✓✓✓✓✓	Scott ✓✓ ✓✓ ✓✓	Scott ✓✓✓✓✓✓✓	21
Shelby ✓✓	Shelby ✓✓ ✓✓	Shelby ✓✓✓✓✓✓✓	Shelby ✓✓✓✓✓	19
Suzie ✓✓✓✓✓	Suzie✓✓✓✓✓✓✓	Suzie ✓✓✓✓✓✓	Suzie ✓✓✓✓✓✓✓	29

(Continued)

Figure 21.1 (Continued)

B. Focus of Conversation

- Separate your CDC journals according to the *Focus of Conversation* recorded.
- Review each *Focus of Conversation*.
- List at least five topics depicted in the *Focus of Conversation* in the table below.
- List the first name of each beginning teacher under each of the topics that represents the *Focus of Conversation* that has been discussed during the *CDC Cycle*. If you have spent more than one session discussing one standard, put a ✓ by the name of the teacher.

Topics representing Focus of Conversation:				
Cooperative Learning	Strategies	Classroom Management	Lesson Design	Differentiated Instruction
Greg ✓✓✓	Aiden ✓✓✓	Aiden ✓✓✓✓✓✓	Aiden ✓✓✓	Gary ✓✓✓✓✓
Jack ✓✓✓✓✓	Anna ✓✓	Anna ✓✓✓	Anna ✓✓✓✓✓✓✓	Greg ✓✓✓✓✓✓✓
Karen ✓✓✓✓✓	Butch ✓✓✓✓	Butch ✓✓✓✓	Butch ✓✓✓	Jack ✓✓✓✓✓✓
Mika ✓✓✓	Charisa	Charisa ✓✓✓✓✓✓	Charisa ✓✓✓	Karen ✓✓✓✓✓✓
Malin ✓✓✓✓✓	Dakota ✓✓✓✓	Dakota ✓✓✓✓✓✓✓	Dakota ✓✓✓	Mika ✓✓✓✓✓✓✓
Sandy ✓✓✓	Gary ✓✓✓✓	Gary ✓✓✓✓	Gary ✓✓✓	Malin ✓✓
	Greg ✓✓✓✓✓	Greg ✓✓✓✓✓✓✓✓	Greg ✓✓✓✓✓	Sandy ✓✓
	Jack ✓✓✓	Jack ✓✓✓✓✓✓	Jack ✓✓	Scott ✓✓✓✓✓✓
	Karen ✓✓✓✓	Karen ✓✓✓✓✓	Karen ✓ ✓✓	Shelby ✓✓✓✓✓✓
		Mika ✓✓✓✓✓	Mika ✓✓✓✓✓	Suzie ✓✓✓✓✓✓✓
		Malin ✓✓✓	Malin ✓✓✓	
		Sandy ✓✓✓✓✓✓✓	Sandy ✓	
		Scott ✓✓ ✓✓ ✓✓	Scott ✓	
		Shelby ✓✓✓✓✓✓	Shelby ✓✓	
		Suzie ✓✓✓✓✓✓✓	Suzie ✓✓✓✓✓	

C. Equity of Time

- Review your monthly schedules recording the time spent with each beginning teacher. In the header row, identify the possible hours for each month. List the first name of each beginning teacher in the first column.
- List the number of hours spent with the beginning teacher under each month.
- In the last column, list the total number of hours spent and the number of possible hours that could have been spent over a six-month period depending on the number of days in school.

First Name of Beginning Teacher	Possible Hours Met per Month						
	1st Month = 4 hours	2nd Month = 8 hours	3rd Month = 8 hours	4th Month = 6 hours	5th Month = 6 hours	6th Month = 6 hours	Total = 38 hours
1. Aiden	4	8	8	6	5	6	37
2. Anna	4	8	8	5	6	6	37
3. Butch	4	8	8	6	6	6	38
4. Charisa	4	4	4	2	3	2	19
5. Dakota	4	4	5	4	4	5	26
6. Gary	4	2	3	3	2	3	18
7. Greg	6	10	10	6	10	6	48
8. Jack	4	8	8	6	6	6	38
9. Karen	4	8	8	6	6	6	38
10. Mika	4	8	8	6	6	6	38
11. Malin	4	4	4	3	3	3	21
12. Sandy	4	8	8	6	6	6	38
13. Scott	4	8	8	6	6	6	38
14. Shelby	4	8	8	6	6	6	38
15. Suzie	8	9	9	7	8	5	48

| Figure 21.2 | Description of Data |

Step 2: Description of the Data
- Review the three data pieces completed above.
- List the first names of teachers under each category and a short description of what you observe about that teacher.

Professional Teacher Standards	Focus of Conversation	Time in Hours
1. Aiden – working on implementing lesson design and assessment	Classroom management and lesson design	37
2. Anna – working on assessment	Lesson design	37
3. Butch – working on managing classroom	Strategies, classroom management, differentiated instruction	38
4. Charisa – needs to work on classroom management and assessment	Classroom management	19
5. Dakota – working on implementing lesson design and assessment	Classroom management and lesson design	26
6. Gary – working on assessment	Strategies, classroom management, differentiated instruction	18
7. Greg – working on all four standards	Strategies, classroom management, lesson design, differentiated instruction	48
8. Jack – working on implementing lesson design and assessment	Cooperative learning, classroom management, differentiated instruction	38
9. Karen – working on classroom management, implementing lesson design, and assessment	Cooperative learning, strategies, classroom management, lesson design, differentiated instruction	38
10. Mika – working on assessment	Classroom management, lesson design, differentiated instruction	38
11. Malin – do not have enough data	Cooperative learning	21
12. Sandy – working on implementing lesson design	Classroom management	38
13. Scott – working on classroom management, implementing lesson design, and assessment	Classroom management and differentiated instruction	38
14. Shelby – working on implementing lesson design and assessment	Classroom management and differentiated instruction	38
15. Suzie – working on all four standards	Classroom management, lesson design, differentiated instruction	48

Figure 21.3 Analysis of Data

Step 3: Analysis of Data

- List the name of any teacher who is an answer to the following:
  - Do you see any clusters of beginning teachers in any one category?
  - Do you see any beginning teachers who stand alone in any one category?
  - Is there any group of beginning teachers that you can identify as standing out more than any others?
  - Are there any teachers that seem to be stuck on one standard or one focus? Are there any teachers with whom you are not spending two hours per week?
  - Are there any teachers with whom you are spending more than two hours per week?
  - Are there any teachers with whom you have not had adequate planning, data collection, and reflective conferences?
  - Write any other descriptions to be considered.

Professional Teacher Standards	Focus of Conversation Write in Areas from Step 1 B.	Equity of Time
Designs Instruction Aiden Sandy Jack Dakota Shelby Malin? Greg Suzie	**Cooperative Learning** Greg Mika Jack Malin Karen Sandy	**Less than 2 hours per week:** Charisa - 19 Dakota - 26 Gary - 18 Malin - 21
Maintains Learning Environment Butch Karen Charisa Malin? Greg Scott Suzie	**Strategies** Aiden Charisa Greg Anna Dakota Jack Butch Gary Karen	
	Classroom Management All 15	
Implements Instruction Aiden Karen Scott Dakota Malin? Shelby Jack Sandy Suzie	**Lesson Design** All 15	**More than 2 hours per week:** Greg Suzie
Assessment Aiden Gary Malin? Anna Jack Scott Charisa Karen Shelby Dakota Mike Suzie	**Differentiated Instruction** Gary Mika Shelby Greg Milan Suzie Jack Sandy Karen Scott	

| Figure 21.4 | Diagnosis of Data |

Step 4: Diagnosis of Data

A. *Professional Teacher Standards* and *Focus of Conversation* Data

- Using the information from Step 2: Description of the Data and Step 3: Analysis of Data will assist you in determining which category best describes your beginning teachers. Place each teacher in one of the following:

Novice	Emergent	Proficient	Accomplished
Seeks rules and regulations, duplicates lessons in textbook, and tries to use previous learned formats, dependent on surviving the role of teacher.	Moves toward understanding basic classroom procedures, begins to apply new strategies while still dependent on textbook, rules, and regulations.	Implements strategies and classroom procedures to meet the academic needs of students, assessment drives instruction; decisions are made during the lesson that impact student learning.	Organizes multiple levels of classroom procedures simultaneously, meets the various developmental and academic needs of students through multifarious strategies, groups and regroups students based on skill levels.
	Aiden *Dakota* *Greg* *Suzie* *Malin*	*Anna* *Charisa* *Gary* *Sandy* *Anna* *Butch* *Jack* *Karen* *Mika* *Scott*	

B. Equity of Time Data

- Look at the beginning teachers with whom you are not spending two hours per week.
- Look at the beginning teachers with whom you are spending more than two hours per week.
- What are the reasons you are not spending more time with those teachers?
- What are the reasons you are spending more than two hours per week with those teachers?
- Is the time you are spending or not spending making a difference?

Less than two hours per week:	Reason:
Charisa	*Sick each day we have been scheduled to meet.*
Dakota	*Teacher has an attitude, I really don't like to meet with him*
Gary	*School conflicts during our meeting time: fire drill, pep rally*
Malin	*Skips out on meetings.*
More than two hours per week:	**Reason:**
Greg	*Very needy. Calls and emails all of the time requesting me.*
Suzie	*Phenomenal teacher, love her to pieces!*

| Figure 21.5 | Action Plan for Meeting Beginning Teachers' Needs |

Step 5: Action Plan for Meeting Beginning Teachers' Needs

A. *Professional Teacher Standards* and *Focus of Conversation* Data

- Look at the names of the teachers in each column from Step 4. Use the information from Step 3 to create strategies that you will use to support transformation of their practice.
- How might you support each group to transform their practice?
- What are some next steps?
- Write an action plan for each group of beginning teachers in order to support transformation of their practice.

Novice	Emergent	Proficient	Accomplished
	Aiden, Dakota, Greg, Malin, Suzie: *Work on planning for instruction to check the components of their lesson plan which will assist them in implementing instruction and classroom management*	*Anna, Butch, Charisa, Gary, Jack, Karen:* *Work on strategies for the classroom, then move into differentiated instruction* *Mika, Sandy, Scott, Shelby:* *Work on analyzing student work and based on that work, discuss and assist teachers to implement differentiated instruction*	

- What evidence can you collect that would document their growth?

Novice	Emergent	Proficient	Accomplished
	Look at lesson plans, collect data on time on task, collect data on questioning skills, complete CDC Journal Records with each conference	*Look at differentiated student groups after student work analysis, collect data on time on task, review differentiation as product, process, or content and collect data on each during classroom observations*	

(Continued)

| Figure 21.5 | (Continued) |

B. *Equity of Time* Data

- Write the first name of the beginning teacher in the first column with whom you are not spending two hours per week, an action plan in the next column, a timeline for change, and type of documentation for change.

- Repeat the process of those with whom you are spending more than two hours per week.

Less than two hours per week	Action Plan	Change Timeline & Documentation
Charisa	I thought she was proficient doing ok so I didn't worry about her – I will make sure she has 2 hours per week	March/Calendar
Dakota	Has an attitude and is emergent in his practice – I will spend 2 hours/week no matter what	March/Calendar
Gary	Is proficient but deserves the 2 hours/week – I will be more committed to the time	March/Calendar
Malin	Is emergent and needs assistance but does not recognize that I can help – I will be more persistent and schedule the time	March/Calendar
More than two hours per week:	**Action Plan:**	**Change Timeline & Documentation**
Greg	Will cut down on the hours and tell him his two hours is up for the week but I can schedule him for next week	March/Calendar
Suzie	Will cut down on the hours and tell her her two hours is up for the week but I can schedule her for next week	March/Calendar

HOW TO USE THE DIFFERENTIATED MENTORING TOOLS

The mentor supervisor introduces the concept of differentiated mentoring six months after school begins. By that time, the mentors have collected enough information to make some decisions regarding the needs of their beginning teachers. The supervisor describes each step, taking enough time for the mentors to process the information. Before the first session, the mentor supervisor asks all mentors to bring all of their documentation with them to the session including their monthly summaries of time spent and calendars, their CDC Journal Records, and their data collection tools. None of the specific information is to be shared with the supervisor so confidentiality is upheld. These documents are for the mentors' eyes only to see how they can further assist their teachers in transforming their practice. Each step will be taken one at a time, allowing each mentor the time it takes to organize the documents they brought with them.

Step 1: Organization of CDC Journal Records and Time Spent

The first step involves organizing the CDC Journal Records by looking at the professional teaching standards and the focus of conversation. The mentor will also identify the *equity of time* spent with each of their beginning teachers. It is important to first organize the information before you can begin to analyze and diagnose needs. The directions are as follows:

Step 1A: Professional Teaching Standards

- Separate your CDC Journal Records according to the professional teaching standards recorded. (See Chapter 4.)
- Review each professional teaching standard.
- List the first name of each beginning teacher under each of the standards that have been discussed during the CDC Cycle. If you have spent more than one session discussing one standard, place a checkmark by the name of the teacher.
- Write the total number of CDC Journal Records for each teacher. If you meet with your beginning teacher every week for six months, you will have a total of 24 journals. Not every calendar week is viable for conferencing so look at the total weeks possible and use that number as your possible number of journal records. Write that number at the top of the column.

Step 1B: Focus of Conversation

- Separate your CDC Journal Records according to the focus of conversation recorded.
- Review each focus of conversation.

- List at least five topics depicted in the focus of conversation.
- List the first name of each beginning teacher under each of the topics that represents the focus of conversation that has been discussed during the CDC Cycle. If you have spent more than one session discussing one standard, put a checkmark by the name of the teacher.

Step 1C: Equity of Time

- Review your monthly schedules recording the time spent with each beginning teacher. In the header row, identify the possible hours for each month.
- List the first name of each beginning teacher in the first column.
- List the number of hours spent with the beginning teacher under each month.
- In the last column, list the total number of hours spent and the number of possible hours that could have been spent over a six-month period depending on the number of days in school.

Step 2: Description of the Data

The mentors review the three data pieces they have just organized. The mentors then list the first name of each teacher under each category of professional teaching standards, focus of conversations, and time in hours. The mentor supervisor asks each mentor to write a short description of what they observe about that teacher. As the mentors examine the data, they will begin to look for patterns that exist.

Step 3: Analysis of Data

The mentor supervisor asks the mentors the following guided questions:

- Do you see any clusters of beginning teachers in any one category?
- Do you see any beginning teachers who stand alone in any one category?
- Is there any group of beginning teachers who you can identify as standing out more than any others?
- Are there any teachers who seem to be stuck on one standard or one focus?
- Are there any teachers with whom you are not spending two hours per week?
- Are there any teachers with whom you are spending more than two hours per week?
- Are there any teachers with whom you have not had adequate planning, data collection, and reflective conferences?

By reflecting on these questions, the mentors will begin to see their beginning teachers in a different way. They will begin to see patterns of their own performance as they look at the performance of their beginning teachers.

Step 4: Diagnosis of Data

The mentor supervisor asks the mentors to place their beginning teachers in one of the following categories using the descriptions they wrote in Step 2 and Step 3:

- Novice: Seeks rules and regulations, duplicates lessons in textbook and tries to use previous learned formats, dependent on surviving the role of teacher.
- Emergent: Moves toward understanding basic classroom procedures, begins to apply new strategies while still dependent on textbook, rules, and regulations.
- Proficient: Implements strategies and classroom procedures to meet the academic needs of students, assessment drives instruction; decisions are made during the lesson that impact student learning.
- Accomplished: Organizes multiple levels of classroom procedures simultaneously, meets the various developmental and academic needs of students through multifarious strategies, groups and regroups students based on skill levels.

Looking at equity of time in Step 3, the mentor supervisor asks the mentors to look at the beginning teachers with whom they are not spending two hours per week and to look at the beginning teachers with whom they are spending more than two hours per week. The mentor supervisor then asks these guiding questions:

- What are the reasons you are not spending more time with those teachers?
- What are the reasons you are spending more than two hours per week with those teachers?
- Is the time you are spending or not spending making a difference?

Step 5: Action Plan for Meeting Beginning Teachers' Needs

The mentors continue to follow the process by writing the first name of the beginning teacher in the first column with whom they are not spending two hours per week, an action plan in the next column, a timeline for change, and the type of documentation for change. The mentors will repeat the process of those with whom they are spending more than two hours per week. The process for Step 5 is as follows.

The mentor supervisor asks the mentors to use the information from Step 3 to create strategies they will use to support transformation of their beginning teachers' practice. The following guiding questions assist the mentors in their thinking:

- How might you support each group to support transformation of their practice forward?
- What are some next steps?

Each mentor then writes an action plan for each beginning teacher in order to support transformation of their practice. It is important to remember that each teacher is equally important and each teacher has individual needs.

DIFFERENTIATED MENTORING TOOLS IN ACTION

Lori, the mentor supervisor, calls an all day session for meeting with the mentors. Each mentor brought his CDC Journal Records, his monthly calendar which summarizes all of the activity and time spent with each beginning teacher, as well as any data collection tools. Lori explains that all documentation is confidential and only the first names of each beginning teacher will be used. No one is to share the names or the documentation with anyone else.

Organizing the data takes one hour. The mentors complete Steps 1–4 within a three-hour period. Lori is most concerned with the action plan each mentor needs to complete for each beginning teacher in order to support transformation of the teachers' practice.

Lori directs the mentors to Step 5: Action Plan for Meeting Beginning Teachers' Needs. She asks each mentor to write the first name of the beginning teacher in the first column that they are not spending two hours per week, an action plan in the next column, a timeline for change, and type of documentation for change. Lori asks them to repeat the process for those with whom they are spending more than two hours per week. Lori asks them to think about, "Why are you not spending the required number of hours with that teacher? What will you change so you will spend the two hours per week with each teacher?" (Figure 21.6).

The mentors discuss with each other some of the reasons that occur. "Some teachers need more time than others."

Lori responds by asking them, "Has spending more time with that teacher transformed his or her practice?" The mentors have to admit the teacher's practice has not changed. Lori and the mentors brainstorm some suggestions for those that constantly request more time such as, "I will be more than happy to assist you, but this week's calendar is full. What time

| Figure 21.6 | Differentiated Mentoring Analysis of Beginning Teacher Development |

Step 5: Action Plan for Meeting Beginning Teachers' Needs

A. *Professional Teacher Standards* and *Focus of Conversation* Data

- Look at the names of the teachers in each column from Step 4. Use the information from Step 3 to create strategies that you will use to support transformation of their practice.
- How might you support each group to transform their practice?
- What are some next steps?
- Write an action plan for each group of beginning teachers in order to support transformation of their practice.

Novice	Emergent	Proficient	Accomplished
Angela – work on writing an objective and completing a task analysis before designing a lesson plan	Briana, Tom, George All have issues with classroom management so I will start by reviewing the templates for lesson design and go back over planning for instruction so that the lesson is in alignment Cynthia and Kelsy have problems delivering their lesson so we will take one section at a time and analyze what part of the lesson is a problem for them and have them create a script for them to follow.	Rebecca, Kimberly, Tyler, Dean, Simon, Elizabeth, Luke, Debby, Jerry, Ellie, Trudi Since they are all proficient, I will work individually with them to find out what there next interest might be: differentiated instruction, task analysis, cooperative learning groups, etc. Individual conferences will determine what our action plan will be for the remainder of the year.	There was no one in this area of development.

- What evidence can you collect that would document their growth?

Novice	Emergent	Proficient	Accomplished
Objective worksheet, task analysis, lesson plans	CDC Journal Records to document conversations and focus conversations for what is needed. Also, use classroom data collection tool for scripting and keeping time for how much time is spent on each section of the lesson plan.	Individual conferences documented with CDC Journal Records and action plans for follow-up on an individual basis.	There was no one in this area of development.

(Continued)

| Figure 21.6 | (Continued) |

B. *Equity of Time* Data

- Write the first name of the beginning teacher in the first column with whom you are not spending two hours per week, an action plan in the next column, a timeline for change, and type of documentation for change.
- Repeat the process of those with whom you are spending more than two hours per week.

Less than two hours per week	Action Plan	Change Timeline & Documentation
Briana Tom George	*Each one is unique but they all do not want me in their classroom. I will make an appointment and show up each time for two hours per week and attempt to follow the CDC Cycle. Since they have already seen the Breaking Confidentiality Protocol (see Chapter 5), I will follow the process and tell them I am speaking to the administrator about their actions.*	*I will discuss the plan of action with the teachers at our next meeting. I plan to contact their administrator as soon as I notify each individual.* *CDC Journal Records and weekly calendar. Document breaking confidentiality.*

More than two hours per week	Action Plan	Change Timeline & Documentation
Cynthia Kelsy	*I will use the following each time they call: "I will be more than happy to assist you, but this week's calendar is full. What time would be convenient for you next week?"* *I will also begin to suggest individuals on their campus they might seek for additional assistance.*	*I will implement my plan at our next meetings.* *Weekly calendar—two hours per week only*

would be convenient for you next week?" The mentors agree that will be a strategy they can use.

The mentors share with Lori that some of the beginning teachers do not keep their appointment or they have a resistant attitude. Lori and the mentors brainstorm some strategies. One strategy that emerges is for the mentors to keep the appointment and follow the CDC Cycle. If the beginning teacher persists in not meeting and following the expectations, the mentor will follow the process for the Breaking Confidentiality Protocol. The mentors share with Lori that they did this within three months of the program. The teachers followed the expectations for one and a half months but then they were back at breaking appointments and not meeting the expectations of the program. Lori encouraged the mentors to present the protocol once again, provide the documentation to the teacher, and immediately follow the process since the teacher once again broke the agreement.

Each mentor looks at the names of the teachers in each column from Step 4: Novice, Emergent, Proficient, and Accomplished. Lori tells them to use the information from Step 3 to create strategies that they will use to support transformation of their beginning teachers' practice. She asks them some guiding questions, "How might you support each teacher to transform his or her practice forward? What are some next steps?" They brainstorm the possibility of using a task analysis or creating cooperative learning groups or using differentiated instruction. Lori asks each mentor to write an action plan for each beginning teacher in order to support transformation of his or her practice. They discuss the importance of each teacher and how each teacher has individual needs in the same way as students in a classroom have individual needs.

NOTES FOR IMPLEMENTATION

Differentiated mentoring is usually introduced during the fifth or sixth month of the school year. This timeline depends on the experience of the mentors. As each student in a teacher's classroom is unique and has individual needs that are to be met, so does each individual beginning teacher. As the mentor determines what specific needs teachers have, the mentor can plan for the rest of the school year in order to support the transformation of each and every one of her beginning teachers' practice.

Figure 21.7 Differentiated Mentoring Analysis of Beginning Teacher Development

Mentor: _____ Date: _____

Step 1: Organization of *CDC Journal Records* and Equity of Time Spent

A. Professional Teaching Standards

- Separate your *CDC Journals Records* according to the *Professional Teaching Standards* recorded.
- Review each *Professional Teaching Standard*.
- List the first name of each beginning teacher under each of the standards that has been discussed during the *CDC Cycle*. If you have spent more than one session discussing one standard, put a ✓ by the name of the teacher.
- Write the total number of *CDC Journal Records* for each teacher. If you meet with your beginning teacher every week for six months, you will have a total of 24 journals. Not every calendar week is viable for conferencing so look at the total weeks possible and use that number as your possible number of journal records. Write that number at the top of the column.

Designs and Plans Instruction	Creates and Maintains Learning Environment	Implements and Manages Instruction	Assesses Learning	Possible # of *CDC Journal Records* =

B. *Focus of Conversation*

- Separate your CDC journals according to the *Focus of Conversation* recorded
- Review each *Focus of Conversation.*
- List at least five topics depicted in the *Focus of Conversation* in the table below.
- List the first name of each beginning teacher under each of the topics that represents the *Focus of Conversation* that has been discussed during the *CDC Cycle.* If you have spent more than one session discussing one standard, put a ✓ by the name of the teacher.

Topics representing *Focus of Conversation:*				

(Continued)

Figure 21.6 (Continued)

C. Equity of Time

- Review your monthly schedules recording the time spent with each beginning teacher. In the header row, identify the possible hours for each month.
- List the first name of each beginning teacher in the first column below.
- List the number of hours spent with the beginning teacher under each month.
- In the last column, list the total number of hours spent and the number of possible hours that could have spent over a six-month period depending on the number of days in school.

First Name of Beginning Teacher	Possible Hours Met per Month						
	1st Month =	2nd Month =	3rd Month =	4th Month =	5th Month =	6th Month =	Total =
1.							
2.							
3.							
4.							
5.							
6.							
7.							
8.							
9.							
10.							
11.							
12.							
13.							
14.							
15.							

Step 2: Description of the Data
- Review the three data pieces completed above.
- List the first names of teachers under each category and a short description of what you observe about that teacher.

Professional Teacher Standards	Focus of Conversation	Time in Hours
1.		
2.		
3.		
4.		
5.		
6.		
7.		
8.		
9.		
10.		
11.		
12.		
13.		
14.		
15.		

(Continued)

| Figure 21.6 | (Continued) |

Step 3: Analysis of Data

- List the name of any teacher who is an answer to the following:
  - o Do you see any clusters of beginning teachers in any one category?
  - o Do you see any beginning teachers who stand alone in any one category?
  - o Is there any group of beginning teachers that you can identify as standing out more than any others?
  - o Are there any teachers that seem to be stuck on one standard or one focus?
  - o Are there any teachers with whom you are not spending two hours per week?
  - o Are there any teachers with whom you are spending more than two hours per week?
  - o Are there any teachers with whom you have not had adequate planning, data collection, and reflective conferences?
  - o Write any other descriptions to be considered.

Professional Teacher Standards	Focus of Conversation Write in Areas from Step 1 B.	Equity of Time
Designs Instruction		Less than 2 hours per week:
Maintains Learning Environment		
Implements Instruction		More than 2 hours per week:
Assessment		

Step 4: Diagnosis of Data
A. *Professional Teacher Standards* and *Focus of Conversation* Data

- Using the information from Step 2: Description of the Data and Step 3: Analysis of Data will assist you in determining which category best describes your beginning teachers. Place each teacher in one of the following:

Novice	Emergent	Proficient	Accomplished
Seeks rules and regulations, duplicates lessons in textbook and tries to use previous learned formats, dependent on surviving the role of teacher.	Moves toward understanding basic classroom procedures, begins to apply new strategies while still dependent on textbook, rules, and regulations.	Implements strategies and classroom procedures to meet the academic needs of students, assessment drives instruction; decisions are made during the lesson that impact student learning.	Organizes multiple levels of classroom procedures simultaneously, meets the various developmental and academic needs of students through multifarious strategies, groups and regroups students based on skill levels.

B. Equity of Time Data

- Look at the beginning teachers with whom you are not spending two hours per week.
- Look at the beginning teachers with whom you are spending more than two hours per week.
- What are the reasons you are not spending more time with those teachers?
- What are the reasons you are spending more than two hours per week with those teachers?
- Is the time you are spending or not spending making a difference?

Less than two hours per week:	Reason:
More than two hours per week:	**Reason:**

(Continued)

Figure 21.6	(Continued)

Step 5: Action Plan for Meeting Beginning Teachers' Needs

A. *Professional Teacher Standards* and *Focus of Conversation* Data

- Look at the names of the teachers in each column from Step 4. Use the information from Step 3 to create strategies that you will use to support transformation of their practice.
- How might you support each group to transform their practice?
- What are some next steps?
- Write an action plan for each group of beginning teachers in order to support transformation of their practice.

Novice	Emergent	Proficient	Accomplished

- What evidence can you collect that would document their growth?

Novice	Emergent	Proficient	Accomplished

B. *Equity of Time* Data

- Write the first name of the beginning teacher in the first column with whom you are not spending two hours per week, an action plan in the next column, a timeline for change, and type of documentation for change.
- Repeat the process of those with whom you are spending more than two hours per week.

Less than two hours per week	Action Plan	Change Timeline & Documentation

More than two hours per week	Action Plan	Change Timeline & Documentation

22

Reflecting on One's Practice

PURPOSE FOR REFLECTING ON ONE'S PRACTICE

Beginning teachers, teachers with new assignments, and mentors transition through the Transformational Learning stages during a single school year. This translates into what can be an amazing evolution of practice from the first day of school to the last day of school. As summer approaches it is wise for those engaged in this process to break from the rush to the end and to reflect on their experiences (Figure 22.1).

In Chapter 1 we stated that beginning teachers need to "see themselves in their practice as they really are and reflect on their experiences over a period of time." Taking the time to formally reflect at the end of the year to identify celebrations and continuing challenges provides both closure and ensures lessons learned during the year will not be forgotten. With eight months of student and teacher observable data in hand, beginning teachers and mentors can use the following tools to record these reflections, converting them into artifacts of the year's practice: *A Look Back: Then and Now, Transformational Learning stages: Reflection for Beginning Teachers, Transformational Learning stages: Reflection for Mentors, Beginning Teacher New Year Action Plan: Continuing the Transformation,* and *Mentor New Year Action plan: Continuing the Transformation.*

These end-of-the-year reflections compliment the three cycles of transformative assessment: role focused, practice focused, and learner focused

Figure 22.1   Transformational Learning Stages

Stage 1: Role Focused

Teacher
- Chapter 4: CDC Journal Record
- Chapter 5: Beginning Conversations
- Chapter 7: Professional Teacher Growth Process

Mentor
- Chapter 1: Transforming Practice
- Chapter 2: CDC Cycle
- Chapter 3: Foundations for Mentoring
- Chapter 4: CDC Journal Record
- Chapter 5: Beginning Conversations
- Chapter 6: Administrator and Mentor Conversation
- Chapter 8: Professional Mentor Growth Process

Stage 2: Practice Focused

Teacher
- Chapter 11: Observing a Master Teacher
- Chapter 12: Student Data Mapping
- Chapter 13: Planning for Instruction
- Chapter 14: Lesson Design
- Chapter 15: Videotaping as a Process for Reflection
- Chapter 17: Probing Higher Level Thinking

Mentor
- Chapter 9: Collecting Evidence: Teacher and Student Behaviors
- Chapter 10: Collecting Evidence: Teacher and Student Verbal Interactions
- Chapter 11: Observing a Master Teacher
- Chapter 12: Student Data Mapping
- Chapter 13: Planning for Instruction
- Chapter 14: Lesson Design
- Chapter 15: Videotaping as a Process for Reflection
- Chapter 16: Collecting Evidence: Student Engagement
- Chapter 17: Probing Higher Level Thinking

Stage 3: Learner Focused

Teacher
- Chapter 18: Analyzing Student Work
- Chapter 19: Planning for Differentiated Instruction
- Chapter 20: Analyzing Student Assessments
- Chapter 22: Reflecting on One's Practice

Mentor
- Chapter 18: Analyzing Student Work
- Chapter 19: Planning for Differentiated Instruction
- Chapter 20: Analyzing Student Assessments
- Chapter 21: Planning for Differentiated Mentoring
- Chapter 22: Reflecting on One's Practice

as well as the self-assessment of practice described in Chapter 7 for teachers and Chapter 8 for mentors. This process of transformational learning develops lifelong learners who continuously seek ways to improve their practice and impact the lives of students.

DESCRIPTION OF REFLECTING ON ONE'S PRACTICE

The A Look Back: Then and Now (Figure 22.2) is a simple tool designed to guide a reflective discussion between the beginning teacher and mentor. Mentors can also use this tool when reflecting with another mentor. Recollections of behaviors exhibited at the beginning of the year are recorded for the following categories: I felt, I said, I did, and I thought. Behaviors exhibited at the end of the year in these same categories are identified and recorded. This tool can be used to stimulate recall in preparation for using the Transformational Stages: Reflection for Beginning Teachers or Transformational Stages: Reflection for Mentors tools.

The Transformational Learning stages: Reflection for Beginning Teachers (Figure 22.3) or Transformational Learning stages: Reflection for Mentors (Figure 22.4) tools provide a formal structure for reflecting on a school year's worth of data and experience. Beginning teachers and mentors identify a celebration and challenge for each of components from the Transformational Learning stages. In addition, they identify an overarching celebration and challenge for each of the three stages.

The Beginning Teacher New Year Action plan: Continuing the Transformation (Figure 22.5) and Mentor New Year Action plan: Continuing the Transformation tools (Figure 22.6) provide a structure for transforming the year-end Transformational Learning stages reflections into a professional action plan for the following school year.

HOW TO USE THE REFLECTING ON ONE'S PRACTICE TOOLS

During the second-to-last reflective conference, the mentor provides the beginning teacher with a copy of the A Look Back: Then and Now, Transformational Learning stages: Reflection for Beginning Teachers, and the Beginning Teacher New Year Action plan: Continuing the Transformation tools. With the mentor's guidance, the beginning teacher completes the A Look Back: Then and Now. Together they review the Transformational Learning stages: Reflection for Beginning Teachers, and the Beginning Teacher New Year Action plan: Continuing the Transformation tools. The beginning teacher may ask questions to clarify her understanding of the stages and components. The beginning teacher completes the reflection and action planning on her own. These may be included in a professional

(Text continues on page 327.)

Figure 22.2 A Look Back: Then and Now

Beginning of the Year		End of the Year
- OVERWHELMED - Unsure why I decided to take this job	I Felt	- TIRED - Proud for making it through the year
- Way too much - Used a loud voice	I Said	- Succinct directions - Used a regular voice and tried not to raise mine as the students raised theirs
- Did not plan enough instruction - Worked all the time even on weekends	I Did	- Planned enough instruction even a little too much sometimes - Took time each weekend to do an activity I enjoyed
- What made me think I could teach anyone drama? - What if our performances are terrible? -What if the kids hate me? - I want them to like me, but I am worried they will not take me seriously as a teacher since I am only 4-7 years older than them	I Thought	- I did pretty good job with the students I had - I have much to learn - I need to find a mentor to talk to - Remember I am their teacher not their friend

Figure 22.3 Transformational Learning Stages: Reflection for Beginning Teachers

For each component identify one celebration and one remaining challenge.
For each stage identify an overall celebration and one remaining challenge.

	Transformational Learning Stage		
	Stage 1: Role Focused	**Stage 2: Practice Focused**	**Stage 3: Learner Focused**
Component Celebrations	☆ *Relationship with my mentor*	☆ *Designing lesson plans*	☆ *Reflecting on my practice*
Component Challenges	✓ *Classroom management strategies from CDC Journal Record*	✓ *Planning for instructional strategies*	✓ *Analyzing student assessments* ✓ *Plan differentiated lessons*
Overall Celebration and Challenge	☆ *Relationship with my mentor* ✓ *Review CDC Journal Records to see what I still need to work on*	☆ *Lesson plan design* ✓ *Student data mapping*	☆ *Reflection* ✓ *Analyzing student work*

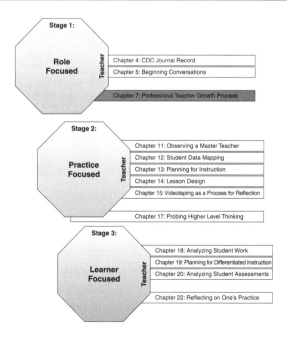

Figure 22.4 Transformational Learning Stages: Reflection for Mentors

For each component identify one celebration and one remaining challenge.
For each stage identify an overall celebration and one remaining challenge.

	Transformational Learning Stage		
	Stage 1: Role Focused	**Stage 2: Practice Focused**	**Stage 3: Learner Focused**
Component Celebrations	☆ *Attaining knowledge regarding mentoring*	☆ *Classroom data collection tools*	☆ *Differentiating my beginning teachers*
Component Challenges	✓ *Knowing when to use the correct stance and mentor language*	✓ *Identify beginning teachers' learning styles*	✓ *Work on analyzing student assessments*
Overall Celebration and Challenge	☆ *Knowledge gained* ✓ *Analyzing CDC Journal Records and making mentoring decisions based on data*	☆ *Implementing classroom data tools* ✓ *Create teacher data maps according to characteristics*	☆ *Differentiating my mentoring skills based on my teachers* ✓ *Identifying additional strategies for use when I differentiate my teachers*

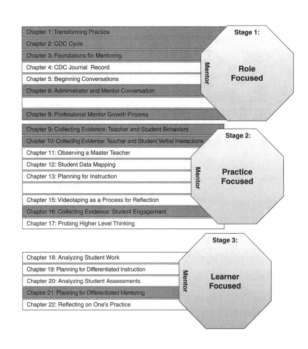

Figure 22.5 Beginning Teacher New Year Action Plan: Continuing the Transformation

- Referring to your *Transformational Learning Stages Reflection* sheet, select the challenges you wish to address each quarter and record them below.
- You may also make note of your celebrations to ensure you continue that practice in the coming year.
- Make sure you store this where you can find it after the summer.

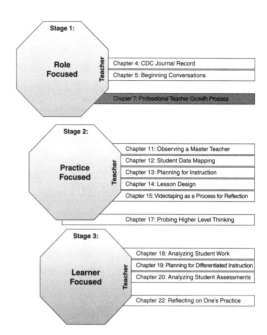

First Quarter	Second Quarter
- *Identify two students in each class to teach new students classroom routines* - *Ask department chair who to call at the district office for various purposes* - *Learn two new instructional strategies*	- *Learn two new instructional strategies* - *Use one new method for differentiating instruction* - *Develop a more efficient and valid strategy for evaluating students performance*
Third Quarter	**Fourth Quarter**
- *Learn two new instructional strategies* - *Use one new method for differentiating instruction* - *Have lesson plans written for two weeks at a time*	- *Learn two new instructional strategies* - *Create a system for conducting a detailed analysis of student work using a variety of different types of assignments and/or assessments*

Figure 22.6 Mentor New Year Action Plan: Continuing the Transformation

- Referring to your Transformational Learning Stages Reflection sheet, select the challenges you wish to address each quarter and record them below.
- You may also make note of your celebrations to ensure you continue that practice in the coming year.
- Make sure you store this where you can find it after the summer.

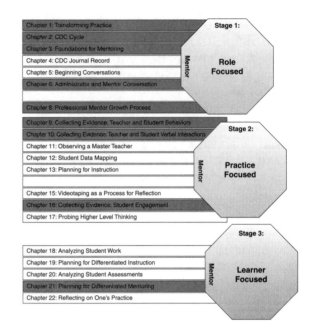

First Quarter	Second Quarter
- Consciously practice showing neutral feelings - Collect all profiles during the first two weeks of school - Practice mentor stances and mentor language - Create teacher data maps to identify beginning teachers' characteristics such as learning styles more quickly	- Identify strategies for working with beginning teachers that are not moving their practice forward; they are stuck - Develop system to track the types of situations I run into and the tool that worked the best - Track what is happening with my teachers to prepare for differentiating
Third Quarter	**Fourth Quarter**
- Focus on analyzing data from logs and making mentoring decisions based on that data - Develop various strategies to use when I differentiate my teachers	- Reflect on my own skills to see if I am performing at a higher level than last year - Create a system for conducting a detailed analysis of student work using a variety of different types of assignments and/or assessments

portfolio. During their last reflective conference the mentor asks the beginning teacher if they would like to share their reflection and action plan.

The mentor supervisor presents the A Look Back: Then and Now, Transformational Learning stages: Reflection for Mentors, and the Mentor New Year Action plan: Continuing the Transformation during the mentors' last professional workshop of the school year. They are provided time to complete these tools during the meeting. They should have all their beginning teacher data and professional growth plans with them to reference.

REFLECTING ON ONE'S PRACTICE TOOLS IN ACTION

During the last mentor workshop, the mentor supervisor has mentors work in pairs to complete A Look Back: Then and Now (Figure 22.7). Her goal is to get them thinking about the year as a whole and how much their practice has developed since the beginning of the year. After each one of the partners completes the tool, the mentors share what they thought was the most interesting change in their own mentoring practice.

NOTES FOR IMPLEMENTATION

Through the professional growth planning process and the CDC Cycle, both beginning teachers and mentors reflect on their practice and use the observations to move their practice forward. In many cases, these reflections are directly related to a specific lesson or particular skill. This end-of-year reflection and planning process enables both to look at their practice holistically. Because beginning teachers may just feel relieved to have survived the year, it is vital that they are encouraged to take the time to complete these end-of-year reflections. One strategy is to compile these tools as culminating documents in their professional portfolios. Another practice is to have a day of celebration at which beginning teachers share what they thought was the most interesting change in their own teaching practice.

Figure 22.7   A Look Back: Then and Now

Beginning of the Year		End of the Year
- Odd not having my own classroom to get ready!	I Felt	- It is still strange being in a different place each day, but I am beginning to like it
- Telling my beginning teachers you can just do it this way	I Said	- There are many ways of addressing this issue such as … Which one do you think would work the best for you?
- Bought fast food between conferences and ate in the car	I Did	- At least twice a week made my own healthy lunch and ate lunch with another mentor or one of my beginning teachers
- Why in the world did I agree to take this job?!!	I Thought	- Wow! I cannot wait until next year. I have so many ideas to try with my beginning teachers

Figure 22.8 A Look Back: Then and Now

Beginning of the Year		End of the Year
	I Felt	
	I Said	
	I Did	
	I Thought	

Figure 22.9 Transformational Learning Stages: Reflection for Beginning Teachers

For each component identify one celebration and one remaining challenge.
For each stage identify an overall celebration and one remaining challenge.

	Transformational Learning Stage		
	Stage 1: Role Focused	**Stage 2: Practice Focused**	**Stage 3: Learner Focused**
Component Celebrations			
Component Challenges			
Overall Celebration and Challenge			

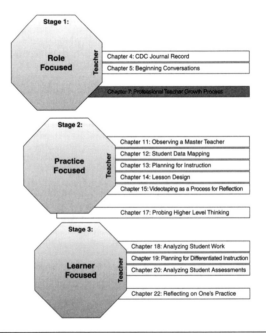

Figure 22.10 Transformational Learning Stages: Reflection for Mentors

For each component identify one celebration and one remaining challenge.
For each stage identify an overall celebration and one remaining challenge.

	Transformational Learning Stage		
	Stage 1: Role Focused	**Stage 2: Practice Focused**	**Stage 3: Learner Focused**
Component Celebrations			
Component Challenges			
Overall Celebration and Challenge			

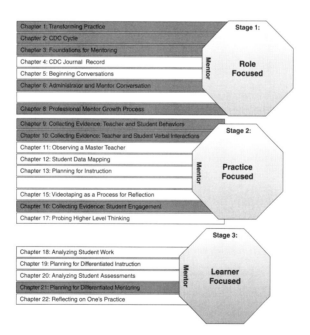

| Figure 22.11 | Beginning Teacher New Year Action Plan: Continuing the Transformation |

- Referring to your *Transformational Learning Stages: Reflection for Beginning Teachers* tool, select the challenges you wish to address each quarter and record them below.
- You may also make note of your celebrations to ensure you continue that practice in the coming year.
- Make sure you store this where you can find it after the summer.

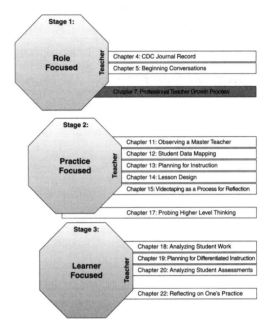

First Quarter	Second Quarter

Third Quarter	Fourth Quarter

Figure 22.12 Mentor New Year Action Plan: Continuing the Transformation

- Referring to your *Transformational Learning Stages Reflection: Reflection for Mentors* tool, select the challenges you wish to address each quarter and record them below.
- You may also make note of your celebrations to ensure you continue that practice in the coming year.
- Make sure you store this where you can find it after the summer.

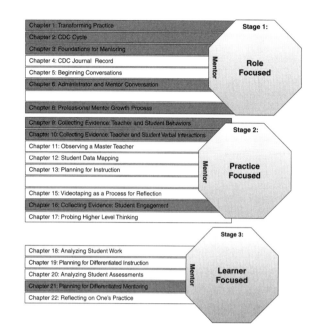

First Quarter	Second Quarter

Third Quarter	Fourth Quarter

Resources

Resource A: Research Summary

Research Connecting Full-Time Mentors, Induction, Mentor Responsibilities, Professional Development, Quality Teaching, Student Achievement, Teacher Development, and Teacher Retention	
Full-Time Mentors	
Researcher	**Findings**
Huling-Austin, 1992	1. Mentors are an important element of a successful induction program.
Moir & Gless, 2001	2. New teachers who participate in systemic professional development through an organized program with full-time mentors remain in the profession at a higher rate than teachers who do not.
Induction Program	
Researcher	**Findings**
Algozzine, Gretes, Queen, & Cowan-Hathcock, 2007; Howe, 2006; Killeavy, 2006; Stansbury & Zimmerman, 2000	1. The topics of professional development for new teachers include: a. Instructional strategies b. Classroom management c. Interactions with parents and community members d. Time management strategies e. Relationships with administrators and peers f. Diverse and unfamiliar cultures g. Professional isolation h. Self-understanding through reflection

Horn & Sterling, 2002	2. Nine common elements were identified in a literature review for an induction program: a. Orientation b. Time c. Adjust working conditions d. Formal mentoring e. Professional development opportunities f. Opportunities for collegial collaboration g. Teacher assessment h. Ongoing program evaluation i. Induction continuum
Stroot, Fowlkes, Langholz, Paxton, Stedman, Steffes, & Valtman, 1999	3. New teachers who receive induction support move beyond basic management concerns and make better use of: a. Instructional time b. Improve planning skills c. Unit preparation d. Better communication with parents and colleagues
Varah, Theune, & Parker, 1986	4. An induction program is an effective way to: a. Develop excellent staff b. Retain new teachers c. Provide documentation for classroom accountability through quality teaching d. Increase performance of the organization

Mentor Responsibilities	
Researcher	**Findings**
Algozzine, Gretes, Queen, & Cowan-Hathcock, 2007; Arends & Regazio-DiGilio, 2000	1. Mentors conduct formative observations.
Arends & Regazio-DiGilio, 2000	2. Regular, face-to-face contact between the mentor and the new teacher is vital.
Dagenais, 1996	3. Mentors discuss strengths and areas of concern during regular meetings with the beginning teacher; then formulate an action plan to strengthen the novice's instruction and environment.

Professional Development	
Researcher	**Findings**
Arends & Regazio-DiGilio, 2000	1. Mentors increase knowledge of adult learner characteristics.
Corcoran, 2007; Ganser & Koskela, 1997; Fieman-Nemser, 1996	2. Mentors must receive formal well-designed professional development for effective mentoring.
Freiberg & Driscoll, 2000	3. Professional development implements ongoing research-based instructional strategies.
Garten, Hudson, & Gossen, 1994	4. Mentors must develop an understanding of new teacher characteristics.
Huling-Austin, 1992	5. Mentors build a trusting relationship with each beginning teacher.
Ingersoll, 2007; Lovo, Cavazos, & Simmons, 2006; Wong, Britton, & Ganser, 2005	6. Professional development opportunities are sustained, well structured, and delivered in multiple formats: a. Job embedded b. One on one c. Conversations d. Classroom visits e. Minicourses f. Workshops

Ingersoll & Smith, 2003	7. Mentors must understand the research-based rationale for supporting new teachers.
Lopez, Lash, Schaffner, Shields, & Wagner, 2004; Anderson & Pelliceer, 2001	8. Ongoing professional development for mentors is a key component of an induction program.
Moir & Gless, 2001	9. Professional development opportunities address and align with professional standards.
	10. Mentors acquire a variety of coaching techniques
	11. Mentors develop multiple methods of classroom observation skills.
Stansbury & Zimmerman, 2000	12. New teachers have the opportunity to develop and implement a professional growth plan.
Walsdorf & Lynn, 2002	13. Mentors need to develop skills for identifying the needs and concerns of novice teachers.
Wong-Park, 1997; Dianda, Ward, Quarta, Tushnet, Radio, & Bailey, 1991	14. Mentors collect and analyze evidence of student learning and effective instruction.

Quality Teaching

Researcher	**Findings**
Allen & Casbergue, 2000	1. Effective teachers incorporate reflective practice.
Covino & Iwanicki, 1996	2. Quality teachers develop an increased depth of understanding about the content and how to teach it to students.
Darling-Hammond, 2000	3. Collegial settings tend to help teachers improve throughout their careers.
Glass, 2001; Durall, 1995	4. Effective teachers learn and use various strategies to meet students' needs.
Hanushek, Kain & Rivkin, 2004; Wang, Coleman, Coley & Phelps, 2003; Jordan, Mendro, & Weerasinghe, 1997; Sanders & Rivers, 1996	5. A link between high levels of achievement and the quality of instruction exists.
Ingersoll, 2007	6. Schools must develop and retain quality teachers.

Reynolds, 1992	7. High quality teachers learn how to maximize their usage of instructional materials, manage the classroom, and have working relationships with others.
Rivkin, Hanushek, & Kain, 2005	8. Teacher quality increases significantly during the first three years of teaching.

Student Achievement

Researcher	Findings
Darling-Hammond, 2000	1. A link exists between high levels of achievement and the quality of instruction.
Horn, Blair, & Metler-Armijo, 2008	2. First year teacher student achievement scores are equal to or greater than veteran teacher student achievement scores over a two year pattern having a full-time mentor.
Villar, Strong, & Fletcher, 2005	3. Greater student achievement gains are realized as a result of intensive induction sustained over two years.

Teacher Development & Performance

Researcher	Findings
Berliner, 1994	1. Five stages of teacher development from novice to expert
Danielson, 1996	2. Four levels of teacher performance from unsatisfactory to distinguished
Fuller & Bown, 1975	3. Three stages of teacher development, differentiated by teachers' main preoccupations
Moir, Freeman, Petrock, & Baron, 1997	4. Three stages of novice teachers' development from emerging phase to integrating phase
Moir, Freeman, Petrock, & Baron, 1997	5. Continuum of five stages of teacher abilities from beginning to innovating

Teacher Retention	
Researcher	**Findings**
Horn, Lussier, Metler-Armijo, & Blair, 2007	1. Retention increases for beginning teachers with a full-time mentor.
Ingersoll, 2007	2. Teachers do not leave the profession due to lack of content knowledge but rather to job dissatisfaction and lack of support with the system.
	3. The majority of teachers leave the profession within five years.
Ingersoll & Kralik, 2004	4. Induction and mentoring are a means of reducing high teacher turnover.
Veenman, 1984	5. The more problems a teacher encounters, the more likely he or she is to leave teaching.

Resource B: Practices and Tools Introduced Throughout the Chapters

Chapter Introduced	Practices and Tools
Section I: Role Focused Stage	
Chapter 1	1. Transformational Learning Stages
	2. Managing Transformational Learning
Chapter 2	3. Conference Data Conference (CDC) Cycle
Chapter 3	4. Mentor Stances
	5. Mentor Roles
	6. Mentor Language
Chapter 4	7. Conference Data Conference (CDC) Journal Record—NCR
Chapter 5	8. Mentor–Beginning Teacher Confidentiality Agreement—NCR
	9. Breaking Confidentiality Protocol
	10. Teacher Profile—NCR
	11. Mentor Profile—NCR
	12. Community and School Resources—NCR
Chapter 6	13. Administrator and Mentor Journal Record—NCR
Chapter 7	14. Framework of Professional Growth Teacher Practice Standard 1
	15. Professional Practice Teacher Self-Assessment Checklist Standards 1–3
	16. Establishing Professional Teacher Growth Priorities
	17. Professional Teacher Growth (PTG) Plan—NCR
	18. Professional Teacher Growth Plan Data Summary—NCR
	19. Professional Teacher Growth Plan Reflection

Chapter 8	20. Framework of Professional Growth Mentor Practice Standard 2
	21. Professional Practice Mentor Self-Assessment Checklist Standards 1–3
	22. Establishing Professional Mentor Growth Priorities
	23. Professional Mentor Growth (PMG) Plan—NCR
	24. Professional Mentor Growth Plan Data Summary—NCR
	25. Professional Mentor Growth Plan Reflection
Section II: Practice Focused Stage	
Chapter 9	26. General Seating Chart—NCR
	27. On Task/Off Task Seating Chart—NCR
	28. Lesson Pacing Seating Chart—NCR
Chapter 10	29. General Scripting—NCR
	30. Focused Scripting—NCR
	31. Question-Response-Question Scripting—NCR
Chapter 11	32. Veteran Teacher Observation Planning and Reflection—NCR
	33. Veteran Teacher Observation Data Collection—NCR
Chapter 12	34. Student Data Map Characteristics
	35. Student Data Map Standardized Assessment: Multiple Content
	36. Student Data Map Standardized Assessment: Single Content
	37. Student Data Map Teacher-Created Assessment
Chapter 13	38. Learning Objectives Worksheet
	39. Task Analysis Part I
	40. Task Analysis Part II
	41. Lesson Element Alignment
Chapter 14	42. Basic Lesson Plan
	43. Inquiry Lesson Plan
	44. Essential Elements Lesson Plan

Chapter 15	45. Video Preparation Checklist
	46. Videotaping Guidelines
	47. Videotaping Reflection
Chapter 16	48. Logging Student Engagement
	49. Logging Engaging Behavior
Chapter 17	50. Questioning Skills: Levels of Knowledge
	51. Questioning Skills: Levels of Knowledge Totals
	52. Questioning Skills: Student Response
	53. Word Bank for Questions Used to Gather Information
	54. Word Bank for Questions Used to Analyze Data
	55. Word Bank for Questions Used to Promote Action
Section III: Learner Focused Stage	
Chapter 18	56. Analysis of Student Work Steps 1–5—NCR
Chapter 19	57. Instructional Groups for Differentiated Instruction
	58. Differentiated Lesson Plan Organizer
	59. Lesson Plan Differentiation Template—NCR
Chapter 20	60. Formative Assessment of Student Practice—NCR
	61. Formative Assessment Protocol
	62. Assessing Student Learning
Chapter 21	63. Differentiated Mentoring Analysis of Beginning Teacher Development Steps 1–5
Chapter 22	64. A Look Back: Then and Now
	65. Transformational Learning Stages: Reflection for Beginning Teachers
	66. Transformational Learning Stages: Reflection for Beginning Mentors
	67. Beginning Teacher New Year Action Plan: Continuing the Transformation
	68. Beginning Teacher New Year Action Plan: Continuing the Transformation
NCR = No Carbon Required paper. NCR copies are made for the mentor and the beginning teacher to provide each with a copy of the tool.	

Resource C: Framework of Professional Growth

Teacher Practice

CONTENTS

INTRODUCTION TO THE FRAMEWORK OF PROFESSIONAL GROWTH TEACHER PRACTICE

The *Framework of Professional Growth Teacher Practice* is a continuum of professional teaching standards based on different levels of mastery as described by performance criteria. This work first began in 1975 under the direction of Fuller and Bown followed by David Berliner in 1994 as he labeled a teacher's developmental performance from novice to expert. The framework is based on their work and others such as, Charlotte Danielson (1996), the Santa Cruz New Teacher Project (2001), the mentors Kristin Metler-Armijo, Tammy House, Misty Arthur, Carrie Carlisle, Michelle Pogue, Shahla Nye, Jamie Bolster (2002), and Patty J. Horn, Heidi C. Blair, Kristin Metler-Armijo, Rick Vanosdall (2005). The *Framework of Professional Growth Teacher Practice* was established in 2007 by the authors to reflect the diversity of students and to meet the changing needs of beginning teachers and revised in 2010.

The Framework of Professional Growth Teacher Practice addresses four standards:

1. Managing the Learning Environment

2. Designing and Planning Instruction

3. Facilitating Student Learning

4. Assessing Student Learning

The Framework is organized to describe five levels of development. These levels are labeled *Novice, Emergent, Proficient, Accomplished,* and *Master*. Each framework level addresses what a teacher should know and be able to do relative to each of the professional teacher standards. They represent developmental levels of a teacher's performance. As teachers move into the profession, move from one grade level to another, or move into a new content area their developmental level of performance changes. The framework was designed to accommodate these various levels of teacher development throughout a teacher's career.

HOW TO USE THE FRAMEWORK

Use the Framework by reading across each row of descriptors from left (Novice) to right (Master). As you read each descriptor, reflect on your classroom performance. The rubric is cumulative as you move from left to right. You cannot move to the next level unless you have met the criteria described in the previous level. Continue to move across the rubric until you come to a level that describes and documents your current level of performance in the classroom.

The *Professional Growth Self-Assessment Checklist* is used in conjunction with the *Framework of Professional Growth Teacher Practice* to provide teachers a means of keeping a written record of their determined level of current practice by placing a N (Novice), E (Emergent), P (Proficient), A (Accomplished), or M (Master) by the performance criteria to indicate how they self-assessed their practice.

GLOSSARY OF TERMS

Framework
A rubric describing different developmental levels of performance.

Performance Criteria
Descriptions of teacher practice within a standard that represents the responsibilities and expectations of a teacher.

Levels of the Framework
Each framework level of the performance criteria represents the developmental levels of a teacher's performance relative to each of the professional teacher standards.

Novice: Seeks rules and regulations, duplicates lessons in textbook, and tries to use previous learned formats, dependent on surviving the role of teacher.

Emergent: Moves toward understanding basic classroom procedures, begins to apply new strategies while still dependent on textbook, rules, and regulations.

Proficient: Implements strategies and classroom procedures to meet the academic needs of students, assessment drives instruction, decisions are made during the lesson that impact student learning.

Accomplished: Organizes multiple levels of classroom procedures simultaneously, meets the various developmental and academic needs of students through multifarious strategies, groups and regroups students based on skill levels.

Master: Moves smoothly throughout the day utilizing a knowledge of teaching to the extent that all students' learning needs are met, instruction is at a high level of proficiency in all areas of teaching, promotes independence within student responsibilities, data is analyzed and used in daily teaching decisions formally and informally.

Standard
Public statements developed by "experts" of what a teacher should know and be able to do.

STANDARD 1: MANAGING THE LEARNING ENVIRONMENT

The teacher:	NOVICE	EMERGENT	PROFICIENT	ACCOMPLISHED	MASTER
1. Establishes expectations for student behavior	Communicates rules and consequences. Establishes basic routines and procedures.	Establishes clear high expectations for student behavior. Creates specific routines and procedures. Responds appropriately to disruptive behaviors and uses some strategies for maintaining students' productive behavior.	Monitors and uses strategies that reinforce behavior expectations, routines, and procedures. Uses strategies that prevent or lessen disruptive behavior and reinforce expectations for behavior. Transitions are seamless and without disruptions.	Maintains a positive environment through use of consistent routines and procedures, engagement, and behavior reinforcement. Encourages students to develop self-monitoring and reflective skills. The classroom is consistently conducive to learning.	Fosters an environment in which students show ownership of routines and procedures, are continually engaged, and reflect on learning and behavior. The classroom is exceptionally focused on learning.
2. Establishes and maintains a respectful and nurturing learning environment	Establishes mutual respect with individual students. Acknowledges some incidents of unfairness and disrespect.	Establishes standards of respect. Models equitable and respectful relationships. Uses some strategies to respond to unfairness and disrespect.	Promotes caring and respectful interactions between all students. Responds to all incidents of unfairness and disrespect equitably. Encourages students to respect differences.	Reflects adherence to established standards of mutual respect. Frequently recognizes students' efforts with positive, constructive remarks. Responds to students' disrespect and implements consequences.	Provides opportunity for the students to monitor their own behavior and offers suggestions for maintaining a positive, caring environment conducive to learning. Students demonstrate caring attitudes for one another.
3. Promotes student responsibilities and self-discipline	Promotes student responsibility for self. Creates opportunities for individual students to have classroom responsibilities. The teacher acts as a professional role model and demonstrates integrity and ethical behavior.	Uses some strategies and activities to develop students' self-discipline and responsibility to others recognizing their rights and needs. Students share in classroom responsibilities.	Promotes positive student interactions as members of large and small groups. Provides some opportunities for student leadership within the classroom.	Engages students in individual and group work that promotes responsibility to the classroom community. Supports students to take initiative in classroom leadership recognizing individual and others' rights.	Facilitates an environment in which students take initiative socially and academically. Promotes and supports student leadership beyond the classroom.
4. Recognizes and values differences among individuals	Acknowledges individual differences among students.	Develops some strategies to address individual differences among students.	Uses a variety of strategies to address individual differences among students.	Promotes caring, respectful, and equitable relationships among students with individual differences.	Fosters a safe, inclusive, and equitable learning community. Students actively participate in maintaining a climate of equity, caring, and respect.

PERFORMANCE CRITERIA

348

STANDARD 1: MANAGING THE LEARNING ENVIRONMENT (Continued)					
The teacher:	NOVICE	EMERGENT	PROFICIENT	ACCOMPLISHED	MASTER
5. Facilitates collaboration among learners	Directs learning experiences through whole group and individual work with possibilities for interaction and collaboration.	Varies learning experiences in large groups that result in student productivity and collaboration. Promotes positive student interactions.	Provides learning experiences utilizing individual and group structures to develop productivity and collaboration. Establishes expectations for appropriate group interactions including listening and responding skills.	Uses a variety of learning experiences to assist students in developing independent working skills and group productivity skills. Expectations for appropriate group interactions are consistently reinforced.	Integrates a variety of challenging learning experiences that develop students' individual responsibility for learning, collaboration, productivity, and cooperation. Reinforces appropriate independent and group participation consistently.
6. Establishes an environment for student success	Displays current topics of study in an organized manner. Structured learning experiences are evident.	Develops learning tasks relevant to the students' interests and needs.	Provides the opportunity for students to select learning tasks to meet their interests and needs.	Supports students in making appropriate choices for learning. Frequent use of motivational techniques such as praise and student success is evident.	Provides consistent, multiple opportunities for student success and student choices are evident. Students take an active part in creating learning activities that support their own learning, interests, and make challenging curriculum choices.
7. Utilizes active participation strategies	Uses basic questioning and discussion strategies.	Implements questioning and discussion strategies that engage students. Makes attempts to include all students.	Utilizes a variety of questioning and discussion strategies that encourage full participation. Expects all students to consistently participate in classroom activities.	Maintains highly motivating and engaging curriculum. Models and encourages students to take on active roles as learners.	Fosters a challenging environment in which students accept responsibility for being an active participant in all classroom activities.
8. Arranges and manages the classroom environment for student success	Arranges room for teacher accessibility to, or visibility of, students. Room displays relate to the curriculum. Movement and access may be restricted by barriers.	Maintains organized use of materials for instructional needs. Arranges and manages room for easy movement and access to resources for varied learning experiences.	Organizes materials to promote student understanding of basic concepts and skills. Room displays are used in learning activities. Designs movement patterns and access to resources to promote individual and group engagement.	Manages room and resources to assist students in developing independent working skills with the use of displays that are integral to learning.	Uses total physical environment as a resource to promote individual and group learning. Integrates a variety of challenging learning experiences that develop students' independent learning, collaboration, and choice. Students are able to contribute to the changing design of the environment.

PERFORMANCE CRITERIA

349

STANDARD 2: DESIGNING AND PLANNING INSTRUCTION

The teacher:	NOVICE	EMERGENT	PROFICIENT	ACCOMPLISHED	MASTER
1. Utilizes academic standards to plan instruction	Aligns instruction to academic standards.	Aligns instruction to academic standards and the standards are referenced within the instructional plan.	Aligns the instructional plan to academic standards. Standards are referenced and follow a logical sequence.	Provides assessment activities aligned with the standards and the instructional plan.	Develops aligned instructional plan within a comprehensive integrated teaching plan.
2. Utilizes student assessments to plan instruction	Develops lessons that align with student assessments to plan for the class as a whole.	Develops most concepts and skills through a series of lessons that are aligned with student assessments.	Plans instruction based on student assessment to meet the varying needs of learners.	Plans differentiated instruction based on analysis of student work.	Provides opportunities for students to self-assess their own learning and create individual learning goals.
3. Plans instruction to meet the diverse needs of learners	Includes a few instructional strategies that address not only academic, but physical, mental, social, cultural, and/or community differences among learners.	Selects additional resources and materials to enhance the learning for students with diverse needs.	Develops assessments aligned with the diverse needs of students.	Uses a wide range of relevant strategies, materials, and assessments that address physical, mental, social, cultural, and/or community differences among learners.	Uses knowledge of student differences to advance individual learning.
4. Links learning to students' prior knowledge and experiences	Develops connections to the past experiences of the students.	Asks questions that elicit students' prior knowledge and past experiences.	Implements activities that links learning with students' prior knowledge, experiences and backgrounds.	Uses questions and activities to connect lesson content to real life situations when appropriate. The teacher assists the students in their abilities to integrate what they know with the content.	Provides the opportunity for the students to synthesize learning content with what they already know and develop a gateway to their own learning.
5. Plans short term learning objectives and long term curriculum goals	Aligns short term objectives and long term goals with content curriculum standards.	Identifies objectives for daily lessons for students. Instruction focuses on one objective at a time. Identifies key concepts within content to facilitate student understanding.	Designs and sequences short term objectives to support and organize long term goals appropriate to the content and to the students.	Designs short term objectives that are aligned with long term goals that are relevant and comprehensive across the content.	Designs activities so that students have opportunities to participate in setting, revising, and achieving personal objectives.

PERFORMANCE CRITERIA

STANDARD 2: DESIGNING AND PLANNING INSTRUCTION (Continued)

The teacher:	NOVICE	EMERGENT	PROFICIENT	ACCOMPLISHED	MASTER
6. Includes a variety of methods in instructional plans	Uses a few instructional methods for lessons to make the content accessible to students. Attempts to relate content to prior lessons within the subject matter.	Matches one or more appropriate methods to subject matter to effectively communicate concepts. Connects lessons to previous learning.	Matches methods appropriate to subject matter to encourage student understanding and critical thinking.	Develops and uses multiple methods that challenge all students. Assist students to construct their own knowledge. Capitalizes on opportunities to make connections while teaching.	Uses a repertoire of methods that are appropriate to subject matter. Utilizes strategies that challenge and support all students to independently apply and think critically about the subject matter.
7. Includes a variety of technology, materials, and resources in instructional plans	Includes instructional materials, resources, and technologies for specific lessons to support student learning.	Includes a variety of instructional materials, resources, and technologies to present concepts and skills.	Selects instructional materials, resources, and technologies to present concepts and skills relevant to content and students' interests.	Selects, adapts, and creates a range of relevant materials, resources, and technologies to enrich learning.	Analyzes, adapts, and creates a wide range of relevant instructional materials, resources, and technologies to extend students' understanding.
8. Develops learning experiences that are developmentally appropriate for learners	Lessons reflect basic knowledge of student development.	Applies knowledge of student development when planning learning experiences.	Builds learning experiences appropriate for the students' developmental level. Objectives are at the correct level of difficulty.	Uses comprehensive knowledge of content area(s) and student development levels to ensure that all students understand key concepts, themes, multiple perspectives, and relationships.	Develops a variety of learning experiences based on the individual students' developmental levels.
9. Develops learning experiences that address the cognitive levels of learners	Identifies key concepts in the content area. Lessons reflect a basic knowledge of student cognitive levels.	Applies knowledge of student cognitive levels when planning learning experiences.	Builds learning experiences with students' cognitive levels and abilities in mind.	Provides learning experiences that includes all cognitive levels for all students.	Uses comprehensive knowledge of content cognitive levels to ensure that all students understand new knowledge and skills.
10. Plans for experiences that align with learning objectives that accurately represent content	Plans for daily lessons and activities that are appropriate for the objectives.	Plans for daily and weekly lessons with attention to short term objectives and student academic standards that accurately reflect content.	Provides learning experiences which accurately reflect content and consistently support the development of new knowledge and skills.	Plans, sequences, and aligns learning experiences appropriately to objectives. Develops learning experiences which accurately reflect content and consistently support the development of new knowledge and skills.	Designs a variety of experiences that are comprehensive and cohesive across the content areas aligned with the objectives. Consistently supports student application and evaluation of knowledge and skills.

PERFORMANCE CRITERIA

STANDARD 3: FACILITATING STUDENT LEARNING

The teacher:	NOVICE	EMERGENT	PROFICIENT	ACCOMPLISHED	MASTER
1. Utilizes a lesson plan to guide student learning	Directs learning experiences and monitors student progress within a specific lesson as planned. Assistance is provided as requested by students. Instruction focuses on one objective at a time. Follows lesson as planned.	Adjusts lessons based on informal assessment of student understanding and performance having taken note of student confusions.	Supports students in developing skills during the lesson implementation. Monitors and adjust activities to particular groups of students. Makes modifications during lessons to address confusions and individual student performance.	Consistently monitors and adjusts instruction to meet all students' needs during lesson implementation. Uses assessments of student understanding throughout the lesson to influence changes during instruction.	Introduces new learning objectives within the lesson implementation as the need arises among students. Involves all students in monitoring their own progress. Uses strategies to ensure that learning is transferred beyond the classroom.
2. Communicates high expectations for learning	Shares learning objectives aligned with standards and expectations for each lesson with students.	Models, articulates, and links learning objectives and expectations based on student academic standards to student learning.	Connects learning objectives and student expectations to course content and clearly communicates this to students and families.	Integrates learning objectives into all learning activities. Establishes, reviews, and revises learning objectives with students on an ongoing basis.	Establishes clear and appropriate learning objectives based on student academic standards, with consideration of students' learning needs. Involves students in developing individual objectives to support learning.
3. Demonstrates skill, knowledge, and thinking processes	Communicates skills and knowledge to be learned during whole group instruction and cooperative learning.	Demonstrates some of the thinking processes, skills, and knowledge to be learned during whole group instruction and cooperative learning.	Actively demonstrates the thinking process, skills, and knowledge to be learned within all learning activities.	Consistently demonstrates the thinking processes, skills, and knowledge related to learning objectives in all settings. Involves students in modeling opportunities.	Facilitates activities that promote peer modeling of thinking processes, skills, and knowledge related to learning objectives.

PERFORMANCE CRITERIA

The teacher:	NOVICE	EMERGENT	PROFICIENT	ACCOMPLISHED	MASTER
4. Uses correct grammar, mechanics, and developmentally appropriate language to communicate with learners	Uses appropriate and developmentally correct language with students. Uses correct grammar and mechanics. Writes legibly.	Models appropriate and developmentally correct language with students. Directions are clear and concise. Models correct grammar and mechanics in student assignments.	Actively models appropriate and developmentally correct language with students, colleagues, and parents. Communication is redirected when appropriate. Actively models correct grammar and mechanics in all written and oral communications.	Consistently models appropriate and developmentally correct language with students, colleagues, and parents. Written and spoken language enriches the lesson. Consistently models correct grammar and mechanics.	Facilitates appropriate and correct language with students, colleagues, and parents. Facilitates correct grammar and mechanics among students.
5. Uses instructional strategies that are appropriate to the developmental levels of learners	Uses a few developmentally appropriate instructional strategies to make the academic standards accessible to learners.	Uses instructional strategies to effectively communicate concepts appropriate to the learners' developmental levels.	Strategies are appropriate to subject matter and are aligned to learners' developmental levels.	Uses multiple strategies that assist students to individually construct their own knowledge and think critically at the appropriate developmental levels.	Uses a repertoire of instructional strategies that are appropriate to subject matter and the learners' developmental levels. Utilizes strategies that challenge and support all learners to independently apply and think critically about the subject matter.
6. Uses strategies to address the diverse needs of learners	Uses a few instructional strategies which recognize the diverse cultural needs of learners.	Varies instruction to increase learner participation. Selects strategies, resources, and visuals with some consideration of learners' diverse academic, linguistic, and cultural needs.	Elicits learner participation through a variety of instructional strategies intended to align with learners' diverse academic, linguistic, and cultural needs.	Uses a repertoire of strategies and differentiates instruction to align with learners' diverse academic, linguistic, and cultural needs.	Uses an extensive repertoire of strategies to meet learners' diverse academic, linguistic, and cultural needs. Ensures the fullest participation for all learners.

PERFORMANCE CRITERIA

353

STANDARD 3: FACILITATING STUDENT LEARNING (Continued)

The teacher:	NOVICE	EMERGENT	PROFICIENT	ACCOMPLISHED	MASTER
7. Promotes critical thinking	Focuses questions on facts and key concepts to support learning content. Learners use a skill or procedure to solve a problem.	Asks critical thinking questions to relate facts and key concepts of content. Learners begin to construct meaning to the content.	Engages learners through activities and questioning strategies that develop skills in identification and use of key concepts. Supports all learners in using problem solving skills.	Engages learners in analysis and provides opportunities for learners to evaluate and consider multiple perspectives. Supports learners in making judgments based on clearly defined criteria and standards.	Facilitates regular opportunities for learners to design and implement inquiries. Facilitates learners to analyze, draw conclusions, and consider multiple perspectives to create a problem solving structure within one's own knowledge.
8. Makes connections between learning and real life situations	Recognizes the value of students' life experiences during lessons.	Connects learning objectives and goals to real life experiences and interests.	Implements activities that help student make connections between real life experiences, learning objectives, and goals.	Uses questions and activities to extend students' abilities to integrate real life situations with the learning objectives.	Supports students' synthesis of knowledge obtained by real life situations to develop their own learning objectives and goals.
9. Uses a variety of instructional strategies to engage learners	Provides a single approach to learning with limited opportunity for student engagement.	Directs learning experiences through whole group and individual work with possibilities for interaction and student engagement.	Uses multiple teaching strategies and develops learning experiences utilizing individual and group structures to ensure that most of the students are actively engaged in learning most of the time.	Provides opportunities to explore different approaches to learning. Students are engaged in the content in a variety of ways to develop knowledge and skills.	Provides opportunities to explore different approaches and solutions to problems. Students are expected to defend their reasoning with evidence. Invites participation, discussion, and inquiry. All students are actively engaged.
10. Uses instructional time to maximize learning	Instruction reflects some learning time.	Provides time for students to complete learning activities. Uses strategies to pace and adjust instruction to ensure continual engagement of some students during some of the class time. Transitions between activities are smooth.	Provides adequate time for presentation and for completion of learning activities.	Classroom procedures and transitions are efficient. Instruction provides opportunities for all students to be engaged and successful.	Presents, adjusts, and facilitates instruction so all students have time for learning success. Provides opportunities for all students to be engaged and reflective. Supports students to self-monitor time on task.

PERFORMANCE CRITERIA

STANDARD 3: FACILITATING STUDENT LEARNING (Continued)

PERFORMANCE CRITERIA	The teacher:	NOVICE	EMERGENT	PROFICIENT	ACCOMPLISHED	MASTER
	11. Ensures students apply new knowledge and skills	Ensures all students have practice opportunities.	Incorporates a variety of practice opportunities. Communicates possible ideas and situations for application.	Uses a variety of meaningful practice opportunities. Involves students in application opportunities.	Challenges students to demonstrate new knowledge through application in a variety of areas. Promotes choice in application activities.	Ensures students transfer new knowledge and skills into different contextual situations.
	12. Uses technology and instructional resources	Uses limited technology and instructional resources for specific lessons to support student learning.	Uses a variety of technology and instructional resources to present content and support student learning.	Integrates technology and utilizes a variety of instructional resources on a regular basis.	Analyzes, adapts, and creates a wide range of relevant technologies and instructional resources to extend students' understanding and provide equal access.	Provides opportunities for students to use technology and instructional resources to acquire new knowledge and skills to demonstrate understanding of what was presented.

STANDARD 4: ASSESSING STUDENT LEARNING

The teacher:	NOVICE	EMERGENT	PROFICIENT	ACCOMPLISHED	MASTER
1. Aligns formal and informal assessments to instruction	Uses one informal or formal assessment to monitor student progress toward learning objectives.	Uses several formal and informal assessments to monitor student progress towards learning objectives.	Uses a variety of assessment tools for monitoring student progress towards learning objectives. Alignment is evident.	Collects, selects, and reflects upon student assessment data to align short and long term instructional plans to support student learning.	Provides opportunities for students to explain thinking, make application to other situations, and provide consistent feedback in alignment with instruction and objectives.
2. Designs student assessments to measure progress	Uses basic assessments aligned to the objective being taught.	Uses a variety of assessment tools to assess student learning and monitor student progress.	Uses formal and informal assessments to gather data on student knowledge and skills.	Incorporates performance based assessment routinely to measure student progress. Assessment opportunities are provided for students to explain their thinking.	Uses a variety of complex assessments to measure student progress. Students use self-assessments to design their own learning.
3. Promotes student self-assessment	Uses assessments that focus mainly on completion of work and/or the correct answer.	Provides students with feedback on work in progress. Some student involvement in assessing work.	Presents guidelines for assessment to students. Assists students in reflecting on and assessing their own work.	Integrates student self-assessment and reflection into some of the assessment activities.	Engages all students in self-assessment and in monitoring their progress over time.
4. Maintains records of student performance and respects privacy of student records	Maintains records of student performance. Recognizes legal responsibility and district policy of confidentiality and privacy.	Maintains confidentiality and privacy with all students, parents, and colleagues.	Keeps up to date and accurate student records. Respects confidentiality and privacy of student records and performances.	Develops a student communication system that reports individual student progress while maintaining privacy and confidentiality.	Ensures that each student knows his progress in meeting established instructional objectives. Encourage students to maintain privacy and confidentiality.
5. Communicates growth progress to students and parents	Provides students and parents with documentation regarding progress through school mandated procedures.	Provides students with specific feedback about their current progress as they engage in learning activities. Parents and support personnel are contacted as needed.	Provides students with specific feedback on how to improve their work. Establishes regular communication with parents and support personnel. Uses a system for communicating with parents in regard to individual student assessments towards meeting the standards.	Engages students, parents, and support personnel in regular discussions regarding student progress and improvement plans. Ongoing information is provided from a variety of sources.	Involves students, parents, and support personnel as partners in the assessment process. Provides comprehensive information about students' progress and improvement plans.

PERFORMANCE CRITERIA

Resource D: Professional Practice Teacher Self-Assessment Checklist

Use the *Framework of Professional Growth Teacher Practice* to determine your level of performance. Use this tool by placing an **N** (Novice), **E** (Emergent), **P** (Proficient), **A** (Accomplished), or **M** (Master) by the performance criteria to indicate how you self-assessed your practice in the framework. Think about the evidence you have to document that level of practice.

☐ Fall
☐ Winter
☐ Spring

Standard 1: Managing the Learning Environment		Standard 2: Designing and Planning Instruction		Standard 3: Facilitating Student Learning		Standard 4: Assesses Student Learning	
	1. Establishes expectations for student behavior		1. Utilizes academic standards to plan instruction		1. Utilizes a lesson plan to guide student learning		1. Aligns formal and informal assessments to instruction
	2. Establishes and maintains a respectful and nurturing learning environment		2. Utilizes student assessments to plan instruction		2. Communicates high expectations for learning		2. Designs student assessments to measure progress
	3. Promotes student responsibilities and self-discipline		3. Plans instruction to meet the diverse needs of learners		3. Demonstrates skill, knowledge, and thinking processes		3. Promotes student self assessment
	4. Recognizes and values differences among individuals		4. Links learning to students' prior knowledge and experiences.		4. Uses correct grammar, mechanics, and developmentally appropriate language to communicate with learners		4. Maintains records of student performance and respects privacy of student records
	5. Facilitates collaboration among learners		5. Plans short term learning objectives and long term curriculum goals		5. Uses instructional strategies that are appropriate to the developmental levels of learners		5. Communicates growth progress to students and parents
	6. Establishes an environment for student success		6. Includes a variety of methods in instructional plans.		6. Uses strategies to address the diverse needs of learners		
	7. Utilizes active participation strategies		7. Includes a variety of technology, materials, and resources in instructional plans.		7. Promotes critical thinking		
	8. Arranges and manages the classroom environment for student success		8. Develops learning experiences that are developmentally appropriate for learners		8. Makes connections between learning and real life situations		
			9. Develops learning experiences that address the cognitive levels of learners		9. Uses a variety of instructional strategies to engage learners		
			10. Plans for experiences that align with learning objectives that accurately represent content.		10. Uses instructional time to maximize learning		
					11. Ensures students apply new knowledge and skills		
					12. Uses technology and instructional resources		

Name: **Date:**

Resource E: Framework of Professional Growth

Mentor Practice

Aligned with the Teacher Induction Program Mentor Standards

CONTENTS

INTRODUCTION TO THE FRAMEWORK OF PROFESSIONAL DEVELOPMENT MENTOR PRACTICE

The Framework was originally developed in 2004 by the authors and the mentors for use in the teacher induction partnership program to support mentors who were working with first and second year teachers. The Framework is being implemented as part of a successful ongoing collaboration between the teacher induction professional development program and the mentors to assess practice and set professional goals.

The Framework addresses six standards:

1. Establish and Maintain Mentoring Relationships

2. Demonstrate Diverse Mentor Roles

3. Use Effective Communication Skills

4. Implement Transformative Assessment

5. Catalyst for Instructional Practices

6. Model Professional Growth

The Framework is organized to describe three levels of development. These levels are labeled *Emerging, Applying,* and *Integrating.* Each developmental level addresses what a mentor should know and be able to do in relationship to each of the six standards through supporting teachers. The levels represent a mentor's developmental levels of practice.

HOW TO USE THE FRAMEWORK

Read across each row of descriptors from left (Emerging) to right (Integrating) as the professional criteria become more complex. As you move from left to right, locate the descriptor that best defines your current mentoring practice. These practices described are cumulative from left to right, so each level to the left of that identified must be met.

The Framework provides a common language for developing a professional growth plan in an environment of collegial support. The Framework is best used as a guide for reflective conversations between mentors, supervisors, and administrators regarding professional growth. It is intended to help mentors interpret their practice and make informed decisions about their ongoing support of teachers.

GLOSSARY OF TERMS

Framework
A document describing different developmental levels of practice or knowledge

Performance Criteria
Descriptions of mentor practice that represents what a mentor should know and be able to do in supporting teachers

Levels of the Framework
Developmental point of mentor practice that represents what a mentor should know and be able to do in supporting teachers

Emerging: A level of development in which the mentor still relies on more experienced colleagues for support but is moving toward becoming more self-directed and independent in his or her practice

Applying: A level of development in which the mentor is able to successfully collaborate with a teacher in support of the teacher's practice and easily applies what he or she has learned about mentoring

Integrating: A level of development in which the mentor's behavior is consistently innovative and creative in all areas of mentoring and professional development. The mentor easily integrates what he or she has learned. A leader in the school, district, and local community, the integrating mentor conducts professional development classes for continuing teachers, and attends conferences and workshops that further develop their professional growth.

Standard
One of the six areas of mentoring practice that comprise the Framework

Mentor Standard 1: Establish and Maintain Mentoring Relationships
Mentors demonstrate the skills necessary for establishing and maintaining productive, supportive relationships

Performance Criteria	Emerging	Applying	Integrating
1.1 Work collaboratively to utilize school and community resources.	Mentor collaboratively assists the teacher in locating information regarding *School and Community Resources*. Discusses the importance of the contacts and resources as needed by the teacher. Mentor knows and shares school specific routines and procedures.	Mentor encourages teachers to utilize School and Community Resources in order to assist them in meeting the needs of their students in developing a plan of action and identifying necessary follow-up.	Mentor follows up to see if resources are being used and are beneficial to teacher. Seeks additional resources together with the teacher as needed.
1.2 Establish a confidential relationship.	Mentor shares with the teacher the *Mentor–Teacher Confidentiality Agreement* as written guidelines established for confidentiality with administrators, colleagues, and others.	Mentor maintains confidentiality when questioned by others. Confidentiality is demonstrated with administrators.	Confidentiality extends beyond the realm of the teacher. Others confide in the mentor and confidentiality remains consistent.
1.3 Use the *Conference Data Conference (CDC) Cycle* to provide a variety of experiences for the teachers through the use of mentor language, tools, and reflection.	Mentor uses an instructive stance in the *Conference Data Conference (CDC) Cycle and CDC Journal Record*. Mentor shows an awareness of mentor language.	Mentor uses a collaborative stance in the *CDC Cycle and CDC Journal Record*. A variety of data collection tools are used to foster reflection.	Mentor uses facilitative stances with the *CDC Cycle and CDC Journal Record*. Mentor facilitates growth experiences through multiple strategies (e.g., modeling, collecting and reflecting on data, and accompanying teacher on veteran teacher observations).
1.4 Identify and address the professional needs of the teacher based on teacher standards and expectations.	Mentor facilitates the discussion with the teacher on how to use the *Framework of Professional Growth Teacher Practice* to identify performance indicators of practice and develop a *Professional Teacher Growth (PTG) Plan*. Mentor completes a *CDC Cycle and CDC Journal Record* with teacher during most conferences.	Mentor collaborates with the teacher to identify data collection tools that provide evidence of growth. Specific needs are addressed through the *CDC Cycle, Classroom Data Collection, and CDC Journal Record*.	Mentor facilitates the discussion with the Teacher to write a *PTG Plan Data Summary* and *PTG Plan Reflection*. The teacher decides what the next steps will be regarding the *PTG Plan*. The Mentor serves as a leader for the teacher and serves as an example to assist the teacher in making connections toward practice, reflection, and change.
1.5 Encourage teachers to become independent as they grow professionally.	Mentor primarily uses an instructive stance when working with teachers.	Mentor moves between instructive and collaborative stances when working with teachers.	Mentors use instructive, collaborative, and facilitative stances consistently when working with teachers. The facilitative stance takes precedence toward the end-of-year sessions.
1.6 Demonstrate empathy towards the needs of the teachers.	Mentor listens attentively, maintains a calm demeanor, and maintains eye contact when meeting with teachers.	Mentor listens, paraphrases, and asks clarifying questions when conferencing with teachers. Mentor maintains positive body language.	Mentor engages teachers in reflective problem solving and uses a variety of question stems when conferencing with teachers.

Mentor Standard 2: Demonstrate Diverse Mentor Roles

Mentors demonstrate diverse roles effectively in mentoring relationships

Performance Criteria	Emerging	Applying	Integrating
2.1 Work collaboratively with teachers and others.	Mentor meets regularly with teachers as established by the district.	Mentor works together with the teachers to follow the *CDC Cycle and Journal Record* procedures.	Mentor works collaboratively with teachers and other school and district personnel to accomplish district and site based goals.
2.2 Facilitate discussion with the teacher regarding analyzing classroom observation data and reflecting on teacher and student behaviors in order to accelerate the teacher's practice.	Mentor collects classroom data based on the discussion with the teacher during the *Planning Conference*. During the *Reflective Conference* the mentor allows the teacher to begin to analyze the data.	Mentor leads the discussion with the teacher to identify the impact of instructional practices on student behavior and learning as evidenced by the collected data.	Mentor regularly uses the *CDC Cycle and Journal Record* procedures to assist the teacher in the identification of effective instructional practices, reflection, and determining next steps.
2.3 Model differentiated mentoring stances (instructive, collaborative, and facilitative).	Mentor identifies the three stances of mentoring and begins to use them in practice.	Mentor demonstrates the use of instructive, collaborative, and facilitative stances when conferencing with others.	Mentor demonstrates the use of the instructive, collaborative, and facilitative stances and uses each appropriately.
2.4 Differentiate mentoring based on andragogy to meet the diverse needs of teachers.	Mentor has a basic understanding of adult learning theory and strategies.	Mentor utilizes some differentiated adult learning strategies in working with the teacher.	Mentor differentiates adult learning strategies when interacting with the teacher during the *CDC Cycle and Journal Record* procedures.

Mentor Standard 3: Use Effective Communication skills
Mentors demonstrate effective communication skills

Performance Criteria	Emerging	Applying	Integrating
3.1 Use a variety of communication tools with teachers and school community to respond professionally to verbal and written communication.	Mentor uses *CDC Journal Records* to communicate with teachers and the *Administrator and Mentor Journal Record* with administrators.	Mentor uses journal records on a regular basis. Mentor uses appropriate form of communication in response to other school personnel.	Mentor uses appropriate forms to communicate with teachers, administrators, and others on a regular and timely basis (e.g., journal records, email, telephone, website, etc.).
3.2 Use appropriate non-verbal behaviors.	Mentor is aware of the nonverbal behaviors of teachers, administrators, and self.	Mentor observes and responds appropriately to nonverbal behavior of others.	Mentor uses appropriate non-verbal behaviors to build rapport with others and to promote change in the behavior of others.
3.3 Use active listening skills.	Mentor uses body language and eye contact consistent with active listening.	Mentor summarizes teacher's comments.	Mentor uses paraphrasing appropriately and asks clarifying questions when needed during conversations with others.
3.4 Use questioning techniques and strategies that address a variety of cognitive levels.	Mentor uses open-ended questions when conferencing with others.	Mentor plans questions in advance when conferencing. Mentor asks reflective questions	Mentor knows when to use various questioning stems during conversations. Mentor monitors and adjusts questioning stems to focus the conversation.
3.5 Develop a positive working relationship with school and district personnel.	Mentor has basic knowledge of school and district personnel. The mentor actively introduces herself to the school staff. Mentor attends mentor trainings and administrator meetings when invited.	Mentor meets monthly with site administrators. Mentor documents conversation with an *Administrator and Mentor journal record.*	Mentor follows up on administrator concerns. Mentor knows who to call within the school and district personnel for different situations. Mentor regularly attends district mentor meetings and follows district expectations.

Mentor Standard 4: Implement Transformative Assessment

Mentors utilize transformative assessment tools and strategies to promote growth and reflection in the teacher

Performance Criteria	Emerging	Applying	Integrating
4.1 Clarify the role of observation and transformative assessment.	Mentor explains the concepts of observation and transformative assessment to teacher and others.	Mentor uses data from observations when working with teachers to demonstrate the role of observation and transformative assessment.	Mentor models the observation and transformative assessment model continuously when working with teachers.
4.2 Use a variety of data collection strategies and tools.	Mentor uses one or two data collection strategies and tools regularly.	Mentor uses two or three data collection strategies and tools regularly to document the teacher's area of focus.	Mentor uses more than three data collection strategies and tools regularly to document the teacher's area of focus.
4.3 Assist in the ongoing development and implementation of the *Professional Teacher Growth* (PTG) Plan using the *Framework of Professional Growth Teacher Practice.*	Mentor assists teachers in developing *Professional Teacher Growth* (PTG) Plan.	Mentor collects data to assist teachers in meeting the goals as established in the *Professional Teacher Growth* (PTG) Plan.	Mentor collaborates with teachers to determine if a new *Professional Teacher Growth* (PTG) Plan is needed.

365

Mentor Standard 5:   Catalyst for Instructional Practices

Mentors demonstrate the ability to serve as a catalyst for teachers in developing and implementing research-based instructional practices

Performance Criteria	Emerging	Applying	Integrating
5.1 Assist teachers in using the professional teacher standards to design, implement, manage, and assess instruction.	Provides teachers with a copy of professional teaching standards and reviews the document with them.	Mentor refers to professional teaching standards at the bottom of the *CDC Journal Record* during conferences.	Mentor uses the language of the professional teaching standards during conversations with teachers.
5.2 Support teachers in using district curriculum and the student academic standards to design, implement, manage, and assess instruction.	Mentor collaborates with teachers in designing curriculum while designing lessons that use state standards, district curriculum, and site expectations.	Mentor facilitates the discussion with teachers to align academic standards, lesson design, and assessment.	Mentor facilitates the conversation with teachers to self-assess how his instruction impacts student learning.
5.3 Support teachers in designing long and short term instructional goals based on student assessment data to meet the needs of all learners.	Mentor ensures teachers receive assessment data necessary for designing instruction to meet the needs of all learners. Mentor reviews the advantages of establishing a timeline for long and short term goals.	Mentor collaborates with teachers in analyzing assessment data and to develop and pace long and short term instructional goals.	Mentor collaborates with teachers to evaluate whether long and short term instructional goals met the needs of all learners based on benchmark data collected.
5.4 Assist teachers with evaluating instructional activities to meet the needs of all learners.	Mentor collects data during instructional activities that reflect learner differences.	Mentor works collaboratively to develop instructional strategies and goals based on the data that meets the needs of all learners.	Mentor facilitates the analysis of whether the teacher's instructional strategies are meeting the needs of all learners.
5.5 Assist teachers with evaluating, selecting, and developing various instructional resources and materials to meet the needs of all learners.	Mentor collaborates with teachers to select and develop various instructional resources and materials for all learners in the class.	Mentor collects data regarding the effective use of instructional resources for all learners.	Mentor facilitates discussions with teachers regarding the use of various instructional resources and the impact on student learning.

Mentor Standard 6: Model Professional Growth
Mentors demonstrate ongoing personal professional growth

Performance Criteria	Emerging	Applying	Integrating
6.1 Develop and implement a *Professional Mentor Growth* (PMG) Plan using the *Framework of Professional Growth Mentor Practice*.	Mentor develops a professional growth goal and creates a *Professional Mentor Growth* (PMG) Plan.	Mentor identifies the evidence needed to document the progress toward her identified goal.	Mentor reflects on the (PMG) Plan and the gathered evidence. Mentor decides whether to create a new (PMG) Plan dependent on reflection.
6.2 Create and maintain a professional growth portfolio to document the *Professional Mentor Growth* (PMG) Plan.	Mentor submits a growth portfolio with artifacts.	Mentor's professional growth portfolio contains a variety of artifacts that exhibit professional growth. Portfolio is organized.	Mentor's growth portfolio contains reflection of professional growth, and artifacts chosen are relevant to the PMG plan.
6.3 Demonstrate reflective practice.	Mentor discusses their professional practice with peers or a mentor partner.	Mentor identifies professional practices and determines successes and areas for growth.	Mentor reflects on evidence collected and makes changes based on that evidence.
6.4 Demonstrate contribution to the teaching profession.	Mentor shares resources with others. Mentor leads professional development for teachers.	Mentor holds professional development classes for new and continuing teachers. Mentor attends conferences and workshops that further develops his professional growth.	Mentor presents at local, statewide, or national conferences.

Resource F: Professional Practice Mentor Self-Assessment Checklist

Place an **E** (Emerging), **A** (Applying), or **I** (Integrating) by the performance criteria to indicate how you self-assessed your practice in the Framework for Professional Growth.

☐ Fall
☐ Winter
☐ Spring

Standard 1: Establish and Maintain Mentoring Relationships	Standard 2: Demonstrate Diverse Mentor Roles	Standard 3: Use Effective Communication skills
1.1 Work collaboratively to utilize school and community resources.	2.1 Work collaboratively with teachers and others.	3.1 Use a variety of communication tools with teachers and school community to respond professionally to verbal and written communication.
1.2 Establish a confidential relationship.	2.2 Facilitate discussion with the teacher regarding analyzing classroom observation data and reflecting on teacher and student behaviors in order to accelerate the teacher's practice.	3.2 Use appropriate nonverbal behaviors.
1.3 Use the *Conference Data Conference (CDC) Cycle* to provide a variety of experiences for the teachers through the use of mentor language, tools, and reflection.	2.3 Model differentiated mentoring stances (instructive, collaborative, and facilitative).	3.3 Use active listening skills.
1.4 Identify and address the professional needs of the teacher based on teacher standards and expectations.	2.4 Differentiate mentoring based on andragogy to meet the diverse needs of teachers.	3.4 Use questioning techniques and strategies that address a variety of cognitive levels.
1.5 Encourage teachers to become independent as they grow professionally.	**Name:**	3.5 Develop a positive working relationship with school and district personnel.
1.6 Demonstrate empathy towards the needs of the teachers.	**Date:**	

Place an **E** (Emerging), **A** (Applying), or **I** (Integrating) by the performance criteria to indicate how you self-assessed your practice in the Framework for Professional Growth.

☐ Fall
☐ Winter
☐ Spring

Mentor Standard 4: Implement Transformative Assessment

4.1 Clarify the role of observation and transformative assessment.

4.2 Use a variety of data collection strategies and tools.

4.3 Assist in the ongoing development and implementation of the *Professional Teacher Growth* (PTG) Plan using the *Framework of Professional Growth Teacher Practice*.

Mentor Standard 5: Catalyst for Instructional Practices

5.1 Assist teachers in using the professional teacher standards to design, implement, manage, and assess instruction.

5.2 Support teachers in using district curriculum and the student academic standards to design, implement, manage, and assess instruction.

5.3 Support teachers in designing long and short term instructional goals based on student assessment data to meet the needs of all learners.

5.4 Assist teachers with evaluating instructional activities to meet the needs of all learners.

5.5 Assist teachers with evaluating, selecting, and developing various instructional resources and materials to meet the needs of all learners.

Mentor Standard 6: Model Professional Growth

6.1 Develop and implement a *Professional Mentor Growth* (PMG) Plan using the *Framework of Professional Growth Mentor Practice*.

6.2 Create and maintain a professional growth portfolio to document the *Professional Mentor Growth* (PMG) Plan.

6.3 Demonstrate reflective practice.

6.4 Demonstrate contribution to the teaching profession.

Name:

Date:

References

Algozzine, B., Gretes, J., Queen, A. J., & Cowan-Hathcock, M. (2007). Beginning teachers' perceptions of their induction program experiences. *The Clearing House, 80*(3).

Allen, R. M., & Casbergue, R. M. (2000). *Impact of teacher's recall on their effectiveness in mentoring novice teachers: The unexpected prowess of the transitional stage in the continuum from novice to expert.* Paper presented at the annual meeting of the American Educational Research Association, New Orleans, LA. (ERIC Document Reproduction Service No. ED441782)

Ambrose, D. (1987). *Managing complex change.* Pittsburgh, PA: Enterprise.

Anderson, L. W., & Krathwohl, D. (Eds.). (2001). A taxonomy for learning, teaching and assessing: A revision of Bloom's Taxonomy of educational objectives. New York: Longman.

Anderson, L., & Pelliceer, L. (2001). *Teacher peer assistance and review: A practical guide for teachers and administrators.* Thousand Oaks, CA: Corwin.

Arends, R. I., & Regazio-DiGilio, A. J. (2000, July). *Beginning teacher induction: Research and examples of contemporary practice.* Paper presented at the annual meeting of the Japan-United States Teacher Education Consortium. (ERIC Document Reproduction Service No. ED450074)

Barkley, S. (2004, December). *Questioning skills for facilitators.* Paper presented at the annual meeting of the National Staff Development Council, Vancouver, Canada.

Berliner, D. (1994). Expertise: The wonder of exemplary performances. In J. N. Mangieri & C. C. Block (Eds.), *Creating powerful thinking in teachers and students* (pp. 161–186). Ft. Worth, TX: Holt, Rinehart & Winston.

Bloom, B. S. (1956). *Taxonomy of educational objectives, handbook I: The cognitive domain.* New York: David McKay.

Bransford, J. D., Brown, A. L., & Cocking, R. R. (Eds.) (2000). *How people learn: Brain, mind, experience, and school* (p. 82). Washington, D.C.: National Academy Press.

Carey, K. (2004). *The real value of teachers.* (Thinking K-12, V01.8, Issue1). Washington, D.C.: Education Trust.

Corcoran, T. B. (2007). *Teaching matters: How state and local policymakers can improve the quality of teachers and teaching.* [CPRE Policy Briefs RB-48]. Philadelphia, PA: Consortium for Policy Research in Education.

Costa, A. L., & Garmston, R. J. (2002). *Cognitive coaching, a foundation for renaissance schools.* Norwood, MA: Christopher Gordon Publishers.

Costa, A. L., & Garmston, R. J. (1994). *Cognitive coaching: A foundation for renaissance schools.* Norwood, MA: Gordon Publishers.

Covino, E. A., & Iwanicki, E. (1996). Experienced teachers: Their constructs on effective teaching. *Journal of Personnel Evaluation in Education, 11,* 325–363.

Dagenais, R. (1996). *Mentoring program standards.* MLRN Professional Articles Division Lincolnshire, IL: Adlai E. Stevenson High School. (ERIC Document Reproduction Service No. ED419776)

Danielson, C. (2009). *Talk about teaching*. Thousand Oaks, CA: Corwin.

Danielson, C. (1996). *Enhancing profession practice: A framework for teaching*. Alexandria, VA: ASCD.

Darling-Hammond, L., & Bransford, J. (Eds.). (2005). *Preparing teachers for a changing world*. San Francisco: John Wiley & Sons.

Darling-Hammond, L. (2000). *Solving the dilemmas of teacher supply, demand, and standards: How we can ensure a competent, caring, and qualified teacher for every child*. New York: National Commission on Teaching America's Future.

Dianda, M., Ward, B., Quarta, K., Tushnet, N., Radio, J., & Bailey, J. (1991). *Support component of the California new teacher project: Second-year evaluation report (1990–1991)*. Los Alamitos, CA: Southwest Regional Laboratory.

Dobbins, R., & Walsey, D. (1992). *Teachers as teacher educators: The impact of nomenclature on roles and relationships in the practicum*. Unpublished manuscript, University of South Australia at Magill.

Durall, P. C. (1995). *Years of experience and professional development: A correlation with higher reading scores*. Unpublished doctoral dissertation, Murray State University, Murray, KY: (ERIC Document Reproduction Service No. ED 386681)

Fieman-Nemser, S. (1996). *Teaching mentoring: A critical review*. Washington, DC: American Association for Colleges of Teacher Education. ERIC Digest, ERIC Clearinghouse on Teaching and Teacher Education.

Freiberg, H. J., & Driscoll, A. (2000). *Universal teaching strategies* (3rd ed.). Boston: Allyn & Bacon.

Fuller, F., & Bown, O. (1975). Becoming a teacher. In K. Ryan (Ed.), *Teacher education: 74th yearbook of the national society for the study of education, Part II* (pp. 25–52). Chicago: University of Chicago Press.

Gagne, R. M. (1985). *The conditions of learning and theory of instruction* (4th ed.). New York: Holt, Rinehart and Winston.

Ganser, T., & Koskela, R. (1997). A comparison of six Wisconsin mentoring programs for beginning teachers. *NASSP Bulletin, 81*(591), 71–80.

Garavuso, V. (2010). *Being mentored: Getting what you need*. New York: McGraw-Hill.

Garmston, R. (2000). Glad you asked. *Journal of Staff Development, 21*(1), 73–75.

Garten, T., Hudson, J., & Gossen, H. (1994). Preparing mentors of first-year teachers: Practitioner/professor collaborative experience. *Teaching Education, 6*(1), 123–132.

Glass, C. S. (2001). Factors influencing teaching strategies used with children who display attention deficit hyperactivity disorder characteristics. *Education, 122*(1), 70–80.

Goldhammer, R. (1969). *Clinical supervision* (Special for the supervision of Teachers). New York: Holt, Rinehart, and Winston.

Hanushek, E. A., Kain, J. F., & Rivkin, S. G. (2004). Why public schools lose teachers. *Journal of Human Resources 39*(2): 326–354.

Hope, W. (1999). Principals' orientation and induction activities as factors in teacher retention. *The Clearing House, 73*(1), 54–57.

Horn, P. J., Blair, H. C., Metler-Armijo, K., & Vanosdall, R. (2005). *Framework of professional growth teacher practice* (Rev Ed.). Phoenix, AZ: Authors.

Horn, P. J., Blair, H. C., & Metler-Armijo, K. (2008, March). *A quality teacher induction program to improve teaching and learning*. Paper presented at the annual meeting of the American Educational Research Association, New York, NY.

Horn, P. J., Lussier, P., Metler-Armijo, K. & Blair, H. C. (2007, February). *Strengthen programs through induction strategies*. Paper presented at the annual meeting of the American Association of Colleges for teacher Education, New York, NY.

Horn, P. J., & Metler-Armijo, K. (2004). *Framework of professional growth mentor practice*. Phoenix, AZ: Authors.

Horn, P. J., & Metler-Armijo, K. (2007). *Framework of professional growth teacher practice.* Phoenix, AZ: Authors.

Horn, P. J., & Metler-Armijo, K. (2009). *Spring 2009 TIP @ NAU Participant Survey Data.* Phoenix, AZ: Authors.

Horn, P. J., & Metler-Armijo, K. (2010 Rev. ed.). *Framework of professional growth mentor practice.* Phoenix, AZ: Authors.

Horn, P. J., & Metler-Armijo, K. (2010 Rev. ed.). *Framework of professional growth teacher practice.* Phoenix, AZ: Authors.

Horn, P. J., & Sterling, H. A. (2002). *Research: Induction programs* [Policy Brief]. Flagstaff, AZ: Northern Arizona University.

Horn, P. J., Sterling, H. A., & Blair, H. C. (2004). *Research: Induction programs.* Flagstaff, AZ: Northern Arizona University.

Howe, E. R. (2006). Exemplary teacher induction: An international review. *Educational Philosophy and Theory, 38*(3).

Huling-Austin, L. (1992). Research on learning to teach: Implications for teacher induction and mentoring programs. *Journal of Teacher Education, 43*(3), 173–180.

Hunter, M. (1989). *Mastery teaching* (Rev Ed.). Pacific Palisades, CA.: TIP Publications.

Ingersoll, R. M. (2007). *Misdiagnosing the teacher quality problem.* [CPRE Policy Briefs RB-49]. Philadelphia, PA: Consortium for Policy Research in Education. Retrieved on January 28, 2010, from http://www.essentialschools.org/pub/ces_docs/about/phil/10cps/10cps.html

Ingersoll, R. M., & Perda, D. (2006). *What the data tell us about shortages of mathematics and science teachers.* Paper presented at the National Commission on Teaching and American's Future Symposium on the Scope and Consequences of K12 Science and Mathematics Teacher Turnover, Racine, WI.

Ingersoll, R. M., & Kralik, J. M. (2004). *The impact of mentoring on teacher retention: What the research says.* Denver, CO: Education Commission of the States.

Ingersoll, R. M., & Smith, T. M. (2003). The wrong solution to the teacher shortage. *Educational Leadership, 60*(8), 30, 4,1.

Jordan, H., Mendro, R., & Weerasinghe, D. (1997) *Teacher effects on longitudinal student achievement.* Dallas, TX: Institutional Research Division, Dallas Public Schools.

Joyce, B., Weil, M., & Calhoun, E. (2009). *Models of teaching* (p.428). Boston: Pearson Education.

Joyce, B., & Showers, B. (1988). *Student achievement through staff development.* White Plains, NY: Longman.

Kegan, R. (2000). What 'form' transforms? A constructive-developmental approach to transformative learning. In J. Mezirow (Ed.), *Learning as transformation: Critical perspectives on a theory and progress* (pp. 35—69). San Francisco: Jossey-Bass.

Kerka, S. (2001). *The balancing act of adult life.* ERIC Clearninghouse on Adult Career and Vocational Education. Columbus, OH. (ERIC Document Reproduction Service No. ED 459 323)

Killion, J. (2008, October). Apply knowledge of learning. *Teachers Teaching Teachers,* 7–9.

Killion, J., & Harrison, C. (2006). *Taking the lead new roles for teachers and school-based coaches.* Oxford, OH: National Staff Development Council.

Killeavy, M. (2006). Induction: A collective endeavor of learning, teaching, and leading. *Theory Into Practice, 45*(2), 168–176.

Lipton, L., & Wellman, B. (2001). *Mentoring matters: A practical guide to learning-focused relationships.* Sherman, CT: MiraVia, LCC.

Lopez, A., Lash, A., Schaffner, M., Shields, P., & Wagner, M. (2004). *Review of research on the impact of beginning teacher induction on teacher quality and retention.* Menlo Park, CA: SRI International.

Lovo, P., Cavazos, L., & Simmons, D. (2006). From BTSA to induction: The changing role of school districts in teacher credentialing. *Issues in Teacher Education, 15*(1).

McTighe, J., & Wiggins, G. (2004). *Understanding by design: Professional development workbook.* Alexandria, VA: Association of Curriculum and Development.

Metler-Armijo, K., House, T., Arthur, M., Carlisle, C., Pogue, M., Nye, S., & Bolster, J. (2002) *Continuum of teacher practice.* Phoenix, AZ: Pendergast Elementary School District.

Moir, E., Freeman, S., Petrock, L., & Baron, W. (1997). *A developmental continuum of teacher abilities.* Santa Cruz, CA: University of California at Santa Cruz, New Teacher Center.

Moir, E., Freeman, S., Petrock, L., & Baron, W. (2001). *A developmental continuum of teacher abilities.* Santa Cruz, CA: University of California at Santa Cruz, New Teacher Center.

Moir, E., & Gless, J. (2001). Quality induction: An investment in teachers. *Teacher Education Quarterly, 28*(1), 109–114.

Moir, E., & Gless, J. (2002). *Launching a new generation of quality teachers: Induction practices that make a difference.* Presented at National Staff Development Council Annual Conference, Boston, MA.

National Commission on Teaching and America's Future. (2007). *High cost of teacher turnover.* Washington, DC: Author.

National Commission on Teaching and America's Future. (2006). *New initiatives from NCTAF: Teacher induction.* Paper presented at the annual meeting of the American Association of Colleges for Teacher Education, San Diego, CA.

New Teacher Center at the University of California, Santa Cruz. (2004, June). *Induction institute.* Santa Cruz, CA: Author.

Nolan, K. Annenberg Institute for School Reform. (n.d.).*Why is looking at student work important?* Retrieved June 29, 2009, from http://www.philaedfund.org/slcweb/prolog.htm

Popham, J. (2008). *Transformative assessment.* Alexandria, VA: ASCD.

Reynolds, A. (1992). What is competent beginning teaching? A review of the literature. *Review of Educational Research, 62*(1), 1–35.

Rivkin, S. G., Hanushek, E. A. & Kain, J. E. (2005). *Teachers, schools, and academic achievement.* Princeton, NJ: Econometrica.

Sanders, W. L., & Rivers, J. C. (1996). *Cumulative and residual effects on teachers on future student academic achievement.* [Research Progress Report]. Knoxville, TN: University of Tennessee Value-Added Research and Assessment Center.

Senge, P. (2006). *The fifth discipline: The art and practice of the learning organization.* USA: Random House Publishers.

Stansbury, K., & Zimmerman, J. (2000). *Lifelines to the classroom: Designing support for beginning teachers.* [Knowledge Brief]. San Francisco, CA: WestEd. (ERIC Document Reproduction Service No. ED447104)

Stigler, J., & Hiebert, J. (1999).*The teaching gap.* New York: Free Press.

Stronge, J., Tucker, P., & Hindman, J. (2004). *Handbook for qualities of effective teachers* (pp. 18, 20). Alexandria, VA: ASCD.

Stroot, S., Fowlkes, J., Langholz, J., Paxton, S., Stedman, P., Steffes, L., & Valtman, A. (1999**).** Impact of a collaborative peer assistance and review model on entry-year teachers in a large urban school setting. *Journal of Teacher Education, 50*(1), 27-41.

Sweeny, B. (2003). *Effective mentoring requires confidentiality.* Kalamazoo, MI: International Mentoring Association.

Tomlinson, C. A., & Edison, C. C. (2003). *Differentiation in practice: A resource guide for differentiating curriculum grades 5-9.* Alexandria, VA: ASCD.

Tomlinson, C.A. (2000). Reconcilable differences? Standards-based teaching and differentiation. *Educational Leadership, 58,* 6-11

Valtman, A. (1999). Impact of a collaborative peer assistance and review model on entry-year teachers in a large urban school setting. *Journal of Teacher Education, 50*(1), 27–41.

U. S. Department of Education. (1999). *A back to school special report on the baby boom echo: No end in sight.* Washington, DC: Author.

Varah, L. J., Theune, W. S., & Parker, L. (1986). Beginning teachers: Sink or swim? *Journal of Teacher Education, 37*(1), 30–34.

Veenman, S. (1984). Perceived problems of beginning teachers. *Review of Educational Research, 54*(2), 143–178.

Villar, A., Strong, M., & Fletcher, S. (2007). *The relation between years of teaching experience and student achievement: Evidence from five years of value-added English and mathematics data from one school district.* Paper presented at the American Educational Research Association annual meeting, Chicago.

Walsdorf, K. L., & Lynn, S. K. (2002). The early years: Mediating the organizational environment. *Clearing House, 75*(4), 190–194.

Wang, A. H., Coleman, A. B., Coley, R. J., & Phelps, R. P. (2003). *Preparing teachers around the world.* Princeton, NJ: Education Testing Services.

Wong, H. K., Britton, T. & Ganser, T. (2005). What the world can teach us about new teacher induction. *Phi Delta Kappan, 86*(5), 379–384.

Wong-Park, M. G. (1997). *The relationship between assessment procedures in teacher support programs and teachers' feelings of support.* (Published doctoral dissertation) La Verne, CA: University of La Verne.

Index

CORWIN
A SAGE Company

The Corwin logo—a raven striding across an open book—represents the union of courage and learning. Corwin is committed to improving education for all learners by publishing books and other professional development resources for those serving the field of PreK–12 education. By providing practical, hands-on materials, Corwin continues to carry out the promise of its motto: **"Helping Educators Do Their Work Better."**